SALES PROMOTION

How to create, implement and integrate campaigns that really work

THIRD EDITION

Julian Cummins & Roddy Mullin

KOGAN
PAGE

First published in 2002
Reprinted 2004

Kogan Page Limited
120 Pentonville Road
London N1 9JN
United Kingdom
www.kogan-page.co.uk

British Library Cataloguing in Publication Data

A CIP record for this book is available from the British Library.

ISBN 0 7494 3864 9

Typeset by JS Typesetting Ltd, Wellingborough, Northants
Printed and bound in Great Britain by Biddles Ltd, *www.biddles.co.uk*

Contents

List of case studies   vii
Foreword   ix
Preface to the third edition   xi

Introduction   1
Sales promotion in action – it adds the fun 1; The extent of
sales promotion 2; Why sales promotion has grown 3; How to
use this book 4

Part I. The context

1. **Starting with the customer**   9
Customers and their behaviour 9; The new marketing mix 11; It's
all in the mind of the customer 13; Managing the brand –
influencing the mind of the customer 14; Sales promotion and
ethics 16; Summary 17

2. **The business and marketing purpose behind sales promotion**   19
Introduction 19; Business and marketing objectives 20; The
promotional mix 22; Value and price 24; Marketing tactics and
strategies 27; The marketing plan 29; Case studies 30; Summary 32

3. **What sales promotions can do**   33
The 10 core promotional objectives 33; Case studies 42;
Summary 44

4. **How to use promotions**   45
    From promotional objective to promotional brief 45; Promotional
    mechanics 49; Case studies 51; Summary 56

5. **How to be creative**   57
    Types of creativity 57; Creative promotions case studies 59;
    Thinking creatively 61; Creative techniques 65; Making the most
    of your idea 67; Case studies 68; Summary 70

6. **How to use suppliers**   71
    Sales promotion agencies 72; Handling houses 77; Point of
    purchase manufacturers 78; Promotional insurers 81; Specialist
    printers 83; Field marketing agencies 84; Premium sourcing
    houses 85; Summary 87

7. **How to implement a promotion**   89
    Budget 90; Timing 92; Communication 92; Logistics 94;
    Legalities 94; A structured process 95; Implementation 99;
    Summary 100

8. **Self-regulation and the law**   101
    UK Codes of Practice 102; UK law 104; EU and international
    law 105; Case studies 106; Summary 108

9. **Marketing accountability and research**   109
    Doing market accountability and research 109; Marketing
    accountability: how to define success, set KPIs, measure and
    evaluate promotions 109; The purpose of marketing
    accountability 110; Keeping evaluation knowledge 111;
    Research 114; Market testing 118; Summary 119

    Part II. Sales promotion techniques

10. **Off-the-shelf offers**   123
    Free accommodation 124; Holiday vouchers 125; Discount
    coupons 127; Two-for-one flights 129; High street vouchers 130;
    Insurance offers 130; Packaged schemes 133; Free film
    promotions 134; Case studies 136; Summary 139

11. **Joint promotions**   141
    Planning principles 141; Sample promotions 145; Referral
    coupon promotions 145; Charity promotions 146; Loyalty
    schemes 149; Phantom partnerships 151; Case studies 152;
    Summary 154

12. **Price promotions** 157
    How prices are set 157; Segment pricing 160; Immediate
    discounts 161; Delayed discounts 166; Coupons 169; Finance
    deals 172; Trade price promotions 175; Case studies 179;
    Summary 183

13. **Premium promotions** 185
    On-pack offers 186; With-purchase premiums 188; Free
    mail-ins 189; Self-liquidators 192; Brand extension
    promotions 193; Business gifts 194; Case studies 197;
    Summary 200

14. **Prize promotions** 203
    Competitions 205; Free draws 210; Instant wins 213;
    Games 214; Probability promotions 216; Case studies 218;
    Summary 223

15. **International sales promotion** 225
    Types of international promotion 225; Localizing the
    global 229; Case studies 231; Summary 234

16. **Self-study questions and feedback** 235
    Self-study questions 235; Summary 238; Feedback 238

    Further information 241

    Index 251

List of Case Studies

Table I.1 Case stud index

Case	Page	Promotion	Type	Business sector
1	30	Nissan	Integrated Marketing	
2	31	Shark	Integrated Marketing	
3	42	Maxwell House	Free draws	Consumer goods
4	43	Bovril	Sampling	Consumer goods
5	43	Sainsbury's	Collector	Retail
6	51	Kleenex Facial	Various	Consumer goods
7	54	Zantac 75	Games	Pharmaceuticals
8	55	Music for Schools	Collector	Confectionary/retail
9	59	Osram	Creativity	
10	59	Sheraton	Creativity	
11	60	Ramada	Creativity	
12	60	Cherry Blossom	Creativity	
13	60	Shell Marketing	Creativity	
14	69	Eversheds	Creativity	Business to business
15	69	Rover Group	Competitions	Motors
16	106	Coca-Cola	Legal	
17	106	Vauxhall Motors	Legal	
18	107	*The Express*	Legal	
19	107	*The Sun*	Legal	
20	108	Balkan Holidays	Legal	
21	136	Tango	Events	Soft drinks

Table I.1   (continued)

Case	Page	Promotion	Type	Business sector
22	137	*The Sun*	Travel	Newspapers
23	138	Passport to the Millennium		
24	139	Hoover	Travel	Consumer durables
25	152	NatWest/BT	Joint promotions	Services
26	153	Shell	Loyalty	Petrol
27	154	Sellotape	Lotteries	Business to business
28	179	Tesco	Price	Retail
29	181	Gale's Honey	Coupons	Consumer goods
30	182	Worcestershire Sauce	Coupons	Consumer goods
31	186	Haagen Dazs		
32	191	SmithKline Beecham		
33	197	Procter & Gamble	Premiums	Consumer goods
34	198	Clearblue One Step	Premiums	Health products
35	199	Electrolux	Premiums	Trade promotions
36	200	Smirnoff	Premiums	Youth markets
37	219	Sarson's	Instant win	Consumer goods
38	219	*The Times*	Fantasy Share Game	
39	220	Worthington Cup		
40	221	Cadbury's Txt 'n' Win		
41	221	Diageo		
42	222	Faber & Faber	Competitions	Bookshops
43	231	Tony Stone Images	Competitions	Business to business
44	232	Umbro	Instant win	Consumer goods
45	233	Visible Vault		

Foreword

Not too long ago, an article in a leading trade magazine raised the question 'Is Sales Promotion Dead?' Sighting integrated campaigns and agencies, it alleged no such discipline existed and the ISP should change its name.

This book explains why such a view exists. So many routes to market have changed or indeed come into existence. So many campaigns are truly integrated, as brands become the powerhouse of marketing. So many agencies have become 'through-the-line' operators as a response to these changes.

Yet despite all these developments the core principles of sales promotion go from strength to strength. Creativity and new digital opportunities have pushed frontiers in its use; the 'sales promotion' agency may now need to embrace other specialities; but the heritage of promotional marketing remains.

Take direct marketing. An increasingly sophisticated technique whether by post, phone or digital means, but it is estimated that 97 per cent of all direct marketing contains a sales promotion element.

This book reveals the changing face of our industry and shows the importance of first principles combines with practical advice. *Sales Promotion* is essential reading for any practitioner needing to stay on top of their game.

Edwin Mutton, Director-General,
The Institute of Sales Promotion Limited (ISP)

Preface to the Third Edition

SO, WHY A NEW EDITION? WHAT'S NEW?

A number of factors have affected marketing and hence sales promotion since the second edition of this book came out in 1998. The impact of the four years has been extensive. For example, the Internet had hardly become universal in 1998; indeed the first Chartered Institute of Marketing (CIM) workshops on Internet user purchases were held in 1997. Now in 2002 there are more e-mails than letters being sent per month. Text messaging hardly featured in 1998; in 2001 some 766 million text messages per month were sent, mainly by the 18–24-year-old age group, and the first conference on advertising through text messages was held in September 2001.

Recent research has indicated the importance of consistency of message and integrated marketing was confirmed as the way ahead. Perhaps the greatest change, which was debated and carried as a motion by the marketing industry's Debating Group in the House of Commons in March 2002, is that customers now have power over global brands.

But what of the advertising industry itself? A quick check of a broadsheet in mid-April 2002 showed there were 38 advertisements (excluding reader offers, announcements and classifieds), of which 17 were offering a sales promotion. So even if you are not a sales promotion enthusiast, others are – and with justification.

The customer is now really aware of marketing

There is increasing real knowledge and a general sagacity of customers in their approach to and perception of marketing, including sales promotions. This applies whether the customer is at that time acting as a business person or a consumer. Customers now know when they are on to a good thing. The reaction to the Hoover promotion practically demonstrated that savvy (see Case study 24), and there are many other examples.

For instance, nowadays business people often prefer to use 'cheap' flights rather than travel business class, recognizing that 'ripping off' their own business may not be a brilliant idea and that business class travel in any case is probably overrated. As consumers, people now arrange their lives so they can take advantage of cheap flights through booking early and on the Internet. Collecting Air Miles matters to some consumers very much; helping charities influences others. These are powerful personal motivators that can be harnessed by sales promotions. Convenience now shares a high spot with value for money. Customers expect to be communicated with in appropriate language, with a consistent brand message that does not patronize. It goes without saying that high quality product performance and service delivery are expected at all times.

What else affects people? There are two things that are presently dominating people's lives: time and quality of life. Time is becoming precious and for routine activities such as commodity shopping, people are prepared to forego the need to examine competitor products or outlets – customers bond with a brand to the exclusion of others, and that brand must offer quality and convenience at an acceptable value level. This includes people bonding with a supermarket chain. For example, in 2001 43 per cent of the top third (ie high spending) Tesco customers did not bother to think of shopping anywhere else. Tesco of course is into sales promotions in a big way and has taken over offering Air Miles from Sainsbury's. Time has also affected products: ready to use, plug in and play, take away, drive away, ready to eat pre-prepared meals are all now big earners – and for all of these, sales promotions can be the trigger to selection and purchase.

Quality of life means the customer consciously assesses and selects products and services that improve lifestyle against personal criteria. This is seen in some advertising messages: 'Go on, spoil yourself, you're worth it', tempting the consumer to go for that quality of life. A particular product or service may cost more, but if it is part of or adds to a person's quality of life, then the customer is prepared to pay. Sales promotions have a part to play here in delivering the glitz, encouraging people to sample or promising to meet the need for what brightens a life.

It is also probably true that the customer has developed an immunity to advertisements generally, probably only noticing those that are offensive (which can backfire on the advertiser), those that offer humour (but do they remember the product or service?) and those that offer a sales promotion, particularly one relating to a relevant need and particularly if it is consistent with the brand perception. If you don't believe that people have become immune to a lot of advertising, ask anyone to recall, from a recently read magazine or newspaper, any advertisements. They may recall one and probably only one that is relevant to them and probably then only one with a sales promotion. A client of ours, contemplating advertising in a TV consumer magazine, called all the advertisers in one issue and found from their marketing departments that at most they had received two responses – even when they had placed a full page advertisement. It was a revelation to the client. It must be near disastrous to those placing the advertisements. Was it the creativity or the medium that was poor?

Marketing integration has arrived

Readers can now benefit even more from this edition of this classic sales promotion book – it now includes marketing integration. Agencies that specialize in sales promotion have recognized the need to integrate sales promotion with other marketing activities. Integrated marketing – which in this book means including sales promotion in the overall marketing process – seeks to move the customer along from knowing nothing about a product/service, to eventually making the purchase and then willingly repeating the purchase thereafter. Where marketing integration produces consistency of communication, research by Professor Merlin Stone shows that it can save 30 per cent of 'lost' sales arising from the differences between the marketing promise, the selling conditions and the operational reality of the service provided. This particularly affects large service providers such as banks, even recently formed ones that offer telephone and Internet banking.

Paul Biggins, Tequila London, and Matt Bell, Tequila Manchester, in an *Admap* article published in 2002 write:

> we take the client's offering and objectives first and then fit the appropriate channels around them, whether DM or SP, on-line or off-line, to realize the best way to communicate a brand. The key area being hit right now is above the line activity. While this is an area we include in our integrated campaigns, it is not our main offering, so we continue to have strong business flow in direct marketing and sales promotion.
>
> Sales promotion skills can be used to make extensive direct marketing even more effective. If you take, for example, the conceptual thinking and creativity of sales promotion combined with highly sophisticated data and direct marketing thinking, you have a very powerful tool. Add to this the power and importance of digital media marketing, as well as the ability to negotiate high-profile sponsorship opportunities, and it all equates to bad news for traditional specialist agencies, which will likely become a relic of the past. We should welcome this new approach, not discriminate against it. It is testament to the dedication of the sales promotion industry that it is helping

to shape and mould change, not sticking to a rigid formula that is no longer relevant or effective.

THE ARRIVAL OF THE NEW MEDIA AND NEW TECHNOLOGY

A lot of changes have affected the environment in which marketing exists. First, there are new media – the Internet, text messaging and interactive TV – to consider. A survey of creative agencies in January 2002 showed that they still largely ignore the new media. The marketing practitioner knows the new media cannot be ignored and, as for all media, they too need sales promotion for success. For example, research by the Henley Centre for Royal Mail shows Internet users buy more readily from a Web site when they have something tangible in their hands, such as a direct mail shot or a press advertisement: a Web site is much more likely to deliver a sale when part of such an 'integrated approach' than a viewing of the Web site alone. A promotion message in transport media, such as a taxi, is most effective when it includes a mobile phone number for instant action, whether by text messaging or by calling a number; and of course you can then respond to the consumer by the same means.

Second, the new technology is making life both more complex and easier. There are second and third generation mobile phones; powerful and affordable PCs, laptops and hand-held devices, with their associated peripherals, software and interoperability; digital cameras and rapid electronic transmission of images – all are readily accessible and affordable.

Sales promotion has to become more accountable and learn from the latest examples. Paul Biggins and Matt Bell again write about this:

Accountability in the marketing community

As with any marketing discipline, accountability is one of the key issues faced by agencies. Clients are taking promotional activity much more seriously – and expecting to be able to measure the results accurately. Whether this is a result of research into changing consumer habits or a change in focus on their part to see a realistic return on investment, it is no longer the poor relation to above-the-line activity, as far as clients' attitudes are concerned.

Consumers also want more from promotions, if these are to elicit any kind of response. Campaigns have to work harder in a much more pressurized market if they are going to be successful in achieving the desired result. It is therefore crucial that agencies are seen as offering measurement solutions that will, in effect, make them more accountable. Many integrated agencies adopt a media-neutral approach to their campaigns, but however important the selection of media is, what is of more importance is delivering a balanced SP and DM planning solution.

What benefit is offered to clients by being media-neutral if there are no measurement systems in place? Clients are more interested in ROI for their campaigns than any hype about their approach to media buying. It is essential that, for the client–agency relationship to grow, these measurement systems are put in place.

The opportunity has been taken with this new edition to include measurement and accountability (see Chapter 9), acknowledging that the marketer now has to offer value for money for all marketing activities. This includes sales promotion. Some say that without measurement and accountability the marketer will fade away.

The Web as a source of information

The Web allows you the reader to keep right up to date. For example, as this book was being written, the Institute of Sales Promotions Web site records uncertainty over tax liabilities resulting from certain reward-based sales promotions. The situation may be resolved by the time the book is printed. Check out the Web site at www.isp.org.uk.

OVERVIEW OF THE BOOK

The first part of the book looks at all the issues that sales promotion practitioners should consider.

Sales promotion is seen as a part of the whole marketing effort, making its contribution in a consistent manner to build the brand or to drive profit through sales. Sales promotion has 'come of age' in that it is now accepted that it has a role to play in overall marketing, and operates within legal constraints and codes of practice. In the past it was seen as 'separate', though advertising, direct mail, telemarketing, etc were used to deliver the sales promotion. What sales promotions can achieve, how they can be implemented, and the importance of creativity, are dealt with in this book.

The second part of the book, dealing with techniques, has been strengthened to include help with measuring success and pointing to examples given on Web sites. International promotions, whether in one or many countries, also appear in this part. Given the speed at which examples can date, sources of recent examples, such as the annual ISP awards, are included.

For those new to this book

Welcome! Sales promotion is a wonderful way to attract the customer. Just think back to the last time you remembered an advertisement from the press or TV. To attract you sufficiently to remember, it probably was near to offensive, was humorous, or made a sales promotion offer. If this rings a bell, you have discovered the truth behind sales promotions: they attract and make advertising memorable. If your brand is not suited to humour or prepared to offend, then only sales promotion remains.

Understanding how customers react nowadays to marketing and particularly to sales promotions is key to success. The rationale, the reasons and thinking behind using sales promotions, the promotion mechanics (how the customer can respond), the production of a sales promotion, are all in the first part of the book. Individual techniques, the offer made, how the offer works, what to look out for (tips) and how to measure the success, are given in the second part of the book.

Reference is made to Web sites where up-to-date codes of practice, the law relating to sales promotion, and examples can be found. Reference is also made to other books dealing with topics that impact on sales promotion, such as creativity, controlling agencies, direct marketing (which covers some of the production of sales promotion), marketing accountability (justifying marketing spend), and the strategic use of sales promotion.

Comment

On a personal note, I'd like to say how much I have enjoyed the opportunity to prepare this third edition of Julian Cummins' book. I doubt I will ever acquire as much knowledge as he has on the subject but I hope I have added the complementary marketing approach now needed to keep a book on sales promotion at the leading edge of the practitioner's toolbox.

I have found in my own company, Helmsmen Limited, that it is often very helpful to have different views and perspectives to solve problems and to keep ahead in business: my heartfelt thanks to Rod Charles and Jim Tiller for their help in business – I hope I have successfully applied the same process to this book, enriching and empowering the reader by the application of experience that differs from Julian's original approach.

I have spent much time looking at the case studies in the earlier edition and have decided to leave most of them in because they are just as useful and valid now. I have updated one or two and added some more, including a couple relating to SMS text messaging. Once again, I stress the benefit of using the Web to see examples. Do also participate in sales promotions – it is an easy way to learn.

I can but commend the reader to this new edition of the book.

Roddy Mullin

Introduction

SALES PROMOTION IN ACTION – IT ADDS THE FUN

No one buys chocolate to be miserable: make your promotions add to the fun.

The same is true of buying any product or service. If the fun goes out of it, so does the spirit that makes buying and selling part of our lives, whether as customers and/or business people. Indeed, of all the marketing tools available to the marketer, sales promotion can most readily be used to give that sense of fun to the customer.

The marketer, however, has other customers to consider: the shareholder, the employee and the management team, which raises serious points too. Some of this book necessarily talks about detailed mechanics – how the customer responds – and the codes of practice that apply. It's also impossible to look at price promotions without some reference to economics. The need for accountability and measuring the success of marketing activities is now with us. A CIM (Chartered Institute of Marketing) report in February 2002 found marketing accountability – the delivery of value for money marketing – the number one subject raised by 69 per cent of the firms surveyed. There's hard graft and detail in sales promotion. At its heart is the serious business of building long-term, profitable customer relationships. Good promotions are not a substitute for serious thinking or for building deep staff and customer relationships; they are, however, a part of the same process.

The best basis for understanding sales promotion is from inside. Get involved in promotions: collect coupons, send in for offers, and seek out special offers. Have a look at how others do it. Put this book down for a few moments and visit the Institute of Sales Promotion Web site at www.isp. org.uk and click on Awards/Events. Look at the winners of the latest competition. Read why the judges awarded the prize. There are some 30 awards to look at. (At the time of writing the Saatchi & Saatchi Army's sales promotion won the top 2001 Award but, just as important, they exceeded the target set for the response, proving the marketing activity was successful.) Now we've seen what a good sales promotion is, read on.

THE EXTENT OF SALES PROMOTION

A cursory check in your supermarket, in your local paper or pub, and in the direct mail sent to both your home and business address, will give an immediate feel of the extent of sales promotion today. Sales promotion is found whenever a supermarket offers 'three for the price of two', whenever a pub offers a happy hour, whenever an insurance or charity mailer offers a free pen for replying, whenever a product offers a free draw, competition or mail-in. In this world of choice a good sales promotion will stop customers for a moment, cause them to think about a brand and product and, if it has the right impact, move the customer to make a decision to follow up the sales promotion. There are hidden benefits – if customers take up your 'three for the price of two' offer they will not be purchasing a competitor product while using yours, and their experience of enjoying a product or service is a great influencer on future purchases. Indeed a second sales promotion delivered with the product or service when the customer takes up the first sales promotion can entice them to make their next purchase of that product or service.

For the customer as consumer at the point of sale, there are now too many choices. Careful placement can influence delivery on the shelves but who knows where your product is? You can pay for specific positioning. But there are, for example, around 1,200 brands of hair shampoo to choose from. What do consumers do? There are busy people who make their buying decisions and choice of brand from the offers available. This is not new. People have always looked for what is 'in season', what is a bargain. Shopkeepers and stallholders in previous centuries would make an 'on the spot offer' to help persuade people to make a purchase – sales promotion is the modern equivalent.

Philip Kotler, the US marketing academic, estimates that 15 years ago the advertising to sales promotion ratio was about 60:40. In 1997, he calculated that in many consumer goods companies, sales promotion accounted for 65 to 75 per cent of expenditure, and had been growing annually for the last two decades. More is now spent in all companies on sales promotion than all other advertising including direct marketing. In March 2002, Edwin Mutton, the Director General of the Institute of Sales Promotion, cited the sales promotion spend as £18 billion in the UK in 2001. The AA and DMIS give a figure of £17 billion for all advertising including direct marketing in 2000 (direct marketing itself is at £10.7 billion according to the 2001 DMA census). So the ratio will soon have reversed to become 40:60.

(You should note that price promotions – a large part of sales promotion – may not always be counted as expenditure, but as lost income. Expenditure on altering packs and products for a promotion may also not be counted as promotional expenditure.)

The amount spent on TV and press advertising was £4.6 and £8.6 billion respectively in 2000. Both these figures include the direct response elements – that is interactive TV and tip-ons or response vouchers – and both are now included in the £10.7 billion direct marketing figure. The amount spent on direct mail was £2 billion and telemarketing £2.4 billion in 2000. NCH, which dominates the coupon redemption business, reports that more than 5 billion coupons were distributed in 2000 (a 20 per cent increase in five years), enough for nearly 250 per household over the year. In a nutshell, sales promotion at £18 billion a year is really big – bigger than the rest put together.

Research in 1986 and subsequently shows that over 70 per cent of the population has taken part in competitions or games on products and services, with almost 60 per cent of the population actively participating in some form of promotion in any given month – whether it be entering a competition, sending in for a free gift or using a money-off coupon. This makes participating in sales promotions one of Britain's biggest active leisure activities. Compare that with, say, the 11 per cent of the UK population participating in golf in any way over the year.

If you are not undertaking sales promotion in your organization, you should be wondering why everyone else is. The figures given above demonstrate that sales promotion is no longer an also-ran in the business of marketing products and services, but one of the most important tools available to companies and a major part of our day-to-day lives. For why it is likely to become even more important in the future, read on.

WHY SALES PROMOTION HAS GROWN

There are six main reasons (not much changed from the previous edition!) for the extensive growth of sales promotion and for managers finding that promotions are essential to building customer relationships:

1. Firms are getting better at what they do. Sales promotion offers a tie-breaker in markets in which most products are excellent. The European

Vice-President of a major toiletries group commented, 'It's no longer enough to have an excellent product at an excellent price; I need a tie-breaker'. Companies everywhere are facing declining real differences between products and services, increased distributor power and faster communication of alternatives. They have to fight harder and faster for every sale.

2. Customers look for more from the brands they buy. Sales promotion offers novelty, excitement and humour at the point of purchase, which customers respond to. Firms are having to rethink the relationship between attitude and behaviour. Trying to create awareness of and a positive attitude to a brand by means of advertising is seen as less effective than encouraging a sale that may lead on to just such a positive attitude to the brand. That encouragement is achieved by sales promotion.

3. The pressure to achieve short-term results is growing. The fortunes of brands and companies are increasingly volatile. Sales promotions can be devised, implemented and take effect far more quickly than other forms of marketing. This is of growing importance as demands for short-term profit performance grow despite people urging a long-term view.

4. TV audiences are fragmenting as the number of channels grows, making it more expensive to reach certain audiences; the decline in community identity at a local level is making it more difficult to reach particular groups (such as the young) via local media.

5. The growth in the sheer number of competing brands and products is leading people to switch off from many of the advertising messages beamed at them.

6. Advertising research has shown that the sales effects of TV advertising over a four-week period are between two and seven times greater when it coincides with promotions. This important finding came from a survey of 21 different brands in eight different consumer goods markets that integrated the shopping behaviour of 9,000 households with TV viewing data. In the case of two out of eleven established brands where the effect of TV advertising with and without promotional activity could be measured, TV advertising was only effective when promotions were also taking place. The same result is now coming from Internet buying surveys. It might be said that the only advertising that works and registers with audiences is that which amuses, offends or offers a sales promotion.

HOW TO USE THIS BOOK

There are two parts to this book: Part I deals with the context of sales promotion and structure and Part II with techniques. They are designed to be read and used differently.

Part I has nine chapters:

- Chapter 1 starts with the customer. It sets out how sales promotions contribute to building long-term customer relationships.
- Chapter 2 deals with the business and marketing purpose behind sales promotions.
- Chapter 3 explains what sales promotion can do.
- Chapter 4 spells out how to use sales promotions, from the identification of a business task to the specification of the promotional brief. These chapters are crucial for understanding what sales promotion can and cannot do.
- Chapters 5 and 6 deal with two crucial inputs into promotional planning: Chapter 5 sets out how to go about identifying the necessary creativity and supplier resources; Chapter 6 deals with sales promotion agencies, handling houses, specialist printers and other suppliers.
- Whether promotions stand or fall turns on the details of their implementation. Chapter 7 describes how to implement a promotion, avoid disaster and ensure that all the elements work together.
- Chapter 8 covers the legal aspects of a promotion, sets out the principles behind the UK Code of Sales Promotion Practice and discusses recent case studies of promotions from the Advertising Standards Authority (ASA). It also discusses the variety of rules that apply in other countries. It is a must as a reference for any promotion you run.
- Chapter 9, on marketing accountability and research, is essential for ensuring that your promotions meet the marketing objectives you set.

If you are tempted to dive straight into the techniques and skip Part I, resist. You can use the techniques to best effect only if you are clear about the why, when and how of sales promotion.

Part II deals with a wide range of promotional techniques:

- Chapter 10 covers offers such as free flights, holidays and film processing that are available 'off the shelf'. It spells out how they work, and how to make the most of them.
- Chapter 11 looks at the important area of joint promotions – teaming up with another firm to your mutual advantage.
- Chapter 12 covers promotions that use discounts, coupons, price reductions, cheap finance and other price-related tools. A massive area of sales promotion, it is one that carries dangers as much as benefits. New in this edition is information on insurance to cover the risk of offers such as those featured in Chapter 10.
- Premiums, whether with a product or available as a mail-in item, are another major area. They are discussed in Chapter 13, along with what to watch for in identifying and sourcing premiums.
- Chapter 14 sets out the range of prize promotions available, including competitions, draws and instant wins.

- International promotions are covered in Chapter 15; these are promotions that take place in a global economy with significant national regulations. Even if your concerns are local, the chapter is full of ideas. In larger companies, promotions span national boundaries.
- Chapter 16 gives a set of self-study questions to help you make the most of this book. It also asks for your comments.

You will find Part II useful for years to come. You may not want to read it all at once. You will probably want to dip into it and refer to it for the nuts and bolts of techniques you may want to use now or in the future. If you are studying for a marketing course, you will find the data you need on the range of techniques available to you.

At the end of the book there is a chapter of further information, listing useful addresses, books, magazines and courses. The organizations listed have a descriptive sentence to explain how they can best help you – most compiled their entry themselves.

There are case studies throughout the book, illustrating the best (and in one case the worst) in sales promotional practice. Use these for ideas for your business sector, and your business challenge. They have been placed at the end of the chapter to which they mainly refer, but they illustrate the many types of sales promotions and their use in different business sectors as well. With many of the case studies there are questions to get you thinking. The problem with including case studies is that they inevitably become out of date. Please do refer to the Institute of Sales Promotion Web site at www.isp.org.uk which, in addition to including examples of sales promotions in its awards section, has links to members' Web sites.

Part I

The Context

Starting With the Customer

CUSTOMERS AND THEIR BEHAVIOUR

Why do you need to start with the customer?

At the heart of every successful business is a close understanding of customer needs and how to anticipate and meet them. For many years, people understood this unconsciously: long before 'marketing' was invented, it was the genius of every great entrepreneur.

When not many alternatives were produced and there was relatively little choice, customers took what they were offered; it was the day of the salesperson. But these days are gone. In an interim period it was thought to be part of the task of a marketing department to make customers aware of the benefits and then for sales to persuade and sell. Now customers have an amazing amount of choice, they generally serve and select the products themselves and the task is to convince them, with little sales person influence, to really want to buy from you and again and again.

When a need or a problem arises the onus was once on the customer to initiate the dialogue and make contact. Now people in firms are going back to seeing customer needs as everyone's concern, not just the concern of a marketing department. Increasingly, firms are sharing responsibility for thinking about customer needs among line managers in every functional discipline. It's not that marketing has gone out of fashion, it is that the customer has come of age and demands attention from all parts of the firm; marketing has been generalized across the firm as a whole – and rightly so.

Identifying your customer

Remember customers are affected by their background, their social or cultural influences; they consider and think of matters in different ways; they have varied economic purchasing power, they have different levels of intelligence; they have prejudices. Clearly you need to understand your existing and potential customers – whoever they are. You need to find out all about them to serve them better, retain their custom and persuade them to buy more. Everyone in your organization needs to know about them. Equally the customer will be finding out about your company; it is a two-way communication. In finding out about each other, you will establish a relationship. Making sure you do that well and that the customer trusts your firm is called customer relationship management (CRM). You should aim to provide a consistent customer experience wherever and whenever the customer touches you.

Identifying your customer and establishing a customer profile – an idealized, averaged, but complete understanding of the way the customers think; what influences the customers; how, when, what and from whom they are prepared to buy. It is really important to grasp this. If you understand the customers, you have a chance to persuade them to buy. If you do not understand them you are less likely to be able to persuade them to buy. Without customers you make no sales; with no sales a business dies.

Marketing is tasked with identifying and knowing the customer. If you discover that there is more than one common type of customer, each with a different approach to buying from you – you have segments. Each of the different, yet identifiable, separate customer groups is known as a segment. Sorting all types of customers by segments is called market segmentation. Market segmentation is only helpful where each segment has a different approach to buying, and is of a size and has the purchasing power, accessibility and future viability from which you will make a profit.

If you are selling to buyers and the buyers are selling on your product or service to customers who are consumers, marketing will need to understand both tiers of customers – that is, the primary buyers and the primary buyers' own buyers, who could be consumers. If you are dealing with business-to-business (B2B) customers, their customers too may be business customers. There are differences within each tier. You need to know and understand them all. There is more on this later when considering sales promotions to the trade, the wholesaler and retailer as well as the customer.

Now the different types of customers have been roughly separated into segments, how do we store all the information and keep it all in mind just in case they call? What you need to understand about customers is not an infinite amount of detail (though some database systems supplied for CRM can now offer this facility); what you need to know is the information about the customer that is relevant to making a sale or relevant to you at that moment, in that part of the sales process. You need to have that knowledge in front of you only when the customer is in front of you or is on the telephone to you. This is part of what is called 'knowledge management' – the provision of timely and relevant information at the moment you need it.

Think from the customer viewpoint

People carry so much baggage from the culture and social environment of their upbringing, their education, their life experience, and it is easy to make assumptions about how others think and are likely to respond to communications with them. Accept the fact that the people you are selling to are unlikely to have the same background as yourself. If you don't, you may have a problem grasping the need for marketing. It is easy to assume that one target group of customers is a segment much like another, to ignore research highlighting differences, and to apply what you have done before – because it's easy, because it may have worked before, because. . . and everyone has such convincing reasons for doing what you have always done and forgetting the research. Don't ignore it: believe and act on your market research.

Before you go any further, for every customer segment that you decide to select as a target (you do not need to target every one), you should apply the following method: Erase from your mind your own thinking and prejudices. Learn to listen, observe and grasp how your target thinks, communicates, comes to conclusions. You need to understand what makes the target tick, react, etc. This method has been described as 'Self-recognition criteria' – accepting that the way you think and react is certainly wrong for any target you are analysing. You should not make any assumptions about the target customer. Find out.

Now that we have an open mind about the customer, let's do just that: find out what makes them tick and how they express their needs.

THE NEW MARKETING MIX

The customer expectation

The basics. Customer needs in any particular area are met by product or service offerings that are a bundle of characteristics – the six Cs. Some the organization controls entirely, and some not. The whole concept (the product and service together) you are offering as a supplier must match what customers need, want and perceive to be the solution to their need, offering greater benefit – ie an advantage – over other suppliers. The description should consider the six Cs the new marketing mix – see the list below. You describe your concept in the language of your customers using their perceptions.

Forget the four Ps; think of the six Cs. This is the marketing mix for now and the future; this is what an organization considers when it is thinking of what to offer the customer – from the customer perspective:

- Cost – a customer considers cost (and cost of ownership) within a value perception. That value perception is personal and includes a quality of life assessment. A customer also puts into the equation the cost of time and travel to make a purchase. The Future Foundation research indicates that consumers will travel for most of their activities and purchases within a 14-mile radius of their home. Sales promotions are often used to affect cost – two for the price of one, 33 per cent free, etc, or in combinations with other products or redeeming vouchers against the full cost.
- Convenience of buying – a mix of place/location, opening hours, cash/cheque/credit card acceptability. Customers are lazy – exercising the brain requires effort and energy – so make it easy for them, convenient for them to buy. Sales promotions can be tuned to enhance convenience.
- Concept – a mix of product and service. Few products are sold without some sort of aftercare service. The quality and fitness for purpose of the concept are assumed to be right. A warranty or return policy is taken for granted. A brand is principally a consolidation of the concept (though the other Cs come into it) into an easy-to-remember space in the mind of the customer. A sales promotion adds fun to the purchase and is remembered as part of the concept, so it too becomes part of the brand.
- Communication – how well the product or service is communicated to the customer. This is where sales promotion really comes into its own, matching communicating – the feel of the brand – with just the right offer and the way it is put across. Customers will not buy if it is too complex, too dull or does not put the concept across in terms they commonly use. This explains why some advertising fails.
- Customer relationship – CRM principles apply. Customers expect to be treated with respect at all times and that all reasonable questions will be answered and problems resolved. Once they have made a purchase of any size or have signed up for a service, they expect to be recognized and remembered. For example, once a customer has had a car serviced at a garage, he or she expects the garage to know all the car's idiosyncrasies when he or she calls. People like to build relationships; you have to accept this. If customers get different answers from different people or departments within the same organization, they tend to trust the people and the organization less. 'Integration' means making sure every part of your business delivers consistent answers. Research shows an integrated approach is worth 30 per cent of sales (or a loss of 30 per cent if you do not practise it). Sales promotion eases the customer relationship forming process – it facilitates building the relationship – often providing a talking point that helps start or recommence the relationship.

- Consistency – the reassurance of ongoing quality and reliability of the other five Cs – brand surety if you like. It is integration and comes from applying internal marketing within an organization.

IT'S ALL IN THE MIND OF THE CUSTOMER

Branding. This is the process of lodging your offer in the customers' mind to remind them you exist just as and when they need you. The 'shorthand' mind retention device is your logo or brand name. If you have it right, the shorthand encompasses the six Cs above. It is a powerful thing, a successful brand and when you achieve brand bonding. . . the world is your oyster; rather, you will sell more. Remember the reminding bit: this means you will need to regularly market to customers.

Buying process and behaviour. That is, understanding that the customer adopts a buying process, different for different purchases and you have the task of finding out what it is and developing a sales process to match. Research shows that many first generation Internet sites forgot the need to match the way their customers buy. A number of models describe how people buy: one is the involvement model.

The involvement model for buying is increasingly being seen as a more realistic description of the way in which consumers buy products and services. The model extends well beyond marketing. The Church, for example, used to think that people started belonging to a church because they believed – often after a conversion experience. However, it is now understood that people belong before they believe. Studies have shown that people become involved in a church because of friends or family. It is often quite casual at first. Only after a period of years do they come to realize that they believe. The process of 'belonging before believing' is about 'behaviour before attitude'.

Sales promotion is, first and foremost, about behaviour. It makes increasing sense in the light of evidence that behaviour precedes attitude. Encouraging someone to try a product or service is often the best way to begin the process by which they become a long-term customer and develop a relationship with your firm. Behaviour and attitude have a complicated relationship with each other. Practical examples illustrate this. Surveys show that far more people think that regular exercise is a good thing (attitude) than actually practise it (behaviour). Surveys also show that people drink more alcohol (behaviour) than they are prepared to admit (attitude). For years, the government urged people to use seat belts (attitude) with only limited effect. They then passed a law making it a crime not to wear them (behaviour). People grumbled at first, but buckled up. Over time, their attitude changed to accord with the behaviour they had become accustomed to. This suggests that marketing campaigns that directly impact on the behaviour of customers succeed, and the desired attitude to the product or service will follow. Advertising campaigns aimed primarily at creating awareness and changing attitudes are less likely to succeed.

The role of influencers. Customers are influenced by others when making purchases and this influence must be understood. You need to know how those around the customers, the people they follow and their perceived status can influence their attitude and their buying behaviour. You can use people in your promotions who embody influence – a public figure, a personality, but remember that they can on occasion fall, so take care when making your selection.

This book considers the customer viewpoint hereafter in terms of the six Cs, accepting branding as shorthand, recognizing that a buying process exists and that behaviour must be studied, and noting the part influencers play.

MANAGING THE BRAND – INFLUENCING THE MIND OF THE CUSTOMER

The bundle of characteristics – the six Cs – the new marketing mix, is your offer, the 'brand' promise. Truly great brands achieve leadership in all dimensions, having superlative quality, unbeatable value and outstanding image in the six Cs offered. Making the most of 'brand equity' – the sum of quality, value and image as customers understand it – is one of a crucial jobs for any manager. As more businesses realize that a company is its brands, so more CEOs and MDs manage the brand. Evidence exists that customers ultimately bond with a brand, not bothering to look elsewhere, as long as that brand delivers the brand promise. Bonding exceeds any loyalty. It has become a CEO deliverable. It gives a value far in excess of the bricks and mortar worth of a company.

The most difficult element of a brand for any firm to manage is the 'psychological' part, that is achieving and retaining ownership of a piece of the customers' mind. Companies often talk about 'creating an image'. They may do so in the minds of the staff who work long and hard to devise it. They only do so in customers' minds when customers adapt, develop and absorb that image as their own. Companies can offer an image, but they cannot make an image. If it is attractive and powerful, and accords with customers' own experiences, it will form part of their image of the product or service. Thoughts and images in our own minds are, thankfully, beyond anyone else's total control.

Customers retain perceptions and images, and their own key senses trigger a brand if the retention has been successful. It is a 'shorthand' memory device, a mix of logo, slogan or a feeling that the customer relates to 'advantage' with regard to a need. If you have such recall in a customer, you are made. But beware: if the concept you are selling does not match the perception, image and experience of the customer, you are far less likely to make a sale. You also need to nurture that retention constantly and favourably reinforce it.

It is quite possible to have different perceptions of your brand in different parts of the globe or even in different parts of one country. Guinness for a time advertised in Africa, unwittingly using a symbol that Guinness improved fertility. Brylcream was thought to be a food delicacy in another African country. A failure of branding you might think – unless of course you are happy to sell with that branding mismatch.

It is also quite possible to reposition a brand. Sometimes this is essential to save a brand that has become dusty and is failing. Failures are often the seed corn of success if the lesson is understood. Lucozade was rebranded as a sports drink from its previous life as an expensive drink for when you were ill. It used to be said that you knew you were really ill when the Lucozade appeared. How different it is now.

The four Ps (the old marketing mix) and why they are no longer relevant

Just in case you are asked about the old four Ps marketing mix, read these paragraphs. There was a time when business was thought of as a series of functions. Marketing was a function; sales was a function; production was a function. Sales promotion was one among many things companies did, one of the responsibilities of a marketing department. Drawn as a hierarchical chart, the marketing manager knew exactly where sales promotion fitted into the scheme of things. Unfortunately, this neat scheme did not really describe how businesses achieve and sustain competitive advantage. It certainly didn't describe the contribution of sales promotion.

Organizationally based marketing traditionally considers the needs of the customer in terms of four Ps: the Product or service, the Place, the Price, the Promotion. (Note: others added Ps for Process, People and Physical evidence to make it seven Ps.) This approach gives the wrong perspective for the marketing needs analysis of the customer in the 21st century and the subsequent decision making about which marketing activities to apply. It is better to approach the needs of the customers (whether buyers or consumers) *in terms of their view* of the four Ps. What you are really doing is applying self-recognition criteria – looking at the Ps – from the customer view. And when you do this, the four Ps become six Cs This is not new, it is an extension of a Philip Kotler preferred viewpoint.

Separate functions, such as finance, production and marketing, continue to exist in firms, and they can be managed well or badly. A good marketing department, however, does not create a competitive advantage on its own any longer. Its work is part of a process that takes place every time someone buys or uses the company's products or services. It is part of the process by which relationships are strengthened, and by which customer and other stakeholder needs are satisfied. Think of it as part of the creation and strengthening of relationships that contribute to the success of the business. The leading management thinker John Kay writes:

> I see the firm as a set of relationships between its various stakeholders – employees, customers, investors, and shareholders. The successful firm is one which creates a distinctive character in these relationships and which operates in an environment that maximizes the value of that distinctiveness.

What characterizes these relationships? Money plays a large part – whether in salaries for staff, dividends to shareholders or invoices to customers. However, there is much more to it than that – like loyalty, expectation and human feeling. Whether people buy a product or work for a firm, they are engaged in a relationship that satisfies their needs to a greater or lesser extent. The task of business is to maximize the value of that relationship. The four Ps approach matched a business structure where relationships did not feature and only hierarchical 'silos' existed.

SALES PROMOTION AND ETHICS

As this chapter deals with the customer, it is right that the duty of care to the customer is covered here.

There is always a temptation in sales promotion, as in many other areas of business, to cut corners, to promise more than you intend to give, to rely on the small print as a get-out. Is this good business if you can get away with it? Some people think so, but they are a declining minority. The reason is that relationships are increasingly seen as central to business success. It is unwise to treat badly those with whom you want to build up a long-term relationship.

In 1996 the Royal Society of Arts published a report entitled *Tomorrow's Company*, with backing from some of Britain's top business leaders. This argued that successful companies are those that have a 'success model' that embraces the interests of all their stakeholders – shareholders, customers, suppliers, employees and community. A study of the United States' most visionary companies in 1996 found that those businesses that were consistently most successful were the ones that did not place profit first, but in second place to a core ideology that often stressed responsibility to others.

Across the world, there is evidence that people prefer to deal with companies they trust. 'The company behind the brand' is increasingly important. Cadbury's has benefited from its association with enlightened social policies throughout its history – a point strongly made in its factory exhibition, 'The Cadbury Experience', visited by 450,000 people a year. Richard Branson's rating as the UK's most admired business leader has helped Virgin diversify from records to air travel to personal finance and drinks.

An ethic of enlightened self-interest guides companies not to abuse customer relationships by subjecting people to sharp sales promotional practice. However, sales promotion practitioners have another and more specific ethical challenge to consider: if sales promotion is effective in changing behaviour, it is a powerful and double-edged weapon that can change behaviour for the bad as well as the good.

Some sales promotion agencies refuse to handle tobacco accounts on the grounds that promotions may reinforce a destructive form of behaviour. Other areas in which behaviour can be influenced to the detriment of wider social interests are the consumption of alcohol and participation in lotteries. On the other hand, sales promotion has been used for purposes that have a positive social benefit. Case study 5 features a promotion for Sainsbury's that helped both schools and the reuse of plastic bags.

What if things go wrong? In 1993, Hoover launched a 'free flights' promotion. There is nothing wrong in that. Free flights are a promotional evergreen (and are described in detail in Chapter 10). What characterized Hoover's promotion in the first instance was the unsustainably generous terms of the offer. What characterized it in the years that followed was the inadequate way in which the company handled its failure. Case study 24 spells out the sorry tale.

Sales promotion in the UK is largely guided by internal self-regulation, policed by the industry via the Advertising Standards Authority. In most of Europe, there are greater legislative controls. The UK government is not convinced that self-regulation works as well as it could or should in every case. The cases of promotional malpractice cited in Chapter 8 indicate that there are legitimate grounds for concern. Every sales promoter needs to take the power to change behaviour seriously, and to think hard about the purposes to which it is put.

SUMMARY

In the 21st century the customer is really aware of marketing and all its facets, including the benefits of a good sales promotion. The offer presented by the marketer must meet the 6C's needs of the customer, match their preferred buying process and fulfil the brand promise.

In the absence of human contact at the decision point – the point of selecting the item to buy – the choice of competing products is daunting. It is then that sales promotion comes into its own. It is the key differentiator between products and services. It must be genuine, ethical and complement the brand it serves. If it offers that something extra, that adds value, carries a real benefit to the customer, then sales promotion is key. It deserves to win.

The Business and Marketing Purpose Behind Sales Promotion

INTRODUCTION

A business task may be to sell more; a business objective specifies a target sales figure. Business objectives define the success of a business task.

Business objectives come from your business vision or mission, or the tasks you see that lie ahead and are usually related to a time period – often a year, sometimes two years. Marketing provides some of the strategic inputs to help decide those business objectives; for example, it can confirm the size and shape of your market and whether it is of a sufficient size for you to make money from it.

From certain business objectives, marketing objectives are derived which, after considering the alternative solutions (each of which may contain many marketing activities, known as a campaign, and possibly including sales promotions), one set of options is selected and forms a marketing plan.

A business objective might be to 'increase volume this year by 10 per cent over last year'. The marketing objective will convert that to a sales target expressed in money terms. Sales promotion in conjunction with other marketing activities is probably in many of the options considered to achieve the sales target. The process of deciding the alternatives provides the context for promotional thinking. Take a sneak preview at Figure 4.1 on page 46, which makes this clearer.

The promotional objective is much narrower in focus. It is concerned with, say, persuading particular people to buy two of your products when normally they would buy one. The promotional objective derives from the business objective you have set and the marketing objectives that followed. It is specifically promotional (see Chapter 4).

Objectives we choose in our personal lives work in a similar way. You may be reading this book because you want to advance your career in business. Learning about sales promotion follows from that, but it is not the only way you could advance your career. Once you have decided you want to learn about sales promotion, you rightly focus on the best means of achieving it – of which reading this book is one.

The next chapter (Chapter 3) identifies 10 promotional objectives that are most commonly addressed by sales promotion, the mechanics available and how to put them together to achieve the behavioural change that you want. Following this process will not guarantee that your sales promotion will be a world-beater. However, it will ensure that it is fit for the task and that it logically connects with business and marketing objectives.

This chapter deals with business and marketing objectives. Chapters 3 and 4 covers promotional objectives.

BUSINESS AND MARKETING OBJECTIVES

This book is not about how to write business plans or marketing plans but to explain how sales promotion activities arise and how they can be used as part of your promotional mix in an integrated fashion to deliver the marketing mix you have drawn up.

Companies sometimes fail to identify that there actually are business tasks to be done. Business tasks come in a variety of forms. They can be: moving offices, setting up a new production line, helping accounts with new software. Thinking clearly about your business and where you want it to be in this coming year and in the future as part of that is not difficult. It is a useful mind clearing process. The paragraphs that follow are purely to illustrate the business process and show how sales promotions are selected and how they end up as part of the marketing plan. First it is important to convert the business tasks to business objectives.

Business and marketing objectives must be SMART: Specific, Measurable, Agreed, Reasonable and Timebound. Check each objective, whether it is a business, marketing or promotional objective, as you write it to see that it meets each of the SMART criteria.

Illustrative business objectives

It is useful here to look at an example. Suppose you are a director of a small sports equipment business. You have business tasks that are to grow the business, modernize, update, relocate and you feel the need to tackle the new media – competitors are doing so; finally, you want to have a better position in the sports sector than your nearest competitor. The SMART business objectives, in order of priority, for a company in sports/leisure might be to:

- sell the existing range of products, with the revamped basic product, to achieve the increased target sales (a figure in £s is included here) within the calendar year. (This objective effectively defines the market share your firm is going for);
- move the headquarters offices and three regional sales offices to new premises in the summer lay-off (no direct marketing implications here, but plenty of indirect ones!);
- grow the customer base by 10 per cent, that is 40 new long-term customers by the end of the year;
- establish the new media, with interactive TV and Web site operating in the next six months;
- achieve a profile at the end of the year that places the perception and image of this firm and its products above those of your direct competitor (list of attributes, benefits, features to be agreed by end January);
- upgrade the machinery in the B production shop to retain labour costs while increasing production by 10 per cent (no marketing impact unless the new machinery is delayed in introduction and there is no product to sell!);
- introduce a new financial accounting software package to be in operation at the start of the financial year (again no marketing implication here – but software glitches occur and it may affect invoices and sales and. . .);
- take a stand at the main relevant sport exhibition;
- raise the awareness to 80 per cent by the end of the year, among those that play, watch or train in the sport, of the purpose of your business and the concept – products/services – it provides.

Not all the business objectives affect marketing. But from these business objectives you can then draw up marketing objectives, which might be:

- To achieve the sales targets set (figure in £s) including sales of one re-launched product in the year ahead.
- To increase consumer and customer awareness and understanding of the products and their purpose so that unprompted recall is higher than for your competitor's products at the end of the year.
- To relaunch the product at the main exhibition.
- To use the new media – Internet and interactive TV – within six months.
- To grow the customer database by 10 per cent (this gives a precise number of customers) with new customers matching your existing long-term customer profile (which you have researched!)
- To maintain the company brand values.

Clearly sales promotions are likely to play a major part in all the objectives except the last. Not all marketing objectives are best met by sales promotional solutions. It may be that advertising is the answer or that there is a fundamental problem with the brand's price, distribution or physical characteristics. No promotion will solve that. However, there are various tasks that are particularly suited to promotional solutions.

Some promotional activities may be inherited and should be questioned. A spring promotion may be run simply because there has always been a spring promotion. This may well be a waste of time and money.

A clearly defined marketing objective is the justification for spending time and money on promotional activity, or any marketing activity for that matter. It is often said that advertising brings the horse to water and sales promotion makes it drink. Consumers may be predisposed to buy a whole range of products and services now or in the future:

> *Sales promotion focuses their attention on a particular product, at a particular time, in a particular place and provides the incentive to buy at that moment.*

Sales promotions can be planned for implementation at a specific time, but they can also be considered and introduced as contingencies. Problems and opportunities inevitably arise during the year and to keep a business or marketing objective in place you may need to take additional action. Among the problems may be competitors taking business from you, stocks being slow to move, distribution being lost, sales being sluggish or an expectation that any of these may happen in the near future. Opportunities also come in a variety of forms: to take market share and volume from a competitor, to build awareness in a particular target market, to back up new distribution, to support other marketing activity at point of sale, to build on trial gains. International events, such as those of 11 September 2001, may change customers' interest in buying.

Every sales promotion must start by being related to one or more marketing objectives that will be achieved by their implementation. Time spent in thinking through the objectives, and relating them to your overall marketing strategy, is never wasted. Once the marketing objectives have been determined, how are they to be achieved? Through use on their own or in combinations of the marketing tools available to you in what is known as the 'promotional mix'.

THE PROMOTIONAL MIX

How does sales promotion fit with the rest of the communications mix? The promotional mix is generally divided into four different tools:

1. *advertising:* paid-for space and time in broadcast, print media or the new media (Web sites, interactive TV, SMS) and other paid-for communications. Do not forget outdoor advertising, which includes ambient and transport media in addition to posters (and balloons);
2. *sales promotion:* incentives and offers that encourage people to behave in a particular way at a particular time and place, usually delivered by one of the other three tools;
3. *publicity:* information and opinion about your products or services carried by third parties;
4. *direct marketing:* personal presentation to customers or prospects to which they can respond directly through filling in coupons, posting tip-ons, contacting call centres, e-mails, etc. The new media – interactive TV, text messaging and e-mails – are a part of direct marketing. Personal selling is now a part of direct marketing called 'field marketing', where a personal presentation of your products or services is made to customers, prospects or intermediaries carried out through a shop, a Web site or exhibitions, demonstrations, personal selling at customer premises and through merchandising. (Note that field marketing used to be considered separately from direct marketing but is now a part of it.)

This division of communications tools within the promotional mix helps in a number of ways. It gives a rough and ready definition of what each marketing tool is able to contribute to the mix, and helps companies to decide which will be most useful in achieving particular marketing objectives. For example, an industrial company is likely to put most emphasis on direct marketing. A company requiring short-term sales may put a priority on sales promotion. A company with a startling new product may go for publicity as its best bet. It also helps companies work out the balance between the different tools. Most of the time, there isn't one tool alone that will do the job, and a balance is needed between all four. This is why it is called 'integrated marketing'.

The logic of this way of thinking becomes clear when you look at how promotional offers are communicated. They invariably use one or more of the other communications tools. It is rare to see a piece of direct mail without an incentive for an early reply. It is rare for companies not to try to achieve media coverage, that is publicity, of their promotions. It is increasingly common for promotions to be featured in advertising. Hybrid communications – combining sales promotion with advertising, direct mail, publicity and personal selling – are not the exception but the rule.

A sales promotional offer does not cease to be a sales promotional offer because you use advertising, publicity, personal selling and direct marketing to get it across to your target market. Does that mean, though, that they are all promotions and nothing else? Of course not: they are promotions-in-advertising, promotions-in-publicity and so on.

Sales promotion is particularly helpful when your firm is making short-term changes to one or more parts of the whole marketing mix – that is, to the six Cs – and communicating that to customers. Examples are when a different-coloured Smartie is included in the pack for a short time, or KitKat is produced in a mint flavour (a change in the concept). It can alter the cost to the customer, for instance when a lager brand is sold as '33 per cent extra free' or when a product is sold with a 10p off flash. It can announce a change in convenience, for example when Guinness is sold at summer fêtes, well away from its normal licensed trade outlets – all in the interests of influencing behaviour now. If you book a flight on Easyjet on the Internet you receive an instant discount which may have been the subject of newspaper publicity or an advertisement or a direct mailshot driving the customer to the Web.

For completeness, the selection of the appropriate parts of the promotional mix has a further dimension: the selection of the appropriate communication channels. For example, advertising may be selected from the promotional mix and the press selected over TV, with newspapers preferred over magazines and the broadsheets selected over the 'red-tops', and *The Guardian* and *The Independent* finally chosen. These two papers would then be entered into the channel plan.

This way of thinking about the promotional mix does reflect the way sales promotion should be used. At last it does justice to the role sales promotion plays in creating and building customer relationships and putting across all the six Cs. At last marketing books are paying attention to sales promotion and one day it will equal the interest and understanding of the people who have been doing the job for real for years. The key point about sales promotion is that it can be effective in every part of the promotional mix and can be used for every element of the marketing mix. If used well it can spice up any element of the six Cs alongside any promotional tool.

VALUE AND PRICE

The Institute of Sales Promotion – the body that brings together all the major sales promotion practitioners in the UK – gives this definition:

> *Sales promotion is a range of tactical marketing techniques designed within a strategic framework to add value to a product or service in order to achieve specific sales and marketing objectives.*

The key phrase is 'add value'. 'Value promotions' essentially give an extra benefit. Ways to add value are to offer extra features, such as a free mail-in item, a chance to win a prize, a special container or some other benefit over and above the normal product offering. It often has a positive impact on brand value.

There are sales promotions that cut price, often called a 'price promotion'. Such promotions offer the concept at a reduced price, with a favourable finance deal, on a buy-now, pay-later basis, or with a coupon against the present or future purchase. In doing so, there can be a negative impact on brand value – particularly if it is a 'me too' price offer. Price promotions can seriously undermine the added value that years of advertising have built up. A study has shown that most price promotions, though helping in the short term, end up lowering the price people are prepared to pay for brands. Many advertisers believe that a price promotion is a short-term fix that detracts from long-term brand building. On the plus side a price promotion can put your product in the hands of customers to experience. This can affect behaviour positively and of course during that time they are not using a competitor product.

Value promotions include:

- free draws;
- mail-in premiums;
- container promotions;
- competitions.

Price promotions include:

- money-off coupons;
- pence-off flashes;
- buy one, get one free;
- extra-fill packs.

There is some doubt over where some promotions lie: for example, some believe extra-fill packs ('33 per cent extra free') belong in the 'value', not the 'price' category. If you want to put them there, you will be in good company – but remember that they can reduce the price people are prepared to pay for the standard size, and that can come to the same thing as a price cut.

The logic of value promotions is clear to see. There is evidence that these not only contribute to short-term sales, but to long-term brand value. The 'Hayfever Survival' campaign (Case study 6) is an excellent example. The case for price promotions is more difficult, and there are criticisms made by eminent industry people.

Why do companies use promotions that can undermine brand value? The reason is competition. For most of the post-war period, the detergent manufacturers Procter & Gamble and Lever Brothers have been locked in a titanic battle. Their leading brands have competed for performance superiority, communicated by single-minded product-performance advertising. The classic 'side by side' comparisons of clothes washed in Daz against those washed in another powder were once considered a definitive form of TV advertising. Product innovation has been far-reaching and relentless.

These two giants have also spent massively on price promotion. In the early 1960s, 95 per cent of packs of Procter & Gamble and Lever Brothers' detergents carried a price promotion offer of one kind or another – from a pence off flash to a discount off next purchase. The situation was mad – and known to be mad. One day it stopped: Daz launched a 'near-pack' premium promotion involving plastic flowers (Case study 33). Millions of families collected plastic roses from Daz in the following years. By the late 1970s, however, the majority of detergent packs once again featured pence off flashes and coupons. Retailers have also veered between price and value promotions. Case study 28 looks at 20 years of Tesco's promotional activity, which has swung between the two.

Sometimes price promotions can be catastrophic for the company concerned. In 1996, the electrical retailer Comet made an offer for its competitor, NorWeb. NorWeb held out for more, which was refused, and then began an extensive campaign of 0 per cent finance offers (see Chapter 12 for details of how these work). Comet decided not to match them. Instead, whenever customers asked about finance, it directed them to NorWeb. Comet's margins went up, and NorWeb was crippled by the cost of its promotion. Soon afterwards, Comet was able to buy NorWeb at a lower price than it had offered before.

What do these stories tell us? Price promotions can drag a company or a whole industry into penury. However, they are not the cause of penury. Rather, they are the symptom of a competition that is so intense that it lays hold of every tool at its disposal – even if some of them are self-destructive. Price promotions are not the ideal way of competing. They are sometimes unavoidable in the marketplace. It makes it even more important to understand how they work, and the circumstances in which they can be less rather than more destructive.

One of the things to watch is the evidence from opinion polls that people prefer price cuts to any other form of promotion. Sometimes companies make use of this in their advertising. During the spate of petrol promotions in 1986–87, Jet ran a series of poster ads with the slogan '98 per cent of motorists prefer cheaper petrol'. Not for us, they were saying, all those tacky gimmicks; we just offer lower prices. Shell meanwhile achieved huge gains in market share with its 'Make money' promotion. People may say they prefer cheaper petrol (attitude), but they often buy more expensive petrol supported by promotional offers (behaviour). In 1997, Shell and Esso were taking two very different approaches to this – one with a value promotion, the other with a price promotion (Case study 26). It's interesting to note that Jet was also actively engaged in value promotions, winning a European sales promotion award for its non-price collector promotion.

Keeping the distinction between price and value promotions clearly in mind is essential to making sense of the subject. The core of sales promotion is the attempt to influence behaviour here and now, and these are the two ways you can do it. It may contribute to a change in attitude, but that is not its primary task. A definition you may like to consider would run like this:

sales promotion is a range of price and value techniques designed within a strategic framework to achieve specific objectives by changing any part of the marketing mix, normally for a defined time period.

MARKETING TACTICS AND STRATEGIES

Tactics

Sales promotion has often been seen as one of the short-term, tactical weapons available to businesses. As such, it has enormous strengths, but there is a real dilemma. Change the marketing mix too often, and the brand loses its identity. Change it too little, and more flexible competitors can overtake you. Sales promotion is a tool that cuts across all the components of the brand. That is why the balance of tactics and strategy is so important in using sales promotion effectively.

Business success is always an interplay between short term and long term, tactical and strategic. Companies succeed by thinking about tomorrow, but they fail if, in so doing, they forget about today; the reverse is also true. The best strategy is always adaptive.

Sales promotion shares with direct marketing the benefit that it can achieve short-term effects, that campaigns can be conceived and implemented in a matter of days, and that the result can be seen in a matter of weeks. As such, sales promotion fits well with a 'just-in-time' approach to business, which is already familiar in manufacturing stock control and delivery cycles.

Taking a tactical approach to sales promotion means having up your sleeve a number of promotional concepts that can be put into effect as and when they are called for. Large manufacturing companies approach this by issuing their sales force with a range of promotions in concept form that can be put into effect with particular retailers whenever the sales situation demands. It also means having the imagination, speed and resourcefulness to react quickly to competitive pressure and to seize short-term market opportunities. These are tactics at their best, but does that mean sales promotion is not strategic?

Strategies

Any business activity benefits from being planned in a strategic manner. Strategy, as John Kay points out, is not another word for 'important'. It is about identifying the firm's distinctive capabilities, and translating them into competitive advantage in the relationships the firm has with its customers and suppliers. It's about what you – and only you – do best.

Sales promotion is strategic if it enhances the firm's distinctive capabilities, increases its competitive advantages and builds its long-term relationships. It is the reverse if it undermines them. That can easily happen in sales promotion. A cut-price offer on a prestige brand, a promotion that is badly administered and leaves customers feeling aggrieved, an offer that promises more than it delivers – all these can undermine long-term relationships. A feeble 'me too' offer copied from a competitor can undermine distinctive positioning.

Frequently, the characteristics of a good tactical promotion are the characteristics of a good strategic promotion. A good promotion can be both tactical and strategic: ('Hayfever Survival', Case study 6, is an example). A bad one can be both bad tactics and bad strategy (Hoover's free flights promotion, Case study 24, is an example of this).

There are several reasons for taking a strategic approach to planning sales promotions. It enables one offer to build on the previous one, and to establish a continuity of communication. This makes it possible to communicate long-term psychological values, making promotions work harder. It can produce considerable savings in time and money, and can speed up response times. Strategic planning also enables promotional offers to be fully integrated into the other activities in the marketing programme.

Sadly, even the largest companies do not always do this. This is often because responsibility for sales promotion is pushed down to junior staff, whose time horizons are shorter, who change jobs more frequently and who have not been briefed properly on strategic issues. This is a pity: it makes promotions less effective, and does not reflect the importance of sales promotion in business today. The remedy lies in the hands of senior management. Those charged with responsibility for sales promotion need to understand the relationships they are dealing with.

There are five things you should do in order to establish a strategic approach to sales promotion:

1. understand the strategic framework in terms of competitive advantage and positioning that should underpin every sales promotion, as any other marketing activity;
2. establish guidelines for each product or service, determining the style of sales promotion that will be appropriate to it – this is the same for all marketing activities;
3. ensure that sales promotions are handled or overseen by a sufficiently senior executive so that they are conceived, integrated and implemented professionally;
4. insist that sales promotions are researched and evaluated through marketing accountability measurement in a way that enables you to assess their performance, and compare it to other types of marketing expenditure;
5. plan and budget for your use of sales promotion over the year ahead so that the promotions become integral to your marketing effort and alongside other marketing activities.

Most of this book details how to run promotions one by one. These are the building blocks for strategic promotional planning. It is well worth taking a look at the promotions your company has run over a longish period – say five years – and asking how they have contributed to its long-term differential advantage. Were they good tactics and good strategy? That is the goal to search for.

THE MARKETING PLAN

The promotional mix you select is your marketing plan. You get there by going through a business process of preparing business objectives first. Once objectives are clear then you can draw out marketing objectives and look at all the options in the promotional mix (a very large list) before picking those that you believe suit you and will achieve your objectives. The picking process (selection of the communication tools alongside communication channel planning) is helped by using a customer perspective (both existing customers and prospects) at all times and thinking throughout of the marketing mix, the six Cs, your customers' buying process and their influencers, and your brand.

Overcome the easy-life tendency

The process of drawing up a marketing plan is a useful discipline. As with inherited sales promotions, if you find activities that do not help in achieving your objectives, then discard them. They are often put in because someone found it too easy to repeat last time's plan – beware the lazy approach. A Willott Kingston Smith (WKS) survey found marketers relied too much on agencies to decide for them which promotional tools and channels to use. The consequence is that the promotional mix and the channels selected change little year on year. If an advertising agency is the sole supplier, beware: a number of agencies are traditionalists who have always made their money from press, poster and TV advertising. Their creative people do not have publicity, sales promotion, direct marketing or Web sites 'on their radar' and unless you insist on all parts of the promotional mix being considered, you may not really get a broad view. The WKS survey found that most agencies only pay lip service to communication channel planning. The way to overcome this is to insist on it or change to a newer agency that does.

The WKS survey found a media buyer view that most marketers are incapable of any accountability. Do not be one of them. It is essential to measure the success of achievement of the final list you select for your plan. Allocate responsibility for each activity and objective. With the person responsible for each marketing activity, define success, then set a key performance indicator (KPI) for their marketing activity. Record the KPI and then measure it. The results indicate the success or failure of the marketing activities to allow you to make any necessary changes next time – and/or allow you to select new marketing personnel! (This is covered in detail in another Kogan Page book, *Value for Money Marketing*, Mullin (2001).)

Planning is essential to achieve focus and control cost. It is a human weakness to write plans then leave them in some filing cabinet. A very short document or table is all that is required and if it is on display it will trigger the conscience. It is all too easy to forget what you originally set out to do. A plan allows you to allocate priorities in case a round of cost-cutting means a number of activities fall by the way. It will also provide a record of what you cut and how that affected the outcome when the day of reckoning comes. Equally if the plan succeeds and the KPI is achieved you can praise and celebrate. You also have real, quantified experience for next time.

CASE STUDIES

There are not many case studies around showing integrated marketing at work and the part sales promotion plays within it. The example of the launch of the Nissan Tino along with a new film 'Shrek' is one. It is also an example of a joint promotion. The second case study is about to be launched as this book goes to press and is another example of integrated marketing.

CASE STUDY 1. INTEGRATED MARKETING AT NISSAN

Tequila Manchester worked closely with Dream Works and Nissan on a joint promotion to launch the latest campaign for Nissan in conjunction with the film, 'Shrek'. The promotion was planned by Manning Gottleib Media to deliver quality prospects for the new Tino through response-based communication. They developed a plan to work in line with the cinema experience to target both parents and children – who are now well known to be influencers in family car choice. The promotion filled the whole cinema environment from foyer to screens, exciting and involving the family audience most relevant to Nissan Tino. To do this, the agency executed imaginative creative material combining the car and the Shrek character. This was produced in the form of cinema postcards, cinema posters, and six-foot high cinema 'standees', and used also at various events. The promotion was accompanied by effective data-collection opportunities through postcards that requested data on car replacement details and personal addresses. The promotion managed to capture the essence of both the Nissan Tino and Shrek, with involving and fun creative executions – thereby providing a credible link between the car and an animated film. It was judged highly successful by Nissan.

Can you identify the different promotional tools employed?

CASE STUDY 2. INTEGRATED MARKETING: SHARK

Tequila London is about to launch a high-energy drink, new to the UK, with a dramatic, fully integrated campaign. This is a great challenge for the agency as it is responsible for establishing not only a brand identity but also the means by which it is communicated and sampled to its target market.

The energy drink market has been dominated by one name in the UK – Red Bull. Successive rival launches have failed to make any kind of credible challenge and remain more or less gathering dust on shelves. Why? To reverse this trend there is really only one strategy – impactful, daring advertising that gets talked about. Ideally, with a target age group consisting of 16–21-year-olds, the most potent work will always be irreverent, sexy and provocative. The campaign portrays the drink, Shark, as a social facilitator, playing on a light-hearted parallel between encounters with a shark and a human. In a series of provocative and graphic images, various parts of the body are shown with the telltale signs (love bites, etc) of a human encounter, with the strap line: 'Bring out the beast'.

Shark was launched to the trade at the Birmingham Food & Drink Expo in March 2002. The multi-million pound integrated campaign commenced with heavyweight outdoor activity in Birmingham, targeting both trade and consumers, using 48-sheets and bus sides. The core activity, however, will focus on London from May 2002 onwards. This will include a high-profile TV campaign with spots directed by top director Philip Stoltz. This illustrates the breadth of the approach adopted for this brand launch. The agency is also responsible for product sampling, both in London and key coastal regions, POS material, sales promotion activity, as well as ongoing communications to the trade.

The challenge is to ensure this new product will stand out in a fiercely competitive and crowded market. Offering a truly integrated approach allows a dedicated focus on the key values attributed to the product at every stage of the campaign.

Can you identify the different promotional tools employed?
What is the benefit of an integrated marketing campaign?
What sales promotions might you apply?

SUMMARY

A sales promotion is the culmination of a process. The process starts with the vision of the owners of a business or the leaders of an organization.

Typically for any year that vision is converted into SMART business objectives, of which some affect marketing directly and some affect marketing indirectly; there are a few that have little effect.

SMART marketing objectives can be derived from the business objectives. After considering the alternative marketing activities, some bundled as 'campaigns', choose a 'marketing mix' to achieve the marketing objectives all set down in a marketing plan. Each marketing activity has a determinant of success set with a key performance indicator chosen to measure that success and achievement.

Within some of the marketing campaigns on marketing activities are sales promotion. For each sales prromotion is set a promotional objective from which a promotional brief is prepared. Sales promotions can be either value or price promotions normally effective over a limited period. They are used to add both fun and provide real and clearly perceived benefit to customers. Planning for sales promotions as a strategy and recording their effectiveness over time will reduce the risk of failure and give a business or organization a lead over competitors. Sales promotions can be excellent brand enhancers.

3

What Sales Promotions Can Do

THE 10 CORE PROMOTIONAL OBJECTIVES

There are 10 core promotional objectives that sales promotion typically addresses:

1. increasing volume;
2. increasing trial;
3. increasing repeat purchase;
4. increasing loyalty;
5. widening usage;
6. creating interest;
7. creating awareness;
8. deflecting attention from price;
9. gaining intermediary support;
10. discriminating among users.

1. Increasing volume

The volume of product or service that you sell is, in the long run, dependent on a range of fundamental marketing factors such as quality, cost, distribution and value – defined in customer terms as the marketing mix – your total offer to the customer. Promotions geared to increasing volume can never overcome deep-seated weaknesses, but they can be of considerable value in meeting short-term and tactical business needs.

Companies may need to increase volume in the short term for a variety of reasons: to shift stock of an old model prior to a new introduction; to reduce inventories prior to their financial year end; to increase stockholding by retailers prior to the introduction of a competitor's product, and to lift production on to a new and higher level.

Volume-generating promotions invariably bring in the marginal buyers, those who only buy when a product or service is 'on offer'. These buyers tend to be regarded by many companies with the distaste felt for the morally promiscuous, but they do not form an exclusive group. The more people buy of a particular product category, the more brands within it they tend to buy. We are all promiscuous purchasers to some extent. A volume promotion can bring in marginal buyers to an improved product or service who may well stay with you thereafter.

Almost any promotion that provides an incentive to buy will help to increase volume. Price promotions are often most effective in the short term. They can be aimed at trialists, regular users or new markets; they can put the emphasis on intermediaries or on the final customer; and they can use a very wide range of the offers described in this book. What must be provided is a real and genuine incentive: a low-budget self-liquidator may massage consciences, but it will do nothing to shift volume. Two case studies in this book are examples of non-price volume promotions: Maxwell House (Case study 3) and Faber & Faber (Case study 42).

The variety of techniques available to increase volume carries its own weakness. It is better to be specific about where you expect to find the extra volume. This means linking the increased volume objective with one of the other objectives listed below.

2. Increasing trial

A major source of extra volume is those who have not used your product or service before or not used it for a long time. In the case of retailers, they would be people who have not visited your premises before. Increased trial is also a self-standing objective that is fundamental to the growth of any business.

Potential trialists have, by definition, no personal experience of your product or service. They may be using one of your competitor's products or services or none at all in your category. A number of offers are particularly effective in gaining increased trial:

- providing a free sample or a trial coupon so that people can try out your product or service;
- providing an additional benefit so that your product or service seems superior to others on the market;

- providing short-term financial benefits, such as good credit rates, so that it seems better value than others;
- doing something different and imaginative, such as an open day or special event, that lifts it out of the general run.

Among the examples of trial promotions in this book are 'Bovril's Bang!', Bovril's sampling programme (Case study 4), and the 'Tango Bash' (Case study 21). These both focused on giving reasons for people new to (or lapsed from) the brand to try. Offers such as free extra product or those that require the purchase of large quantities of your product or service are unlikely to attract potential trialists. They will not, after all, want to buy it in volume until they know they like it.

3. Increasing repeat purchase

Repeat purchase promotions overlap considerably with volume promotions as existing customers are most likely to be prepared to bring forward their regular purchases and buy in bulk. Repeat purchase promotions are also effective in achieving other marketing objectives, such as spoiling the launch of a competitive product and getting your customers into the habit of using your product to the exclusion of others. This can be particularly important in markets such as the pub trade and frequently purchased confectionery products where people habitually use a range of different brands, chopping and changing between them from day to day (a pattern known as 'repertoire purchasing').

Here are some of the offers that are particularly effective in increasing repeat purchase:

- coupons on the product giving discounts off the next purchase;
- specific incentives for multiple purchase – for example, 'buy three, get one free';
- collector promotions, such as collecting 10 tokens and sending for free merchandise or a cash refund.

Maxwell House (Case study 3) and Gale's Honey (Case study 29) are both imaginative examples of promotions that target the need to increase repeat purchase. Promotions that are unlikely to be appropriate for increasing repeat purchase include door-to-door coupon drops and straight pence-off flashes. They simply give the regular purchaser a discount without requiring any multiple purchase to take place. This is very nice for the purchasers, but of no use to the promoter.

4. Increasing loyalty

Loyalty to a product or service is a much more subjective and personal quality than repeat purchase. It is possible to buy something on a regular basis
because it is the cheapest and best, without feeling any loyalty towards it.
Loyalty keeps you buying when (perhaps temporarily) it ceases to be the
cheapest and the best.

An example of loyalty occurred in the early 1980s, when Ford replaced
the Cortina with the Sierra. The early Sierras suffered from a number of
teething troubles, and although Ford did lose market share to Vauxhall's
Cavalier, its extent was limited by Ford's high level of loyalty among
motorists and fleet buyers. To paraphrase Winston Churchill: anyone can
support you when you are right, friends are there to support you when you
are wrong.

Most supermarkets in the UK have adopted loyalty promotions. They
are designed to achieve a high level of personal identification and involvement with a company's product or service beyond the collection of points.
They tend to be long running and to become integral to the way purchasers
think about the product or service. There are a number of types of promotion
that work well in building loyalty:

- long-term collector promotions – where a wide range of merchandise
  branded with the product or service can be collected;
- clubs that people can join, and which offer a range of special benefits;
  these are particularly effective for children's products;
- factory visits, road shows and other direct-contact promotions, which
  bring purchasers into personal contact with the people behind the
  product or service.

A good example of a loyalty promotion is Shell's Smart card (Case study
26); the two 'Music for Schools' promotions run by Jacob's Club and the
Co-op (Case study 8) are also relevant. In their different ways, they link
closely to the interests of their consumers.

Immediate cash discounts to those who are not members of the scheme
have no place in loyalty promotions. Their objective is to supersede
immediate cash considerations by appealing to longer-term benefits. This
is one of the major ways in which value promotions can contribute to long-
term brand value.

5. Widening usage

Very often a product or service will be widely used in only one of the many
possible ways it could be used. For example, most households buy honey,
very infrequently, to use as a spread. A minority of households use it in great
quantity as a cooking ingredient. Telling people how to use honey in cooking
is therefore an important objective for honey processors.

Sometimes a company will have to widen the usage of a product or service because its original use is fast disappearing. The transatlantic shipping companies had to do this when people stopped seeing ships as a mode of travel, and had to be persuaded to start perceiving them as a form of holiday. Sales promotions can be very effective in widening the usage of a product or service in a number of ways:

- by physically linking the product or service with something else already in the new usage area: for example, issuing trial samples with another product;
- by offering books or pamphlets that are of value in themselves and explain new ways to use the product or service: for example, a 'cooking with honey' cookbook;
- by creating a non-physical link with something else already in the new usage area, via coupons or joint promotions with another company: for example, coupons from a travel agent for winter ski gear.

Widening usage will almost always be achieved by a combination of promotional tools, including advertising and publicity. There is often huge consumer resistance to overcome – for example, to the idea that you should put Mars bars in the fridge or drink sherry with a mixer. The Lee & Perrins promotion for Worcestershire Sauce (Case study 30) is a good example of extending usage of a very distinctive product.

Pence off or other cash-related promotions will not help at all in this. The right kind of value promotion can encourage purchasers to make the leap and try out the new usage of your product or service. Only when they've done that will they be convinced that what you have said in your advertising is true.

6. Creating interest

This can seem a very woolly objective, and is often avoided in favour of something that seems more specific, such as 'increasing volume'. Many consumer markets are mature and offer limited scope for product differentiation. Providing a reason to buy one product rather than another can be as simple as creating interest and excitement.

It is no accident that our ancestors punctuated the year with a series of festivals, fairs and holy days. Life becomes very boring if it proceeds at a regular, uninterrupted pace. Purchasing products and services is exactly the same. Out of sheer boredom, purchasers can decide to buy something else or go somewhere else. Creating interest in your product or service by means of sales promotion is a way of keeping purchasers with you. It is a matter of ringing the changes, having something fresh to offer, and keeping interest and enthusiasm on the boil.

The principle has long been understood by people who run successful businesses. One of Jesse Boot's colleagues recalled the early days of what became the Boots chemists chain in the 1880s: 'Always, Mr Boot had some-thing striking, something to make people talk about Boots.' Richard Branson of Virgin has similarly had people talking about his companies as a result of a constant stream of striking innovations, stunts, offers and promotions.

Value promotions that create interest are characterized above all by their humour, inventiveness, topicality and style. Examples include:

- being the first to offer a new product or service as a promotional premium;
- linking up with a celebrity or relevant charity;
- finding a totally new way to do something that people enjoy doing.

British Airways' offer of tickets on Concorde in spring 1997 achieved a massive 30 million responses. Older examples include the treasure hunt for a buried hare featured in the book *Masquerade* and later copied (with disastrous results) by Cadbury's Creme Eggs; the telephone Trivial Pursuit game run by Heineken lager; and the enormously successful 'tiger in your tank' campaign by Esso in the 1960s, which had millions of cars driving around with a tiger tail hanging from their petrol cap. Case studies in this book that share these qualities are the promotions by solicitors Eversheds (Case study 14) and Smirnoff (Case study 36).

7. Creating awareness

For new or relaunched products, creating awareness is a key objective. This is a different challenge to that faced by mature brands, where the aim is to maintain interest. It is often assumed that creating awareness is a job for media advertising. Sales promotion, it is said, should restrict itself to nuts and bolts matters such as shifting volume and gaining trial. In fact, there are a number of sales promotions that are very effective at making people aware of products:

- joint promotions with another product or service that is already well known in a particular market;
- link-ups with charities or voluntary groups that have a relevant image;
- the production of books or educational materials for schools and the general public.

Generating awareness is a wholly legitimate business objective, particularly in industries where purchases are infrequent, and for new brands. Major brands – for example, The Body Shop, Haagen-Dazs and Swatch watches – were launched and developed largely through promotional activity. In the case of The Body Shop, it included the active engagement of customers in campaigning against animal testing. Haagen-Dazs used placements in leading restaurants and selective arts sponsorship. Swatch hung giant watches from buildings and early on built a customer club. The 'Tango Bash' (Case study 21) is also an example of this kind of promotion. The ill-fated ITV Digital offered a monkey doll to those who subscribed – probably now a highly valued collectors' item – that increased awareness significantly.

Crucial to such ideas is the understanding that people are selective in the attention they pay to advertising. There are more than 9,500 brands in the UK that advertise enough for their advertising to be recorded by MEAL. How many can you name? Most people run out of names after a few hundred. Promotional activity can cut through this selective attention.

8. Deflecting attention from price

An obsession with price on the part of your customers is dangerous. It can readily lead to price wars, which have a destructive effect on company profitability. Price wars are a form of mutual masochism into which many industries fall from time to time until, weary and impoverished, they find more sensible ways to compete with each other.

The purpose of a great deal of advertising is to replace price considerations with a focus on features such as quality, brand identity, performance and loyalty. That way companies can both compete effectively and achieve attractive margins.

Both price and value promotions are part of the armoury companies have at their disposal to do this. The key is to offer benefits that justify a higher price and cost less than an equivalent price cut. If your product is priced at 10p more than your competitor's and that differential cannot be justified on intrinsic grounds, you can either discount by 10p to achieve price parity or offer an extra benefit that costs you 9p or less and looks at least as attractive.

A very wide range of sales promotional offers can achieve this objective. Among the main ones are:

- variations on price cuts, ranging from 'pence off next purchase' and 'buy three, get one free' to cash-back or cash share-out offers, that appear more valuable than a straight price cut;
- making price comparisons less direct, by offering extra-fill packs, short-term multi-packs, joint packs, or part of the product or service free, for example;
- long-term collector promotions, such as Shell's Smart card promotion (Case study 26) or Green Shield stamps (Case study 28), which can seem more interesting than price cuts. Air Miles do the same.

SMP's promotion for Gale's Honey (Case study 29) is a good example of deflecting attention away from the premium price of branded honey. It is a constant challenge for manufacturers of brands in markets in which retailers' own-label products have taken a significant share. Part of the success of

Kleenex Facial Tissues in the last 10 years has been the extent to which its active promotional campaigns have limited the market share of cheaper own-label tissues (Case study 6).

9. Gaining intermediary support

Some products and services rely very heavily on the support of wholesalers, distributors, agents, retailers and other intermediaries. Others, sold directly to the end-user, rely less heavily on, but still benefit from, the support and recommendation of other businesses. And every business benefits from word-of-mouth recommendation from one satisfied customer to another.

All these people can be regarded as intermediaries. Gaining their support ranges from being absolutely critical to simply important, and there are a number of sales promotion techniques that businesses can use to this end. Among the key ones are:

- specific programmes directed at wholesalers, retailers, agents and distributors to gain distribution, display and cooperative advertising;
- 'member get member' schemes, which reward customers for introducing new people to you: the Institute of Directors does this;
- promotional events aimed at the media and other decision making influencers.

Gaining display is a central objective for promotions run by manufacturers who sell via retailers, wholesalers, distributors or other intermediaries. It is often the display that results in extra sales, but the promotion that secured the display in the first place.

Display can take many forms: extra shelf space, gondola end (the end of a shelving rack), a window bill, the display of door stickers, the use of point-of-sale material, the presence of leaflets, the installation of a dumpbin or special display rack. It is all about achieving extra prominence for your product or service.

A number of promotional offers are effective in achieving display:

- incentives directed at store managers and sales assistants. The same applies to free offers targeted at those who make the orders such as direct ordering of stationery items, which effectively offer a personal gift to the person placing the order;
- price offers that enhance the margin to the intermediary;
- the production of attractive, compelling offers of every kind that the intermediary believes will provide them with an advantage – tailor-made promotions, which run only in one store group, are particularly effective.

There is a close relationship between trade and consumer promotion in the retail trade. If a promotion succeeds with the trade, but lacks a strong consumer element, it may still succeed with the consumer – simply because of the display and volume support of the retailer. However, the reverse is not true: a promotion with a strong consumer element that does not appeal to the trade is unlikely to succeed with either.

Examples of effective promotions to intermediaries include Zantac 75 (Case study 7) and the Electrolux campaign for the X8 (Case study 35).

10. Discriminating among users

A large number of businesses, such as hotels, airlines, train companies and leisure facilities, face three unavoidable market factors. They have a high percentage of fixed costs in providing the service, which do not vary significantly with the number of people using it. Usage varies considerably from time to time. Also, different people are prepared to pay different amounts for the service and accept different levels of restriction. This has been particularly true of air travel.

This last factor enables businesses to manage fluctuations in demand. The price paid for an airline ticket varies depending on the time and day of the flight, the degree of flexibility allowed, how long in advance the ticket was booked, the type of seat purchased, the purchaser's participation in a loyalty scheme and the outlet where it was booked. The objective that airlines and similar businesses share is to maximize the revenue per seat – and that means avoiding giving better terms to those who do not need them at the same time as giving the optimum terms to those who do.

For these businesses, sales promotional thinking is at the heart of marketing strategy, and they use a number of mechanisms:

- customers who are motivated by price are self-selected – they book early or via particular outlets and so on – while those who are less motivated by price do not bother with these aspects;
- the difference between business and leisure travel is marked by requirements to spend a Saturday night away to qualify for leisure pricing; business users are, in turn, given special discounts on leisure flights;
- particular groups are given additional benefits not available to others – for example, families and the retired can buy train tickets at a price not available to a group of adults travelling together.

Pursued to its logical conclusion, discriminating among users allows companies to develop particular packages of product, price, distribution and promotion for different categories of user. The major challenge is to keep the boundaries between them clear, so that those prepared to pay higher prices do not take advantage of lower prices. This in turn means that offers are often deliberately short-term, focusing the benefits on those most motivated to take advantage of them.

CASE STUDIES

Three case studies illustrate the central points made in this chapter about relationships, behaviour and the capacity of sales promotion to change every other part of the marketing mix.

CASE STUDY 3. MAXWELL HOUSE

Maxwell House operates in the highly competitive instant coffee market, dominated by Nestlé's Nescafé. It was relaunched in 1992 with an improved product formulation, a blue packaging theme, the proposition of 'mountain-grown taste' and TV advertising featuring the Maxwell House hot air balloon. However, the brand still faced the pressures that face number two brands generally. How was it to persuade repertoire purchasers (those who buy Nescafé and other brands from time to time) to buy Maxwell House? And how was it to persuade existing users to buy the brand more often?

Triangle Communications' answer was a major promotional event that took place on-pack, on TV and in events round the country. Its title was 'Out of the blue'. The basic mechanic was a free draw. Consumers were invited to win £500,000 of cash prizes by entering via on-pack coupons or 'plain paper' (which means those who had not bought the product could enter by writing in on a piece of paper). Noel Edmonds phoned 100 winners 'out of the blue' from the Maxwell House hot air balloon. The phone calls were featured on TV ads as a live dialogue, giving viewers the responses of winners to hearing they had won cash prizes of £2,000 to £10,000. Meanwhile, the balloon made a series of visits to events around the country, creating a direct link between brand, balloon and offer.

The novelty of the delivery of the free draw created extensive PR coverage: 500,000 entries were received, the brand achieved its highest market share for six years, and in the promotional period its share was 50 per cent more than it had been the previous month.

This was a free draw on a massive scale, but the mechanic was simplicity itself. What characterizes it is the involvement of Noel Edmonds, the novelty of the means of contacting winners, the use of live dialogue on TV and the close link with the brand's mainstream advertising. The promotion won two ISP Gold Awards.

(Agency: Triangle Communications.)

How did Maxwell House integrate the sales promotion into the rest of its marketing strategy?
What were the advantages/disadvantages of the Maxwell House promotion compared to spending the same amount on mainstream TV advertising?

CASE STUDY 4. BOVRIL

Everyone knows Bovril. It's one of those brands you can't remember not knowing. It's not constantly in your mind, though, and people lose the habit of drinking it. For some years, Bovril has had a strategy of reminding people that when you are cold, wet or in flagging spirits, a drink of Bovril cheers you up, sustains and nourishes you. It is one of those messages that can be put across by advertising, but is very much more powerful when it is experienced.

Bovril arranged to offer samples of Bovril at 467 bonfire night parties – they are cold, damp and often wet. Bovril linked with local radio stations and charities organizing firework displays. Kits of paste, cups and promotional material were supplied free. Charities could raise funds by accepting donations for cups of Bovril. Local radio stations were offered the opportunity to provide road shows at the largest events, and to trail the events with both DJ plugs and paid-for advertising.

Two million people attended the sponsored bonfire nights, and over five million were reached by radio coverage. Thus, 520,000 people were sampled with Bovril at a fraction of the cost of door drop methods. Sales rose by 4 per cent over the year.

Bovril did not have to create bonfire night – it was already there. The ingenuity of the promotion was recognizing it as a perfect sampling occasion at exactly the right time in the year to promote sales. The executional skill was to provide charities and radio stations with a reason to be involved in the delivery of the promotion. Extended over time, the promotion offered Bovril a direct link with a popular annual tradition.

(Agency: Promotional Campaigns Group.)

What behaviour was Bovril seeking to change, and how did the promotion seek to change it?
What benefits/disadvantages would media advertising have had over the sampling programme Bovril adopted?

CASE STUDY 5. SAINSBURY'S

Sales promotion's capacity to impact directly on consumer behaviour can be used to good ends and bad. Sainsbury's 'Schoolbags' promotion is an example of a promotion that achieved business objectives along with social and environmental ones.

Sainsbury's faced two unrelated challenges: it needed to increase its appeal to families, which lagged below that of competing supermarkets;

and it needed to tackle the financial and environmental cost of nearly 100 million carrier bags issued every year at a cost of £20 million.

These challenges were brought together by the agency Promotional Campaigns Group in a promotion that provided a reason for families with children both to shop at Sainsbury's and to reuse their carrier bags. The link was raising money to buy equipment for schools.

The mechanic was simple. Customers were offered a 'Schoolbags' voucher at the checkout for every carrier bag they reused. These vouchers could be used by schools to obtain equipment, starting with a pack of crayons for 120 vouchers. Schools were recruited to the scheme via direct mail, and the promotion was advertised in store, on TV and in the press.

The promotion succeeded in all its dimensions. Over 10 per cent of Sainsbury's carrier bags were reused, saving 900,000 litres of oil in their manufacture and £2 million in cost. A total of 12,000 schools (about half the total in the country) and a million families participated. The nature of the mechanic will have ensured a substantial incentive to making repeat visits to Sainsbury's. And the schools benefited too: they claimed about £4 million of equipment.

This promotion is a good example of hitting more than one objective at the same time, and doing so with a simple mechanic that is easy to communicate via a multiplicity of media.

How did Sainsbury's 'Schoolbags' promotion reflect on Sainsbury's core values?

What considerations would be involved in making this promotion a permanent feature of Sainsbury's trading?

SUMMARY

Promotions are primarily tactical in nature, but can be part of long-term strategy. They must be understood in the context of the functional, economic and psychological benefits with which firms seek to meet customer needs. Promotions are a means of influencing behaviour, and alter every part of the marketing mix to do so.

This chapter has set out how sales promotion fits into the central business challenge of building relationships that confer differential advantage. It does so as a process that focuses on behaviour, and in two different ways: price promotions and value promotions.

There are reasonable criticisms of certain types of promotion that undermine rather than enhance brand value. Tacky and dishonest promotions have no place in long-term relationships. The manager who understands the place of sales promotion in the firm's strategy will be best placed to manage the risk of using the many techniques available.

4

How to Use Promotions

FROM PROMOTIONAL OBJECTIVE TO PROMOTIONAL BRIEF

Nobody in business likes giving away something for nothing. So, how do you decide on the objectives for a promotion? How do you work out what it can and cannot achieve? And how do you choose between the many techniques available?

The promotional planning cycle looks like that shown in Figure 4.1, and the stages are dealt with in turn in the next six chapters. As you go round the cycle in your promotional career, you'll find that you get better at each of the six elements.

So, once you have the business and marketing objectives established and know what sales promotions you are going to do as marketing activities within a campaign, you need to write a short brief.

Whether you intend to devise a sales promotional offer yourself or to brief someone else, the first stage is the same. It involves setting down the answers to the six questions below, preferably on paper. It is just as valuable to draw up a brief to yourself as it is as a brief to someone else. And it should be short – any more than two sides of A4 is long-winded:

1. What is the *strategic* nature of the brand – its positioning and differential advantage? This will have come from the six Cs and the marketing mix – the offer.
2. What is the promotional objective? Pick only one – see Chapter 3.

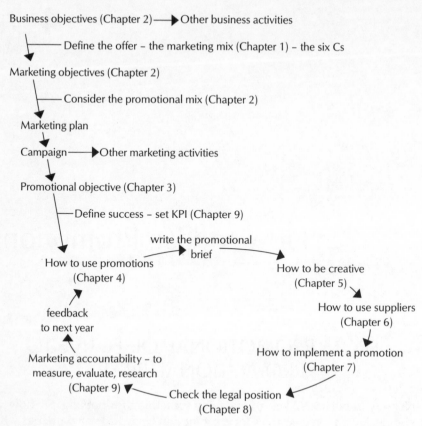

Figure 4.1 The promotional planning cycle

3. Define how you will know it has been a success. Find the particular Key Performance Indicator (KPI) that you need to measure whether you have achieved success. Remember to allocate resource to measure the KPI.
4. Who are the *people* whose behaviour you want to influence? What are they like and what interests them?
5. What *behaviour* do you want them to reinforce or change – in other words, what exactly do you want them to do?
6. What are the *operational constraints* of the promotion – budget, timing, location, product coverage and logistics?

At any given time, it will be possible to specify which of 10 objectives in Chapter 3 most coincides both with your overall marketing objectives and the campaign of which the sales promotion forms part. It is vital to get this right. Sales promotion agencies are sadly familiar with briefs that specify the objectives (often for a small-budget promotion) as 'to increase trial and repeat purchase, increase loyalty and increase trade distribution'. Desirable as it may be to do all these things, it is difficult to shoot at four goals at once.

If your promotional objective does not overlap with any of the 10 in Chapter 3, it may be that you do not have a promotional brief, but a brief for some other kind of marketing activity – or, indeed, for a rethink of your business as a whole.

Taking the promotional objectives seriously (remember, just like business and marketing objectives they should be SMART) means quantifying what the promotion is expected to achieve. For example, if the objective is increasing trial, it is important to specify how many trialists are sought, where they are to be found and the quantity of products or services they are expected to consume. Quantifying the objectives at the beginning enables you to measure and monitor the success of the promotion (a subject explored in Chapter 9).

It is now possible to ask the central promotional question: 'Who do I want to do what?' This is when you move from the marketing objective to the promotional objective. The transition comes when you start thinking about the people who will help you achieve your marketing objective and the things you want them to do so that you can achieve it.

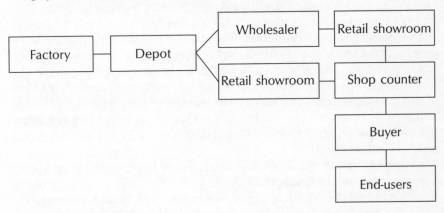

Figure 4.2 Flow chart of the journey of a confectionary item from factory to end-user

Figure 4.2 shows the movement of a confectionary item from factory to end-user. Similar flow charts could be drawn up for the movement of any other product or service; some would be simpler, some more complicated. At each point on the flow chart, there are a number of people. These form the target for promotional activity.

In using the flow chart, it is important to ask yourself four questions:

1. Who holds the key to the business problem? Is it the end-user or the retailer? The buyer or the depot? Is it the customer?
2. What are these customers like? What other things do they do with their time? What are their motivations, interests and desires? What is holding them back from behaving as I would like them to behave?

3. What exactly do I want them to do? Buy one product or more? Use it more frequently or for the first time? Put it on display or tell their friends about it?
4. Who else on the chain has leverage? Some intermediary? Is it a boss or other staff member? Is it children or friends? Who are they with when they are making the decision that I am interested in?

Achieving behavioural change requires a high level of focus on these questions. It is the point at which marketing thinking moves from the general to the particular. It is no longer a matter of market share, penetration, segmentation and the other abstract categories. It is now about Julie Smith and her son Wayne trying to get the shopping done on a busy Thursday afternoon in Tesco in Birmingham, and spending less than a minute passing the gondola on which your product is located. What will make her choose one brand of vinegar rather than another? Will it be a coupon sent door-to-door, a Tesco multi-buy or an on-pack offer (if you can persuade Tesco to take it)? Sarson's vinegar found a particular solution to these questions with its 'Shake on the Sarson's' promotion (Case study 37).

In the office stationery market, it is about the same Julie putting in an order for that week's needs for the small computer consultancy where she works part-time. Julie is now a different kind of customer, taking on the role of a business buyer not a consumer. What will make her choose one brand of sticky tape over another? Will it be an 'extra free' offer, a handy container, a straight discount or a personal benefit for her (if her employers will allow it)? Sellotape's 10,000 Lottery Chances (Case study 27) provides one promotional solution.

In the pub market, it is about the same Julie and her friends having a night out in a large, modern suburban theme pub. What will encourage her to try out one brand of drink in preference to another? What will encourage her to try another within the limits of safe drinking? Colour by Smirnoff (Case study 36) is an example of focusing on the particular characteristics of groups of young people in pubs.

In none of these cases is Julie alone. In the supermarket she is accompanied by Wayne. At work she is answerable to her boss. In the pub she is part of a group of friends. The social relationships of mother, employee and friend are very different and have different impacts on the way Julie will make her decision to choose one brand over another. Understanding the relationships and the contexts is crucial to finding the right means of encouraging Julie to do the thing you want her to do.

Thinking through Julie's needs and interests in relation to your business objectives is the key to promotional creativity, and is the subject of the next chapter.

How will you *evaluate* the promotion and know whether or not it has achieved the task you set for it? Chapter 9 gives you the answer. If you have defined success, set the KPI and measured it, it's easy.

PROMOTIONAL MECHANICS

Thinking about the variety of intermediaries and consumers you may want to influence, their relationships and lifestyles, creates a bewildering number of options. After all, people are varied. The other side of the coin is the distinctly limited number of mechanics that are available in sales promotion.

A 'mechanic' in sales promotion refers to the particular things that consumers have got to do – in other words, a competition is a mechanic and so is a free mail-in. There are surprisingly few mechanics available, and all promotions use one or more of them. In many parts of the EU, law further limits the number of mechanics available to you. Objecting to one of them on the grounds that it has been used before is like objecting to a newspaper ad because newspaper ads have been used before.

The creativity and interest of a promotion does not lie in the mechanic itself, but in its relevance to your promotional objectives and to your target market, in the way you tweak it and vary it, in the content of an offer, and in the way you put it across. For that reason, mechanics are discussed throughout the rest of the book in the context of actual offers.

Sales promotion has already been divided into price and value promotions. Mechanics can also be divided into those that impact immediately at the point of purchase and those that give a delayed benefit. Mechanics can then be classified as shown in Table 4.1.

Table 4.1 Classification of promotion mechanics

Promotional type	Immediate	Delayed
Value	Free in-pack	Free mail-in
	Reusable container	Competition
	Instant win	Free draw
	Home sampling	Self-liquidator
	Free on-pack	Charity promotion
Price	Pence-off flash	Next purchase coupon
	Buy one, get one free	Cash refund
	Extra-fill packs	Cash share-out
	In-store coupon	Buy-back offer
	Finance offer	

Table 4.2 matches 10 key mechanics to the 10 objectives described in the previous section. The matching ranges from 0 (not well matched) to 10 (very well matched). The ratings can be used as a rough guide to suitability. Very often it is the creative execution of a mechanic rather than the mechanic itself that is most effective at creating interest. Clearly, high-cost promotions like

Table 4.2 Linking the objectives to the mechanics: how they match up

Objectives	Mechanics								
	Immediate free offers	Delayed free offers	Immediate price offers	Delayed price offers	Finance offers	Competitions	Games and draws	Charitable offers	Self-liquidators
Increasing volume	9	7	9	7	5	1	3	5	2
Increasing trial	9	7	9	2	9	2	7	7	2
Increasing repeat purchase	2	9	2	9	5	3	2	7	3
Increasing loyalty	1	9	0	7	3	3	1	7	3
Widening usage	9	5	5	2	3	1	5	5	1
Creating interest	3	3	3	2	2	5	9	8	8
Deflecting attention from price	9	7	0	7	7	3	5	5	2
Gaining intermediary support	9	5	9	5	9	3	7	5	1
Discriminating among users	1	9	1	9	9	3	3	5	1

immediate free offers are more effective on almost every criterion than low-cost promotions, such as self-liquidators.

If you have followed this process you will have a clear promotional objective in mind, and you will have had an initial look at the mechanics that could meet it. Now it is time to look at matching the two together in an imaginative and effective way: it is time to see how to be creative.

CASE STUDIES

The three case studies in this chapter have been chosen because they illustrate the selection of promotional objectives and because of the way they make the link between business objectives and promotional mechanics.

Every promotion in this book has something to say about the link between marketing objectives, promotional objectives and mechanics. Use the following questions to identify what it is in particular that these three case studies illuminate: from the evidence presented, how successful were the three promotions in achieving their objectives? What other mechanics could their agencies have considered to achieve those objectives?

CASE STUDY 6. KLEENEX FACIAL TISSUES

This case study covers seven years of the 'Hayfever survival' promotion, run since 1991 by Kimberly-Clark, manufacturers of the leading brand of tissues, Kleenex Facial Tissues. Created by The Blue-Chip Marketing Consultancy, it is a rare story of consistent promotional development.

The original brief was simple and focused: to build a strategic platform to sell Kleenex tissues in the summer. Why hayfever? About 10 per cent of the population suffer from it, concentrated in particular geographical areas and on particular days when the pollen count is high. They are heavy users of tissues, but responsible for a small percentage of volume. Focusing on hayfever gave Kleenex tissues a promotional theme in the summer that used the demands of extreme product usage as a metaphor for best quality, softness and strength. While focusing on the hayfever sufferer, the offer had to appeal to all buyers of tissues.

The promotional offer in 1991 was for a free hayfever 'survival kit' in return for three proofs of purchase. It comprised a toiletries bag containing an Optrex eye-mask, Merethol Lozenge pack, travel pack of Kleenex tissues, money-off coupons for sunglasses and a room ionizer, and a 20-page hayfever guide from the National Pollen and Hay Fever Bureau. It was a partnership promotion, in which Optrex and Merethol provided their samples free. Why should they do so? Because Kleenex tissues could sample the hayfever sufferer in a way that no other brand could. Run on 900,000 packs, the promotion produced a 7.7 per cent response.

The 1997 promotion bore a strong similarity to the 1991 promotion, though now running on nearly 5 million packs and developed to include 'natural remedies'. In return for five proofs of purchase and 50p towards postage, the consumer received a toiletries bag containing an Optrex eye-mask, tube of Halls Mentholyptus, travel pack of Kleenex tissues and a hayfever guide from the renamed National Pollen Centre.

What happened in the intervening five years? It's a fascinating story of how promotions adapt to new needs and new opportunities – and how they can also lose their way.

In 1992, the recession forced a drop in the promotional budget. The toiletries bag was now unaffordable, and consumers were asked for 40p as a contribution towards postage. The contents remained the same but, to pick up on interest in that year in Europe, the guide became a European hayfever guide, with handy tips for travellers. There was also a new opportunity. Vauxhall had just launched the first family-priced car with a pollen filter, the Corsa. One was made available as the prize in a free draw. Despite this addition, the offer was objectively less valuable to the consumer than in 1991, and redemptions dropped to 3.9 per cent.

Kleenex tissues tried a new tack in 1993 – a two-level offer. A new hayfever guide was available for one proof of purchase, and a set of samples for three proofs of purchase and 40p. A strong profile was given to an 0891 (premium rate) 'pollen line'. The creative treatment also changed. From focusing on 'hayfever survival', it now focused on 'those critical days' when the pollen count is at its highest. Extended to 4 million packs, the two-level offer was not a success. Redemption dropped to 0.3 per cent for the guide only, and 1.3 per cent for the sample kit.

This caused a rethink for the 1994 promotion. Providing a clear and uncomplicated incentive to trial and repeat purchase became the priority. The 0891 number was dropped in favour of a link with the *Daily Mail* and Classic FM. The sample pack was slimmed to a new hayfever guide and three samples – Kleenex tissues, Optrex and Strepsils. The central offer was a high-quality AM/FM radio consumers could use to find out the pollen count. It could all be obtained for £3.50 plus five proofs of purchase. The 'hayfever survival' theme was prominently back. Response increased to 1.7 per cent, despite the higher requirement made on the consumer for both proofs of purchase and cash contribution.

This was not to last. In 1995, the focus of the offer changed significantly. The central offer was a 'pollen filter' Vauxhall Corsa to be won in a free draw each week for the 10 weeks of the 'pollen season'. The runners up – 10,000 of them – received hayfever survival kits that included a new hayfever guide. The pollen count information was still there, but reduced in profile. In 1996, the free draw mechanic stayed the same, but 10 'hayfever-free' family holidays replaced the Vauxhalls as the prizes in the free draw. Redemptions were 9.5 per cent in 1995 and 6.4 per cent in 1996. Unlike previous years, they included the option of 'plain paper' entries and did not require even one proof of purchase.

Then, in 1997, the wheel turned full circle. The promotion was a virtual remake of 1991, heavily focused on hayfever survival, offering high-quality samples in a high-quality bag in return for a significant number of proofs of purchase. The major addition was strongly featured pollen count information in partnership with the *Daily Express* and Talk Radio.

What has happened to the brand in this seven-year period? Its share of the branded tissue sector has increased from 50 per cent in 1990 to over 70 per cent in 1996, recording increases every year. Its share of the total market increased to over 40 per cent. Critical to this has been the brand's success in attracting extra volume from the 50 per cent of consumers who buy both Kleenex tissues and own-label tissues. Other factors are undoubtedly present, including product quality and product innovation – notably the launch of Kleenex Ultra tissues in 1995. However, sales promotion has been one of the key marketing weapons throughout this period and must take a major share of the credit.

Did the promotions lose their way in 1995 and 1996, when the mail-in was replaced by a free draw? On the surface, it looks like it, but it is hard to see that a single mechanic could have been maintained without declining returns. A single mechanic would also have been unlikely to have achieved the scale of media coverage the campaign has enjoyed, extending to over 100 publications a year. Operating on-pack, at point of sale, in the media and with third-party endorsers, it has been a thoroughly integrated promotion. The challenge for the future will be to keep the hayfever theme consistently fresh and relevant to both the brand and its consumers.

Three factors that stand out in this case study will undoubtedly help: the ability to seize new opportunities, such as the launch of the Corsa; the proactive relationship with third parties, including pharmaceutical and media partners; and the close partnership that Kimberly-Clark has formed with The Blue-Chip Marketing Consultancy. Unsurprisingly, it is the UK's most acclaimed promotion, winning 11 awards including an ISP Grand Prix and two on a European level. It is a fine example of sales promotion in action.

What changed and what remained constant in the business objectives behind the 'Hayfever Survival' promotions?
How many mechanics did Kimberly-Clark use over the seven years, and why were they used?

CASE STUDY 7. ZANTAC 75

Zantac 75 is a remedy for indigestion and heartburn that was launched in 1994 as an over-the-counter (OTC) version of Zantac, the leading prescription medicine. OTC products are medicines that the consumer buys without a prescription, but not on open shelves. The consumer must ask the pharmacist or pharmacy assistant for them, and will often seek their advice. Just think through the people involved, following the Figure 4.2 example.

The difficulty Zantac 75 faced was that the product story was complicated. There were seven training manuals for sales reps to read. Unless reps could talk knowledgeably about the product to pharmacists, there was little chance that they would stock or display it, let alone recommend it to consumers. The promotional objective was simple: to ensure that reps were fully educated about Zantac 75 and able to present it effectively to pharmacists.

The Promotional Campaigns Group's solution was an e-mail game that took the theme of Zantac 75's world leadership in the prescription market. Each rep chose a world leader from a list that included Margaret Thatcher, Boris Yeltsin and Nelson Mandela. This identity was flashed on their laptop computers every day. Every three days, a new episode of an amusing story about world leaders was sent by e-mail. The script was tailored to each rep's personality to increase involvement. Product learning was reinforced by questions from an imaginary Home Office, Treasury and Foreign Office.

All the reps participated, scoring an average of 90 per cent correct answers. Within four months, Zantac 75 had achieved 100 per cent distribution in independent pharmacists, and within six months it was the second most recommended brand of indigestion remedy in the UK.

Driving people into learning is hard work for learner and teacher alike. This promotion used a novel technique to make learning fun. It focused on product knowledge as the critical issue for the brand at that point in its life, and delivered the goods. Pensions companies that are counting the cost of poorly trained reps could well learn from this case.

How had the manufacturers of Zantac 75 answered the 'Who do I want to do what?' question, and with what result?
How many categories of intermediary were involved in selling Zantac 75 to the consumer, and how did the promotion relate to their different needs?

CASE STUDY 8. MUSIC FOR SCHOOLS

In 1996/7, schools were offered two entirely unconnected opportunities to build their collection of musical instruments. Both picked up on research evidence that schools were short of musical instruments and valued them highly. The promotions from Jacob's Club and the Co-op offer a contrast in objectives and execution round an identical theme.

Jacob's Club is the third biggest chocolate biscuit brand with a 6 per cent market share. It is constantly faced with the challenge of larger brands and new entrants into a highly competitive market. Half its volume is purchased for use in lunchboxes.

Its promotional objectives included achieving a sales uplift of 25 per cent, increasing consumption in lunchboxes, and reinforcing its family/caring image. The promotion devised by Clarke Hooper – printed on 150 million packs – invited consumers to take the wrappers to school. The school could in turn redeem them for musical instruments. Direct mail to 25,500 schools resulted in 30 per cent of them registering. Telephone follow-up increased that to 90 per cent.

The promotion ran from August 1996 to May 1997. Nearly 14,000 schools claimed a total of 36,000 instruments worth over £800,000 at retail price. The entry point was low – a descant recorder worth £6.99 could be obtained for 295 wrappers, a spend of £29. Brand volume rose by 52 per cent during the promotional period, and household penetration rose by two-thirds.

The Co-operative Retail Trading Group (CRTG), which provides buying and promotional support for leading Co-ops, faces a squeeze from more powerful multiple retailers. It has the particular problems that its coverage is not universal (not all Co-ops belong to CRTG) and that its sales immediately before Christmas decline as shoppers go to larger superstores. Its objectives were to retain family shoppers and to reinforce its historically close links with the community.

The Continuity Company's promotion for CRTG was targeted at 16,000 schools near to the 1,300 participating Co-op stores. Recruitment was by direct mail, followed up by postal reminders. A total of 9,000 schools registered. The mail-out to schools included posters, wall charts and A5 leaflets to send home with each child. Co-op shoppers obtained one voucher with every £10 spent, which schools could redeem for instruments. There was a low starting point – just 35 vouchers entitled a school to a £5.99 descant recorder, representing an expenditure of £350.

The Co-op promotion stabilized sales in the period up to Christmas. It also resulted in 190,000 instruments being claimed by schools.

Schools welcomed both promotions – 91 per cent told Jacob's that they would participate again, and 98 per cent said the same to the Co-op. Both have a number of factors in common: not being market leaders; appealing to families; having a broadly sharing/community image; and facing intense market competition. It is not surprising that their promotional analysis led them to very similar promotions. Both succeeded against their objectives, and both attracted considerable PR coverage.

There are a number of details that are different, however:

- Jacob's backed the promotion with TV, the Co-op with press.
- Jacob's used telephone follow-up, which the Co-op did not.
- Jacob's enlisted the support of the Music Industries Association, while the Co-op used the endorsement of celebrities like Richard Baker and Phil Collins.
- Basically similar descant recorders required £29 to be spent on Jacob's Club, or £350 in Co-op stores.

Does it matter that these very similar promotions ran at the same time? It would have done if KitKat and Club or the Co-op and Asda had run them, but Club and the Co-op are in different sectors. Analysis of similar promotional objectives can lead to similar solutions. The executional differences give a good example of how the way in which a promotion is carried out gives the promoter a range of options once the main approach has been decided.

To what extent were the objectives and business context of Jacob's Bakery and CRTG different in the 'Music for Schools' promotions?
How did the 'Music for Schools' promotions address the needs of different influencers on the purchase decision?

SUMMARY

Setting out the brief clearly and concisely is an essential first stage in devising a promotion. If the brief is not clear, your promotion will be built on sand. It is easy to miss out this stage if you are devising a promotion yourself, but it is a mistake. A good brief saves time, and well-defined objectives make the selection of mechanics straightforward.

The objectives and mechanics identified in this chapter do not constitute a rigid grid, but they provide a good checklist for you to develop and apply. The rest of the brief will help you to organize the promotion in detail.

To think through the next chapters, set out a sample brief for a product you know, and use it as a yardstick to judge the promotions discussed in them.

5

How to be Creative

What makes an ordinary promotion outstanding? How do you go about the process of translating promotional objectives into an idea that will achieve behavioural change? This is the art of creativity – the subject of this chapter.

TYPES OF CREATIVITY

Creativity is a much misunderstood word. For some people, it is the opposite of order and structure. It is thought of as the free expression of feeling, of your deepest self. Some talk about creativity as if it is only found in the visual or dramatic arts, such as painting or dance. They have difficulty thinking of the creativity of the engineer or physicist, let alone of the business person. In business, 'creativity' can be understood to mean bending the rules: for example, the 'creative accountant' is a dodgy accountant, not an imaginative and effective accountant.

Advertising people have added to this confusion. 'Creatives' in many agencies are distinguished from the business people, the 'suits'. The background of creatives is normally in visual design, and their hearts may still be there. Awards for creativity given by the Design and Art Direction Association often put a premium on the clever, off-the-wall and fashionable. The Institute of Practitioners in Advertising (IPA) runs Advertising Effectiveness Awards, which reward campaigns that achieve the greatest results for sales and profits. Some – but far from all – also win 'creative' awards.

In sales promotion, creativity does not mean free expression, exciting pictures, clever copy or off-the-wall concepts. It certainly does not mean dodgy practices. It means generating the most effective concept possible. In this, it goes back to the original meaning of creation or creativity. Chaucer writes, in *The Canterbury Tales,* of 'All things as God created, all things in right order'. Bringing into being the wonders of the world out of nothing was what Chaucer had in mind. On a smaller scale, generating something new where nothing was before is at the heart of creativity. It applies as much to the engineer as to the musician. Order, structure and fitness for purpose are not enemies of creativity, but part of it.

Sales promotion, and indeed advertising and PR, communicate with one person at a time, usually the reader of a leaflet, poster, mailshot or press or TV advertisement. But they are not atomized individuals: they are people who build their understanding by means of their interactions with friends, colleagues, families and communities. The more specifically you can define your target audience in both individual and group terms, the more precise will be your creative approach and the more effective your promotion.

If you are going to be responsible for creating a truly effective promotion, you must be really clear about what it is you need to achieve and be capable of imaginative, lateral thinking. If others are to create the promotion for you, then this chapter will help you provide them with the best brief possible.

It is a sad fact of life that as people grow older, fewer and fewer show signs of creative ability. Research has shown that 95 per cent of children show strong creative tendencies, while only 5 per cent of adults show the same traits. We simply become less good at inventing and developing new and original ideas.

This is partly because creativity is the one life skill that has seldom been taught at school or university and partly because our elders and peers stamp it out of us. Remember when you were caught jumping on the settee and told off for doing so? Your mother just saw her child damaging the furniture. You were riding a horse, escaping from the Indians – exercising your creativity.

To create promotions, you do not need to jump up and down on your office chair, however much you might feel like doing so sometimes. You do need to suspend belief and really and truly imagine. Experience shows that the latent creative ability can be liberated in most people. There are many exercises and procedures that can help you become more creative, and later in this chapter we will look at some techniques that can be helpful in a business context. They will help you structure your creative planning to enable you to create a truly great promotion rather than an imitation of someone else's idea.

CREATIVE PROMOTIONS CASE STUDIES

CASE STUDY 9. OSRAM

Truly great ideas stand the test of time. Osram had produced a new light bulb that lasted four times as long as a normal one but cost only twice as much. It was ideal for use in industry where bulbs are often changed all at once, towards the end of their life. Not only would the bulbs be cheaper over a period of time, there would also be considerable savings in labour costs. However, industry was not buying them.

Research indicated that this was because the maintenance department purchased bulbs and were usually instructed by finance departments as to the maximum amount they could pay. Maintenance staff were not allowed to suddenly spend twice as much as normal.

The 'Who do I want to do what?' question led to the answer. Maintenance and financial staff could only agree to buy Osram if they did so together. The solution was to send the chief accountant a cash box and explain that there was information inside the box on how to save more than 50 per cent on bulb replacement. The key was sent to the head of maintenance and this fact was also communicated to the financial officer.

To read the information inside the box, both the financial and maintenance representative had to meet, and they were then in a position to have a short discussion. Was it successful? Of course it was. A neat, elegant solution far more likely to succeed than a simple brochure mailing or trade press campaign. This promotion deservedly won an ISP Grand Prix Award – albeit over 30 years ago.

CASE STUDY 10. SHERATON SECURITIES

Another elegant solution involved, of all unlikely things, a wellington boot. Sheraton Securities wanted to attract commercial property agents to visit their greenfield development site. These agents are inundated with similar requests, and are regularly sent brochures and inducements. Sheraton chose to deliver personally one left wellington boot to 50 selected agents. They then advertised in the trade press 'What possible use is one wellie?', stating that the other boot was to be found on their development site. This humorous and off-beat approach succeeded in bringing the agents along.

CASE STUDY 11. RAMADA

Ramada opened a new hotel in Manchester in the mid-1980s, shortly after the opening of a major competitor. There are many established hotels in Manchester and the Ramada was just not reaching its targets.

There are innumerable ways of promoting hotels, but one of the best of them is to encourage positive recommendations from existing guests. How, though, can you do that? The bizarre solution was to put a plastic duck in each bathroom and tell the guests, by means of a tent card, that they could keep the duck. Alternatively, if they wished, they could have it sent anywhere in the world in its own special crate for only £2.50 plus postage.

This promotion not only succeeded, it made a profit. The cost of the duck and crate were far less than £2.50 and hundreds were sold to intrigued guests. This promotion won a European sales promotion Gold Award.

CASE STUDY 12. CHERRY BLOSSOM

How would you go about sampling thousands of consumers with a new shoe-cleaning pad? Cherry Blossom must have considered door-to-door sample drops, banded offers and all the other techniques. The one they used, however, was to link with the Boy Scouts who, at that time, cleaned people's shoes outside supermarkets during Bob-a-Job week. Simple, cheap and a winner of several awards.

CASE STUDY 13. SHELL'S 'MAKE MONEY'

Many people still remember Shell's 'Make Money' promotion in the 1960s in which customers collected halves of banknotes. They could redeem them for their face value if they collected both matching halves. Obtaining that elusive matching £10,000 banknote half became compulsive, driving out any thought of visiting a competing petrol station. This promotion has been run several times in the UK and throughout the world. It works – it works again and again, and it has been copied over and over. It must be a great promotion.

All these promotions have a number of things in common. They are engaging. It is not immediately obvious what they are trying to achieve (the objectives are not showing). They were original when they were first implemented. They are very carefully targeted. The promotions' creators all clearly identified 'who it was that they wanted to do what'.

The Osram promotion clearly identified that the company wanted the accountants and the maintenance people to meet and discuss the benefits of the new bulb. The developers wanted agents to come to their site. Ramada wanted people to tell their friends and business acquaintances about the new hotel. Cherry Blossom wanted people to try the new product and feel warmly about the company. Shell wanted people to come back to its petrol stations rather than visit those of its competitors.

It is this clarity of thought and of definition of the target audience or, to put it another way, clarity of the promotional objective, that they all have in common. Once that is in place, humour, excitement, style, graphics and copy can be introduced in an appropriate way to enhance the overall offering to the customer. Indeed, it will be easier.

What has clarity of promotional objectives got to do with creativity? Essentially, it is the key to success! Briefs often state that the objective is to increase sales by X or to increase distribution by Y. As discussed in Chapters 1 and 2, these are marketing objectives, not promotional objectives (see Chapter 3). A promotional objective is the answer to, 'Who do I want to do what?' Remember that promotions are about changing behaviour. Setting the right objectives is often truly creative.

THINKING CREATIVELY

Very often, a marketing objective will turn into a number of different promotional objectives as you ask the question, 'Who do I want to do what?' This is not a problem unless you try to achieve them all by the same promotion. Note that we are talking here about a promotion and not a promotional theme. You may decide on a theme that has several different promotions targeted at different audiences. Different people in the distribution chain will be motivated in different ways. The wholesaler, the retailer and the consumer all need to be attended to. Also, the same theme can be worked through different promotions over a period of time.

Let's take a typical brief, one that is often proposed by brand managers of lager beer. 'We want to generate sales of X cans during Y period. Our target market is C1/C2 men and women between the ages of 18 and 25.'

Have you ever met a C1/C2, or indeed anyone aged 18 to 25? The group contains postgraduate students, marketing managers, soldiers, lathe operators, nurses, car mechanics, musicians performing classical and heavy metal music, teachers, truck drivers, jockeys, farm workers, photographic models and so on. How can you possibly attract all members of such a diverse group? The only thing they have in common is that they visit pubs and off-licences and like to drink lager. Think of them as a sociological category and you will end up with a bland promotion. Alternatively, although not a bad promotion by any means, you will focus on the single thing they have in common, giving away lager as an incentive – 10 per cent extra free, buy five get one free, are standard promotions in this market. But is that the best that you can do?

Before you go any further, have you spotted the flaw in the description I have given? I made an assumption, and this is always a very great mistake. I assumed that the 'Who?' was existing lager drinkers. Perhaps the promotion might target non-drinkers or wine drinkers. These approaches could be worth examining!

Never assume anything. In the case of Ramada, the normal action would have been to advertise to people who book hotels. The problem in that case is that these people are all over the world and do not see the same media. It would have been an impossibly expensive strategy.

The first task is to answer the 'Who?' part of the question. In our lager example we can list:

- existing drinkers of the brand;
- lager drinkers who buy other brands;
- ale drinkers;
- wine drinkers;
- people who vary what they drink;
- home drinkers;
- pub drinkers.

However, this list only describes them in relation to their drinking. They have many other characteristics. They may be further categorized into:

- amateur pop singers;
- fashion followers;
- tennis players;
- golfers;
- classical music devotees;
- and many others.

Once we have decided the 'who?' we must define 'what we want them to do'. The list might be as follows:

- existing drinkers of the brand: suggest it to friends;
- lager drinkers who buy other brands: switch brands;
- ale drinkers: switch to lager, our brand;
- wine drinkers: try lager when it's hot;

- people who vary what they drink: be consistent, drink our brand;
- home drinkers: go to the pub;
- pub drinkers: take some home.

It is possible that some groups will have exactly or nearly the same 'what?' as others, so it might be possible to use the same promotion. For example, the same mechanic may well work with ale drinkers and drinkers of other brands. Already we can see the opportunity for creatively engaging these different sorts of people in different ways. Now we have the 'who?' and the 'what?', it's time for the real creativity.

Let's study the second list of amateur pop singers, fashion followers, tennis players and the like. Remember that any one of the people in these categories may also be in one of the other categories. We have, therefore, the grounds for 35 possible promotional objectives, and the lists are by no means exhaustive. Let us take just one example: tennis players who vary their drinks. We can now start to build a picture of real people and work out how to motivate them. We know they are under 25. We know they drink a variety of things. We know they play tennis and are likely to visit the club bar. The answer to the question, 'Who do we want to do what?' is therefore: 'We want tennis players who are not consistent in their choice of drinks to try our lager once a week in their club after their game.'

Now we can begin to devise a worthwhile promotion for these people. We can imagine them as flesh and blood, coming in from the game, looking for a drink. We can imagine the place, the time of day. We can picture their friends, the things they will be talking about. It is far more real, far more focused than trying to attract that sociological category, the C1/C2 person between 18 and 25.

A number of ideas immediately present themselves for encouraging tennis players who are not consistent in their choice of drinks to take a lager once a week after their game. A chance to play tennis with a celebrity? A discount on tennis kit? The chance to collect something for the club?

However, tennis players are just one of our groups. A similar process will lead to similar thoughts about the classical music devotee who never drinks at home and the amateur pop singer who normally drinks beer.

Having categorized the consumers, it is worth looking at the intermediaries – at the publicans, managers of off-licences and supermarkets, cash-and-carry buyers and the rest. Like the consumers, they are immensely varied.

Let's assume that the tennis club idea proved a basis for a promotion themed on sport and leisure, and designed to offer a range of celebrity sports opportunities. Now go back to our tennis club and develop the trade dimension of the promotion. Consider the bar steward. He will now become the 'who'. The 'what?' might be, 'To suggest a cooling lager is best after a game'. It being a club, there may also be another 'who?' – the committee, which might have to give permission to allow the promotion to run. Should the club be given the opportunity to host the celebrity events or another incentive?

If you follow this method of identifying 'who?' and 'what?', you will quickly devise hundreds of different promotional objectives. This is delightful but you are unlikely to have the time to work them all up into full promotions – and you could not afford to run them all anyway. You need only work through those promotional objectives that are most likely to achieve the marketing objective. To do this requires careful assessment of the extent to which your promotional objectives will grip the underlying marketing objective.

There are a number of questions to ask about each of your promotional objectives and the initial promotional ideas that go with them:

- Is the particular audience a reasonable proportion of the total or can the idea at least be attractive to a wider group of people?
- Is it likely to be achievable within the budgetary, legal, timing and other constraints that you face?
- Does it lend itself to simple, clear expression to the trade and to consumers?

In this case, we may conclude that these tennis players form too small a group to be significant, but that there is an opportunity if we add them to a range of other active club sports.

The process of devising a promotion is far from over when you have a flipchart covered with possible promotions. However, to try to be creative without attempting to answer the who?' and 'what?' will usually result in promotions that are less effective than they could be.

In the case of the Ramada promotion, long before ducks or anything else was considered, it was realized that, mainly due to budget limitations, the 'who?' would be the guests and the 'what?' would be telling their contacts about the hotel. It was as simple as that. The statement of the promotional objective in that case and in many others is creative in itself.

In this case, the creative process then had to find a way of getting guests to talk about the hotel. A business hotel is not something one normally talks about – except in negative terms – as they are fundamentally similar across the globe. A true creative leap was required. It was realized that one thing all guests do when they are in a business hotel room is to grab some relaxation time, often by taking a bath or a shower. We should catch them while they are relaxed and are likely to be receptive.

Brainstorming was useful. Could we put a waterproof joke book by the bath? A bathroom karaoke kit? Something useful? Humour seemed appropriate and, eventually, along with boats came that deeply loved creature of children's baths, the duck. Brainstorming was not the only technique used. To devise good promotions, you need to use a range of creative techniques.

CREATIVE TECHNIQUES

Here are five creative techniques that are particularly useful in moving from 'Who do I want to do what?' to an effective promotion.

1. Listing

As we have already seen, making lists is a very useful technique. It was a straightforward process to list all the different types of young lager drinkers, for example.

Lists help you order your thoughts and show up any gaps. They do have one disadvantage, which is that it is often difficult to see the connections between items on a list and particularly on several different lists. One way round this is to use the largest sheet of paper you can find and draw lines to show these connections. For example, you could link rugby players and golfers as people who would be members of a club, and therefore involved with bar stewards.

2. Mind maps

Another way of showing connections is not to write a list, but to draw a 'mind map', which is a formalized way of connecting ideas. Take a sheet of paper and start with one idea. It could be anything related to the subject, for example 'wine drinker'. Then, draw a line from it. Along that line write connected ideas, for example 'sophisticated', 'educated' and 'travelled'. From each of these words draw other lines, and write the words that occur to you. For example, from 'travelled' you might write 'airline tickets', 'currency', 'passport' and 'duty free'. Keep on doing this and the interconnected ideas stay together. Connections also appear that will not at first have struck you. For example, 'duty free' brings you back to 'wine drinker'. Is there a promotional idea in that? Mind map software programs can help here.

3. Brainstorming

Once you have really defined your chosen, practical promotional objectives, you may then decide to brainstorm. Brainstorming is not meant to be a woolly general discussion. Set the objective for the session very clearly and ensure everyone understands it. For the Ramada promotion, it was, 'What can we put in a bathroom, in a business hotel, that will amuse the guests and encourage them to mention how good the hotel is to the person who booked it and to colleagues?', and the related one, 'Is it also possible to provide something that would act as a constant reminder to the guest?'

It is useful to spend just a few moments on a warm-up exercise to get people into the right frame of mind. Perhaps you could examine where else the session could have been held that would increase the creativity level. The best hotel in the world? The most beautiful? Then imagine you are there.

There are no right or wrong answers in a brainstorming exercise. It is important that people are not allowed to feel foolish or they will cease to contribute. They may have that brilliant idea lurking in their heads just waiting to pop out. Use affirmative expressions such as 'Yes, and . . .' rather than 'Yes, but . . .', let alone 'No, because . . .'.

4. The village

A very useful technique is to define all the types of 'who?' and, in your imagination, people a village with them. Imagine the houses they would live in, the places they would meet, the resources they would need, where they would go for fun, where they would shop. Then, aim your promotion to appeal to the village. Think how they would react to it, how it would come up in their conversation. If it does not appeal to most of the villagers, you probably need to redefine your objectives or run more than one promotion.

5. Being someone else

If you feel you are not capable of solving the problem creatively, imagine someone you think could. Imagine a great artist – say, Picasso – or think about the most imaginative person you have met in your life. Then, in your mind ask them what they would come up with.

A variation of this is to mentally take six people out to dinner and ask them what suggestions they have. Imagine a series of different people, the different perspectives they would have on the question and how they would discuss it among themselves. Why not even imagine one of the 'villagers' and ask them?

Practice makes perfect

Thinking about promotions can be turned into a party game, perhaps for use on long car journeys. Think of a product category known to you and list all the brands in it. Then assume an objective and a set of mechanics and match the two together. Examine the following list of confectionery brands and promotional offers:

After Eight	Free Levi's jeans to be won
Yorkie	Win a racehorse
Jellytots	Free Mother's Day lunch to be won

Dairy Box	Win a holiday in LA
Toffee Crisp	Win a visit to Legoland
Drifter	Win a mountain bike
Lion Bar	Win a day out in a tank

Are they well matched? No. Why not give them a better matching, and then see if you can think of even better promotions to encourage repeat purchase for each of these brands?

MAKING THE MOST OF YOUR IDEA

Deciding on your mechanic and theme as the answer to the 'Who is it we want to do what?' question is an important step. Now you must make it work well.

There may be some pitfalls you need to identify. In the case of the Ramada duck it was recognized that if it was left in the bathroom with no explanation it might look as though the room had not been cleaned properly. People who took the duck, something the Ramada wanted them to do as a reminder of the hotel, might feel guilty. If they did so, they would be unlikely to carry the message about the benefits of the Ramada hotel in Manchester.

The problem was solved by printing a small tent card that introduced the duck and explained that it could be taken home or posted anywhere. The duck was also given a distinctive personality and distinctive packaging. Named 'Reggie', he was supplied with a specially constructed cardboard 'crate'.

In the case of Sheraton Securities' wellies, the different sizes of feet had to be taken into consideration.

It is essential to identify problems and practical difficulties – such as ensuring that a sales representative's car can carry sufficient quantities of your latest creative brainwave. More positively, you also have the ability to polish and extend the creative idea. However, beware of so extending the idea that it becomes impossibly complicated.

Mazda ran a competition that offered the chance to win a holiday. The stages involved required some imagination. Consumers were enticed by teaser ads in a newspaper, and directed to another and bigger ad; there they were asked to identify an island; then they had to go to their local Mazda dealer and identify three other photographs; identify another 'special photograph'; complete an entry form and, should they so wish, phone a London telephone number for a clue. The persistent motorist would, however, have noticed that nowhere did a Mazda car appear, and at no stage did the Mazda dealer play a part in the promotion. Creativity? Not of a sales promotional kind.

The golden rule is to keep it simple and keep it relevant. The duck crate is an example of a simple extension that enhanced the promotion, yet the promotion would still have worked without it. That promotion was later extended further by putting the duck on Christmas cards and providing star staff with duck merit badges.

When you devise a promotion, be aware of what is current. You can often create far more interest about the activity at little extra cost. Linking in with a current fad can work. Golden Wonder crisps once offered embroidered jeans patches showing the Wombles. This was just as the characters became famous and as jeans patches became fashionable. It seemed that everyone was eating crisps all day judging by the response.

Be especially careful if you promote overseas. It is vital to know the traditions and expectations of your foreign consumers. In developing countries, cigarettes are often sold singly as 'sticks'. Thus, any promotion using packet tops in such countries will only benefit the retailer.

When you find a promotion that can be extended in many different ways, you know you have a winner. It is always worth polishing and extending an idea until you have bled it dry.

Once you have your promotional concept, there is a lot of work to be done to turn it into an effective operational plan. For this you need suppliers (the subject of Chapter 6) and an effective implementation strategy (the subject of Chapter 7). In doing so, though, never forget the importance of the original idea: one that can extend and extend, one that is elegant and simple, one that you are really proud of. You will hear a voice in your head asking why no one has done it before. You will begin to fret that there must be something wrong. Don't worry. If you have followed the steps above you will have created a memorable promotion that will succeed. Congratulate yourself.

CASE STUDIES

This chapter has been full of examples of creative promotions. Many are from high-profile consumer fields. The two case studies that follow demonstrate that promotional creativity can be found on fairly sticky wickets – in promoting intellectual property law and an ageing car.

CASE STUDY 14. EVERSHEDS

Intellectual property is a dry, complicated but increasingly important branch of law. Most companies – not least sales promotion agencies – need to think very carefully about who owns the ideas, trademarks, designs and copy that their staff and subcontractors create. The trouble is, drawing up the necessary contracts is something that can always be put off until tomorrow.

The leading legal firm Eversheds wanted to promote its 'Intellectual Property Health Check' in 1996. An ordinary brochure would not have broken through the apathy. Instead, they sent a simple letter accompanied by a piece of wood with a hole drilled through it, marked with the Eversheds logo. They offered a prize for the best answer to two questions. What is it? And what intellectual property rights apply?

The engagement of leading business people in the questions was enormous. So too was the response. The object (which turned out to be a wine bottle holder) was genuinely intriguing. The follow-up letter contained winning solutions, an analysis of no fewer than five intellectual property rights that could apply to it and an invitation to arrange a 'Health Check'.

Eversheds deserved to succeed with this promotion. Simple and to the point, it showed that even lawyers could be creative!

How exactly did Eversheds answer the 'Who do I want to do what?' question?
What other promotional solution could you devise that would be as good or better?

CASE STUDY 15. ROVER GROUP

To understand this promotion by the agency Ammirati Puris Lintas, point your browser (Internet Explorer or Netscape) at http://www.mini.co.uk. Such is the nature of Internet sites that what was true in late 1997 may no longer be true, but this is the story as it was at that time.

In 1996, Rover was faced with the question of what to do to stimulate sales of the ageing and much-loved Mini. Sales were to long-established customers, who were declining in number. Could the Mini appeal to a younger generation who may not know it is even available? Potential customers needed to be made aware that they could still buy one, and that Rover's enormous range of options meant that they could virtually design their own.

The solution was found in an interactive Internet site with a monthly competition to design your own Mini with real and fantasy features. Designs were entered on a gallery, where visitors to the site voted for the best design. The winner was rewarded with Mini merchandise, and winning designs were posted on a special page. Everyone won the chance to turn his or her design into a game and download it as a screensaver.

Like any good Web site, it constantly changed. Developments included a walkround film and a concept car section. These helped it to be one of the top 10 UK sites and to be voted Microsoft's site of the month. As well as an ISP Award, it was voted commercial Web site of the year in the UK Yell Awards and best automotive site by *New Media Age*.

In its first four months, the site received 3 million hits, 5 per cent of them turning into brochure requests. Did they convert into sales? The jury is out on this, but the commercial logic is far stronger than on many other sites. The promotional mechanic of a design competition is proving effective in engaging people with the Mini, and with the differential advantage it has over far newer cars: the capacity to design your own.

Think about the 'village' of visitors to this Web site. What other products and services featured on the Internet would they like?
What promotions could you devise to encourage them to visit your own company's Web site (or, if you don't have one yet, a site you know)?

SUMMARY

Creativity is about finding effective solutions. It requires the ability to think laterally and imaginatively, which can be developed with practice. There are several techniques that can be used, including mind maps and brainstorming.

Creative promotions arise out of close attention to the question, 'Who do I want to do what?' Once the process of answering this question is begun, hundreds of possible promotional objectives emerge. A really good idea can be versioned and developed in many ways.

6

How to Use Suppliers

All promotions need suppliers. Complicated national promotions require an army of suppliers: promotional and design agencies, premium sourcing specialists, printers, point-of-purchase manufacturers, handling houses and telephone response companies. Many of these will, in turn, have suppliers that are critical to the success of the promotion. This chapter deals with how to select and use them.

Sales promotion can present a particular difficulty in this respect. A company will normally have a wealth of experience of component suppliers and subcontractors for its core products and services. There will often be long-term supply agreements and careful supplier assessment in accordance with established quality criteria. In sales promotion, the picture is different – discontinuity is the rule. Promotions are different from one to the other so each promotion often needs different suppliers from the last one. Yet, the same requirements of quality assessment and value for money apply. For this reason, many firms try, where possible, to build long-term partnerships.

There are two models of supplier relationship: the 'quotation model', which assumes that you know what you want and can obtain the lowest price and best terms from a range of suppliers by setting out your specification as an invitation to quote; and the 'partnership model', which assumes that you will obtain the best solution by working with a chosen supplier from the earliest stage, incorporating the supplier's skills into the specification. This second model is often called 'partnership sourcing'.

Some organizations – particularly in the public sector – have rules that require them to obtain three quotations for every piece of work. Others believe that the constant use of tenders and quotations keeps suppliers on their toes. The risk in sales promotion is that you never use exactly the same product or service often enough to be able to specify what you want without the help of a supplier. That supplier is most likely to help if you build up a long-term relationship, and bring them into the planning of a promotion from the earliest stage.

SALES PROMOTION AGENCIES

Who they are

Most sales promotions are conducted by people who are not sales promotions specialists – by marketing managers, sales managers, managers of small businesses and by executives in general advertising agencies. In a number of large consumer goods companies, promotions are under the aegis of a sales promotion manager, but even then implementation is often the responsibility of non-specialist sales and marketing executives.

Many of the biggest and most high-profile promotions are developed and implemented by specialist sales promotion agencies. They are often called 'consultancies' because, unlike insurance or advertising agencies, they derive much of their income from fees rather than commission. However, sales promotion firms also derive a proportion of their income from selling artwork, merchandise, print and other services, which is not normal practice among consultancies. The word 'agency' is used here as the description commonly applied to firms engaged in providing marketing advice, consultancy and implementation.

Visit Web sites to find agencies. The DMA, ISP and MCCA Web sites contain listings or contacts to obtain lists. The MCCA offers a Portfolio service to select an agency. They offer a pitch guide. In the main, they are on all lists. Outside these lists, there is a wide variety of agencies that include the words 'sales promotion' in their list of services. Some are advertising agencies, which may or may not employ dedicated sales promotion specialists. Some are purveyors of particular sales promotional vehicles, such as travel or merchandise, and may be very competent, but they are not necessarily impartial about the types of sales promotion they recommend. And some are newer agencies, which may be extremely good, but have yet to qualify for MCCA membership.

How they work

There are many different ways that sales promotion agencies originate, and this is reflected in their continuing diversity of structure. Some began as spin-offs of sales promotion specialists working in advertising agencies; others as the breakaways of advertising agency sales promotion departments;

others from a base in supplying print, merchandise or incentives; and yet others (and this is increasingly the case) as greenfield start-ups that are meeting the growing demand for specialist sales promotion services.

Despite the variety in their size and structure, sales promotion agencies have a number of features in common:

- They charge for creative and conceptual work on a fee basis that reflects their time input. This method of working – comparable to that of solicitors and accountants – means that it can be possible to use them simply for creative thinking and to do the organization and implementation of a promotion yourself.
- They are normally equipped to supply design, artwork, premium sourcing and a host of other services that are needed to make promotions happen. Sometimes these services are supplied in-house, sometimes by subsidiary or associated companies and sometimes they are subcontracted. Agencies will always make a margin on these services, but their prices benefit from economies of scale and can be highly competitive.
- They work on an *ad hoc* or continuing basis. It is conventional for advertising and PR agencies to work with clients on a continuing, contractual basis. Sales promotion agencies like to do this, and increasingly do so, being paid a retainer rather than one-off fees. However, many clients still use them on an *ad hoc* basis, briefing them for particular promotions as and when required.
- They are increasingly involved in a broad range of marketing services. We discussed earlier the reasons for the growth of sales promotion. Most of these apply also to the use of an integrated mix of sales promotion, direct mail, PR and other tools assembled to meet particular needs. The disciplines of sales promotion agencies provide a good basis for providing these integrated marketing services, and many have taken up the challenge.
- Account handlers are heavily involved in the creative process. There is a tradition in advertising agencies for account handlers – the people who meet the clients – to be largely excluded from the creative process. In sales promotion agencies this is not the case. The creation of effective promotions is an interdisciplinary, brainstorming affair, simultaneously conceptual and practical, and the person you meet will play a central role in that process.
- They tend to be of moderate size. This partly reflects the relative newness of the industry and partly their low start-up costs. New agencies tend to be tightly run, enthusiastic and entrepreneurial and almost always run by the people who set them up.
- They are able to give impartial advice on the type of sales promotion that will most meet your particular needs. This is perhaps the most important benefit of their fee basis of payment. They have no particular axe to grind over whether or not the promotion is a competition, an on-pack or a mail-

in or uses travel, clothing or cash. In a world where there are many axes ground, that is a bonus in itself.

Sales promotion agencies earn their living from a combination of fees for time spent and mark-ups on goods supplied. The balance between the two will vary, but most commonly includes a fee for time spent, normally calculated at £35 to £170 per hour (2002 rates), depending on the seniority of the staff involved, and a mark-up on goods supplied (print, artwork, premiums and so on) of 15 to 20 per cent. These two combine to give an overall margin of 25 to 30 per cent (lower for bigger jobs and higher for smaller jobs).

Some agencies have dropped the words 'sales promotion' as the description of their business in favour of 'integrated marketing', 'below-the-line marketing', 'promotional communications' or any combination of these. They describe rather better the increasingly integrated nature of sales promotion and the business that agencies do. The trouble is that client firms do not always understand them. 'Sales promotion' remains a broad description that people understand – as long as you recognize that it includes a great deal else besides.

What to look out for

Choosing the right agency is a difficult process. The MCCA offers a useful service of putting together a portfolio of the work of 10 or so agencies from among its members that can be reviewed at its London offices. Both the ISP and MCCA publish annual awards on Web sites and brochures, detailing the best promotions of the previous year. Also, there is regular coverage of leading agencies in the three specialist sales promotion magazines – *Incentive Today*, *Promotions & Incentives* and *Sales Promotion*. All these offer a good starting point for drawing up a short list.

A relationship with a sales promotion agency normally starts with a pitch. The MCCA and the Incorporated Society of British Advertisers (ISBA) have devised a set of guidance notes for them. They provide a good basis for the often vexed process of competitive pitches, and are obtainable from either the ISBA or MCCA (see the further information chapter at the back of the book for details). The principles are to treat each other with fairness:

- prepare the background information properly;
- don't ask more than three agencies to pitch;
- write a proper brief and allow time for it to be responded to;
- decide quickly and objectively;
- give the losers the chance to learn how they could have done better.

Fees for pitches are a subject of regular dispute. The MCCA's Code of Conduct discourages its members from making speculative pitches. The reason is that promotions are devised for a particular brief and so have no salvage value. Some companies pay agencies a briefing fee, sometimes known as a pitch or rejection fee. Nevertheless, if an agency produces acceptable work, but the promotion is not run for reasons outside its control (for example, you have changed your own plans), it is only right that it should be paid for its work. It is an open question as to whether or not agencies should be paid briefing fees for competitive pitches. Agreeing to pay them intimates that it is recognized that each concept is tailor-made for each brief and has no salvage value. Equally, it is always possible to find smaller, hungrier agencies that will pitch for nothing.

In practice, most agencies are happy to compete against a reasonable number of others for a real piece of business, and all of them are happy to compete for ongoing business. The distinction is one of common sense. If you repeatedly brief half a dozen agencies for single promotions that may not even materialize, they are unlikely to find it profitable to respond. Conversely, if you brief a limited number for promotions that do materialize – and particularly with a view to establishing a long-term relationship – most agencies will respond professionally and effectively.

There are five key attributes that companies normally look for in their sales promotion agencies, and which form a handy checklist for selection:

1. *Creativity.* The capacity to produce promotions that are more imaginative, more effective and more eye-catching than you could do yourself is the fundamental reason for using an agency. Creativity should stand out in an agency's presentation of its work.
2. *Communication skills.* Promotions are produced to meet specific marketing objectives. In the way it presents its work, an agency should be able to demonstrate an understanding of a range of different marketing situations and of the techniques appropriate to communicating effective solutions.
3. *Budget control.* Implementing promotions requires a range of design, artwork, premium, handling and other resources. It is not important that these should all be in-house, but an agency should be able to demonstrate that they are to hand and that it can control them within your budget.
4. *Good service.* A successful promotional relationship requires client and agency to be on the same wavelength. It is important to meet the people you will actually work with – not necessarily the same people as those who make the new business presentation – and get on well with them. Just ask your team if they get on with the prospect agency; is the chemistry ok? If not, don't use them.
5. *Good track record.* The evidence from awards brochures and from the trade press is critical here – and a call to existing clients can also tell you about qualities of service and budget control that might not be obvious from published work. This is probably the best tip.

Having applied these criteria, you may end up with three agencies you feel you could work with. It is then common practice to put a brief to all three, and to make a judgement on the basis of their response.

Once you have run a promotion with a particular agency, you will be able to judge its performance in practice. There are broadly three ways you can work in the longer term:

1. *Occasional supplier.* This is an arm's length approach – the agency is given the minimum information necessary for the job, is always in competition with others and is briefed only when the need arises.
2. *Rota member.* This is a compromise approach, where two or three agencies are put on a rota of agencies used by the client. Rather more information is given and some or all briefs will only be given to one of the agencies on the rota.
3. *Business partner.* Here, a single agency is appointed to work as an extension of the client's marketing department. Marketing plans are discussed jointly from an early stage, and a renewable contract establishes an ongoing partnership.

Agencies understandably dislike the first approach. It makes planning their own business difficult and results in a high percentage of wasted and unprofitable work. Clients that insist on 'occasional supplier' relationships can find that they are presented with off-the-shelf promotions, dusted down and rejigged without too much thought and effort, generally from second-rate agencies.

Clients are understandably wary of the third approach. It does involve putting all their eggs in one basket, and can lead to complacency and staleness on the part of the agency. Retainer fees, paid on a regular monthly basis, are liked by agencies as they provide a regular income. However, they only make sense when there is a steady, predictable flow of work.

For these reasons the second approach is often where client and agency find themselves in mutual agreement. It gives the client flexibility and it gives the agency a reasonable basis for predicting the amount of business it will get. Variants on this approach include using one core agency most of the time, but trying out others for particular briefs or in particular areas where the core agency may lack specialist expertise.

Is it worth letting between a quarter and a third of your budget go to the sales promotion agency? If the agency is any good, the answer is 'yes', and for three good reasons:

1. Part of the agency's margin will be covered by buying promotion items effectively and by its ability to produce promotions cost-effectively.
2. Part will be covered by saving your time in devising, planning and executing the promotion.
3. Most importantly, a good agency will produce a promotion that is measurably more effective.

HANDLING HOUSES

Who they are

Handling houses originated in the need for premiums items to be warehoused, customer applications to be received and processed, and for goods to be dispatched. From this basis, handling houses have grown into sophisticated businesses that offer data capture, database building, in-bound and out-bound telephone call centres, barcode scanning, downloading of e-mail sites and a range of customer interface operations.

The industry body is a part of the DMA, the Response & Fulfilment Council, concerned with providing both industry and consumers alike with a universal professional, effective, legal and value-for-money service for all aspects of response fulfilment, irrespective of the medium of communication.

How they work

Poor handling can destroy consumer confidence in a promotion and the brand behind it, as well as create considerable work for you as you try to limit the damage. Conversely, good handling can create added value in the information collected about participants in promotions, and build consumer confidence through the promptness and accuracy of your response to them. The following 20-point checklist identifies the details to be included in briefing a handling house (see also the DMA Web site for a 'Best practice response handling guide'):

1. *The promotion:* incentive offered, instructions to applicant, any restrictions on entry.
2. *Handling requirement:* how it should be done, turnaround time.
3. *Duration:* start date, close date.
4. *Response forecast:* anticipated volume, variation over time.
5. *Promotion media:* on-pack, press, TV, direct mail.
6. *Application format:* coupons, leaflets, plain paper, telephone.
7. *Point of purchase requirements:* number, type, tolerances, count procedure.
8. *Payment requirements:* amount, coins, cheques, postal orders, credit cards, charge cards, tolerances, need to await cheque clearance.
9. *Bank account:* client's, handling house's, responsibility for charges.
10. *Postage and dispatch:* first class, second class, discounts for bulk mailings, recorded delivery, registered, carrier, cash floats for postage.
11. *Packing:* pre-packed, envelope, padded bag, carton.
12. *Goods storage:* quantities, period, special security.
13. *Insurance:* client's, handling house's.
14. *Application details:* captured manually, computerized, fields required, deduplication, selections, sort criteria.

15. *Reports:* type, frequency, period covered, analysis headings.
16. *Consumer relations:* incorrect applications, correspondence, complaints, returns, exchanges, refunds.
17. *Audit:* retention of applications, record of dispatch dates.
18. *Stock control:* reorder levels, returns, final disposal.
19. *Goods inwards:* delivery dates, counting-in, quality checks, receipts.
20. *Security/confidentiality:* expectations, special requirements.

Thinking through what you need under these headings will ensure that both you and your handling house know what is expected. You can also obtain an accurate quotation for the job. Clearly, these vary depending on the amount of work involved. A typical cost might be 90p for receiving and checking three proofs of purchase and dispatching a model car. For setting up an in-bound telephone call number, receiving calls for a brochure, data capturing and posting the brochure, you might pay £2.00.

What to look out for

If you brief your needs early enough, handling houses are an ally. The main decision you face is one of cost and sophistication. If all you need is the receipt of applications and the mailing of items, there are local facilities in most parts of the country that will do the job for a low cost. However, this is probably missing an opportunity, both in terms of data capture and customer relations. More sophisticated operations cost more.

Points to look for include the audit trails a handling house offers for goods and cash, the scale of its computer operations, the training it gives to telephone staff, the efficiency and security of its warehousing and the nature and timeliness of its reports. All these mark out the sophisticated from the low-cost operation. Whatever type of handling house you use, make sure you have a good contract (see Chapter 4 for further details).

If you are running promotions regularly, it makes sense to build a long-term relationship with a handling house that becomes an extension of the company for both you and your customers.

The DMA Response and Fulfilment Council has produced a Practitioners guide to Response Handling, which can be downloaded from its Web site (dma.org.uk).

POINT OF PURCHASE MANUFACTURERS

Who they are

Drawn from a background in shop-fitting or design, the leading firms are members of the Point of Purchase Advertising Institute (POPAI), set up in the United States in 1936, in Paris in 1989 and in the UK in 1992. Point of purchase manufacturers enable promoters to attract attention, communicate offers and brand image, and increase impulse sales at the point at which the great majority of purchase decisions are made. The activity used to be referred to as point of sale (POS), but the initials created a confusion with electronic point of sale (EPOS). POP is clearer, but watch for the fact that POP is also the acronym for proof of purchase.

How they work

The incorporation of sound, light, movement and promotional offers in a single unit has moved POP well beyond its origin in cardboard dumpbins or PVC shelf-barkers. There are wonderfully creative people called 'cardboard engineers' who make incredible designs. Examples show the inventiveness and scope of POP:

- Cadbury's Creme Eggs enjoy a short but intense season between January and Easter. Advertising is wasted unless there is adequate display. In 1997, Cadbury introduced a dumpbin flashed with a question that echoed the advertising: 'How will you eat yours?' Consumers pressed a button on the dumpbin to release a flashing roulette sequence of lights that stopped at one of five suggested ways to eat your egg.
- Shortly after the introduction of Canadian Moosehead lager to the UK in 1993, the brand faced the challenge of increasing distribution in larger outlets. Standard POP material tends to get lost in them. The solution was an eight-foot relief map of Canada that featured a barcode reader. Consumers received a swipe card with every Moosehead purchase. When swiped through the reader on the map, it set off a swirl of LED lights that ended up in a different destination in Canada each time and a different prize to be claimed from behind the bar.
- Spillers Petfoods developed a 'shelf purrer' to launch its cat food brand Purrfect Selection. The battery-operated device sensed customers within a 12-foot radius and set off a voice message, 'Indulge your loved one with a can of new Spillers Purrfect'.

The primary applications of POP are in sectors that sell via retailers. Leisure outlets such as hotels, pubs and sports clubs are also important. However, POP is increasingly used to communicate brands well away from their normal sales outlets. Interactive displays in shopping centres, airports or anywhere else people gather can sell almost anything. Increasingly, the use of smart-card technology and interactive video and text messaging enables promoters to target particular offers to particular people, capture data about them and communicate product benefits and promotional offers wherever people have the time and propensity to respond. In the future, as people arrive at an airport in a new country, information on where they can buy their favourite brands will be instantly available to them.

Text messaging

SMS, text messaging sales promotions work well with the 18- to 24-year olds who are accustomed to text messaging. These are POP of a new kind. Imaginative displays accompany them. People use text messaging because it is fun: 70 per cent use it for humour, 60 per cent use it to make social arrangements. It removes voice contact, which can give people greater confidence in communication. It is a wireless system and is not linked to a fixed line. The text is limited to 160 characters per screen. It is capable of displaying logos or cartoons on screen and users can download ringing tones (10,000 are doing this each day). The quality of the accompanying sound and graphics is continually improving.

SMS advertising using the mobile Internet is in effect a permission-based lifestyle-centred communication, delivered via a device that is carried by the person and is often permanently on. A text message is short and usually pithy and uses the developed text language. Case studies on Cadbury's Text n' Win (40) and Diageo (41) appear in Chapter 14.

What to look out for

Sales promotion is about influencing behaviour. Consumer behaviour at the point of purchase is the behaviour that matters most. The enormous point of purchase operation to introduce the UK National Lottery was implemented in less than four months, long after other elements of the mix had been put together.

Critical points to look out for in using point of purchase are:

- think early about POP needs and integrate them into your advertising and promotional planning;
- use it to gain exposure in non-standard outlets; there are often great opportunities for joint promotions based on a POP unit;
- make the best use of increasing opportunities for light, sound and movement; there are real benefits to being an innovator in POP;
- think hard about the operational issues, especially who will distribute, site and install the units and (if high-tech) keep them running.

The leading manufacturers in the field are increasingly able to offer an all-in design-to-upkeep service. For details of them, contact POPAI (the address can be found in the further information chapter at the back of the book).

PROMOTIONAL INSURERS

Who they are

Any promotion carries an element of risk. Specialist insurance brokers, among whom the market leader is PIMS, exist to limit that risk. There are four main promotional risks that can be insured:

1. The offer can be so appealing that consumer redemptions vastly exceed your expectations, playing havoc with your budget. This is dealt with by over-redemption insurance.
2. A promotional premium can have met all relevant consumer legislation, and still be faulty. In the worst case, you may need to recall all the premiums in the market and cancel the promotion. You need product liability and recall insurance for this.
3. You can have carefully calculated the number of winners in a prize scheme, only to find that, as a result of a printer's error, you have vastly more winners than you expected. Printers' errors and omissions insurance will take care of it.
4. As promotions increasingly involve events, you will need insurance for the jugglers, fire-eaters and dancers that accompany them.

How they work

Whether you are offering a free mail-in item in return for a number of proofs of purchase, issuing a coupon in the press, sending out direct mail offering a brochure or offering retailers a reward for display, you need to calculate the likely number of redemptions. Only then can you calculate how many mail-in items to buy, how much money to set aside for coupons, how many brochures to print and how many retailer prizes to organize. The calculation is simple:

opportunities × *redemption rate* = *redemptions*

Most promoters will have experience of the likely redemption rates on promotions they regularly run on their own brands, but what if you are wrong? What if you are running a promotion that is new to you or in a product category that is unfamiliar to you? PIMS has a database of more than 5,000 promotions built up over the last 10 years that analyses redemption rates by brand, product category, communication mechanism, reward and promotional technique.

PIMS can first of all advise you of the likely redemption rate – which may vary from 2 per cent to 30 per cent or more. It can then insure against redemption that is higher than this. If the likely redemption rate is 10 per cent, it will typically insure redemption of between 10 and 15 per cent at a cost of 17.5 per cent of the amount you want to insure. It is possible to insure 100 per cent of the risk, but most contracts specify that you carry the risk if redemption is more than twice the expected level.

How do you know what amount to insure? It is very much up to you. If you are running a free mail-in for a model car with a cost of £1, you are most likely to want to insure for the cost of the car and the cost of postage and handling. A typical calculation would look like this:

Offer –free model car with two proofs of purchase.
Opportunities – offer printed on 200,000 packs, so, as two proofs of purchase are required, that gives 100,000 opportunities.
Redemption rate – 10 per cent.
Redemptions – 10,000 (100,000 × 10 per cent).
Cost per redemption – £1.80 (£1 for the model car, plus 80p handling and postage).
Over-redemption insurance requirement – 10 to 15 per cent.
Number of redemptions covered – 5,000 (15,000 – 10,000).
Sum insured – £9,000 (£1.80 × 5,000).
Premium payable – £1,575 (7,000 × 17.5 per cent).

It is worth noting that, at present, insurance premiums are not subject to VAT, though they are subject to Insurance Premium Tax (IPT).

Is it worth it? It all depends on how confident you are that you have estimated the redemption rate correctly, and how capable you feel of carrying the cost of over-redemption. A management benefit is that you can calculate the budget for all your promotions for the year and be confident that you have covered all eventualities. Unsurprisingly, insurance is most often taken out on promotions that are new to the promoter or their agency.

Product liability/recall and printers' errors and omissions insurance can apply either to single promotions or (more economically) to all the promotions you run in a year. For many manufacturers, it can be an extension of existing product liability insurance. The particularities of sales promotion mean it is often best to deal with it separately from the very specific product liability insurance a company will have negotiated for its own products.

Is it a good idea to have this kind of insurance? The tendency for consumers to prosecute companies for things that go wrong is increasing all the time. Many promoters now believe that insuring against it has become a cost of doing business and the price of sleeping easily at night.

What to look out for

There are three things that companies need to do when thinking about the risks involved in promotions:

1. Be absolutely clear about the scale of your risk. Look at existing data on redemptions, look at case studies of promotions that have gone wrong and understand consumer protection legislation. Only then can you make a decision about what to insure and what risk to take yourself.
2. If you are thinking of using an insurer, talk to them early on. Their experience of redemption rates can help in your budgeting, and sometimes show that particular offers are not affordable. They can also help ensure that your contracts with suppliers are as watertight as possible.
3. If you do insure a promotion, make sure you stick to the number of opportunities you have declared. Insuring on the basis of 200,000 packs and then printing 250,000 could invalidate the insurance.

If you do decide to carry the risk yourself, remember that there is a real cost involved. Set aside part of your annual budget to cover the minority of promotions that will, for all your planning, over-redeem or go wrong in some other way.

SPECIALIST PRINTERS

Who they are

Many promotions use standard leaflet, brochure and packaging printers. If you are intending to run an instant win promotion or to use games or scratch cards, you need to enlist the services of a specialist printer. Other printers specialize in the short runs that are sometimes needed for display material or individual-outlet promotions. Others specialize in label leaflets (those that carry a large amount of information in a concertina leaflet the size of a sticker).

How they work

If you are running a game or instant win promotion, you need to know that the right number of winning cards have been printed, that they are evenly distributed, that there can be no leakage of cards from the printers or distributors, that they cannot be counterfeited and that you can verify the winners. This is a tall order and leads to constant innovation in the technologies involved.

Part of the development is in the inks used. Latex overprints are the standard format for game cards. Developments include heat-sensitive inks that reveal a message on being touched, cold-sensitive inks that respond to a cold drink being put on them and microwave inks, which respond in a microwave. Case study 37 discusses an imaginative promotion for Sarson's vinegar – it used an ink that responded to vinegar. Another development is to replace hidden messages with a crack-open card that reveals another card inside. Special inks can increasingly be used on ceramics, plastics and textiles.

Avoiding counterfeiting has led to the development of computer systems for verifying winning tickets. One process is to mark winning tickets with a security number that, when entered into a database, shows the exact layout of the card. Another is to print winning tickets with codes that only show in ultraviolet light or that can be read only when matched exactly to a template. Holograms and three-dimensional technology are also used – and the best techniques, naturally enough, are not even disclosed to promoters.

What to look out for

Make sure you use a printer who really understands this business: winding up, as one retailer did, with 27 winners of its top prize in the first week of a promotion is a cost you cannot afford. Ensure, also, that your printer has errors and omissions insurance that specifically covers games.

Once the material has been printed, look closely at the procedures for packing and distributing winning tickets. If you are including an instant win inside a product (for example, underneath the cap of a bottle), make sure it is safe against tampering, both by retail staff and consumers. Keep up with evolutions in game technology. Games succeed as much by novelty as by the scale of the prizes being offered. It is well worth using a specialist printer's knowledge to be the first in your field to use a particular ink or game device.

FIELD MARKETING AGENCIES

Who they are

Field marketing agencies offer a large number of mainly part-time staff as a long-term extension to your own company's staff or to undertake one-off projects. The DMA's Field Marketing Council, which represents the leading firms, estimates that there are 35,000–40,000 people employed part-time in the business. A large firm may have as many as 15,000 people on its books.

The major firms are increasingly moving towards full-time staff working on long-term contracts for major promoters. They also overlap with handling houses in offering database, storage and dispatch services as well as staff. You can expect a competent agency to provide not just the personnel, but also to plan geographic coverage, create briefing materials, dispatch and control the items needed in the field, monitor and control the staff, analyse the results and even design and produce special uniforms for them.

How they work

Field marketing personnel can be employed to do almost anything that needs people out in the marketplace. They can act as a sales force to smaller outlets, install promotional material, distribute leaflets and coupons, hand out samples, collect consumer data, undertake mystery shopper calls, staff exhibition stands, sell directly to consumers, provide information in shopping centres and airports, and carry out blind product tests. Their application in promotional campaigns is huge.

Prices vary depending on the nature of the work to be done, but are typically based on a personnel cost of £8 per hour (2002 rate). A typical brief may be to call on independent retailers with promotional material and stock. Taking planning, travel, briefing and supervision into account, you could expect to pay £16 per outlet visited for this service (2002 rates).

What to look out for

The critical point to remember is that field staff are part of your firm as far as the people they meet are concerned. There is a balance to be struck between the cost a firm charges and the level of briefing, training and supervision that staff receive. Increasingly, the emphasis is on higher quality, and rightly so. Effective use of field marketing agencies depends, as with every other promotional supplier, on clear briefing and a clear understanding of what you want to achieve.

PREMIUM SOURCING HOUSES

Who they are

Open any of the three promotional magazines and you are confronted by page after page of advertisements for clocks, sweatshirts, electronics, model cars, crockery, books, pens. . . you name it, it's there. The British Premium Merchandise Association (BPMA) acts as the trade association for manufacturers of premiums, and its magazine is an effective advertising feature for its members' products. For any given product area, there are also endless sources of manufacturer information in trade directories and, increasingly, on the Internet.

Why not go direct to these companies to buy the premiums you need? For small quantities, and for standard items, it often makes sense. However, for large quantities, special products and products made in the Far East, it can make most sense to go to a company that is set up to design, source and ship promotional premiums to your specific requirements. These are the premium sourcing houses.

These businesses are not large – few have a turnover of more than £10 million. They typically have extensive contacts in the Far East, a direct or indirect base in Hong Kong, design facilities in the UK, processes for quality checking in the country of origin and other developed countries, and extensive knowledge of international customs regulations, product safety legislation, shipping arrangements and trade finance.

How they work

Premium sourcing houses ensure that promotional items are created, manufactured and delivered to the specific needs of a promotional campaign. Recent examples show the nature of their work:

- Nestlé has a continuing requirement for products that give 'playground cred' to Smarties among 7–9-year olds. The right premium ensures that Smarties remains an attractive product for this age group, and not just something that your kid sister eats. Developments in low-cost consumer electronics meant that it became possible to create the Zapper. This is a Smartie-shaped widget with eight coloured buttons that emits noises of sirens, machine guns and the like, and is cheap enough to offer with five proofs of purchase. The electronics were manufactured in one country, the plastic casing in another. It has been supplied to Nestlé subsidiaries throughout the world.
- Mugs are a promotional evergreen, used by coffee, tea and confectionery manufacturers among others. Traditionally, they have been sourced in the UK, but UK prices are not competitive in world terms. There are numbers of low-cost producers, but their quality has often been inadequate. There are also increasing regulations governing the toxicity of printing inks. Long-term collaboration between a sourcing house in the UK and a Far East factory led to the development of the right mug for KitKat at the right price.
- Another high-profile promotion run by Nestlé was themed on magic tricks. The company had identified a series of injection-moulded magic tricks that it could obtain from China, but was forestalled by quota restrictions on imports from China imposed by the EU. Its premium sourcing house was able to identify a manufacturer in India and help the factory meet unfamiliar quality requirements.

What to look out for

You can expect a premium sourcing house to have extensive contacts with manufacturers throughout the world, and to have a track record in creating and manufacturing products and shipping them across the globe. Pay particular attention to their quality systems. If you value brand reputation, it is not worth skimping on the quality process. Premium sourcing houses registered to ISO 9001 will have demonstrated the capability of their systems. It is seldom worth the risk of dealing with an intermediary company offering products at knock-down prices that cannot demonstrate quality systems.

It is worth bringing premium sourcing into an early stage of the discussion of promotions. In a number of markets – children's products in particular – the choice of premium may be critical to the success of a promotion. A good premium sourcing house will understand marketing as well as premiums. If you form a long-term relationship with a sourcing house, you will often be the first to hear of innovative products that are right for your market.

SUMMARY

Sales promotion agencies, handling houses, POP manufacturers, promotional insurers, specialist printers, field marketing agencies and premium sourcing houses form an infrastructure of businesses with one common thread: making promotions work. There are others, too – including the companies that supply off-the-shelf promotions. The trade press regularly reports on them, not least because they provide a substantial amount of advertising, and that makes much of the reporting uncritical. You need to use the trade press and exhibitions such as Incentive World.

If you do any amount of promoting, you are likely to need all of them at some time. It pays to identify a company in each sector with a solid financial basis, to consult with them at an early stage of promotional development and to build up a long-term relationship. No promoter can hope to develop specialist expertise in each of these fields. It makes sense to use them for their skills. If you decide to put all your promotions to a sales promotion agency, it still makes sense to know whom they are using for specialist services. One weak link in the promotional chain – whether it is handling, premium sourcing or field marketing – is enough to destroy a promotion.

How to Implement a Promotion

If you've followed the process so far, you will understand the crucial ingredients in devising a promotion. You'll be clear that for your product or service:

- there's a marketing objective to be fulfilled for which you can specify a promotional objective, such as increasing volume or gaining trial;
- you know the strategic nature of the brand, its values and customers;
- sales promotion, as the part of marketing that focuses on behaviour, is the right answer to a part of the marketing campaign that includes a need to draw attention at a specific time and at a specific place to a marketing activity;
- you know how to convert the marketing objective into a promotional objective by answering the question, 'Who do I want to do what?';
- you know of the need to define success, pick a KPI and then measure it to confirm that success (more of this in Chapter 9);
- the processes of brainstorming, list making and mind maps have been used to enable you to think imaginatively about promotional solutions;
- you have in mind the suppliers you can use, and the ways in which they can help you devise and implement an effective promotion.

Now it is time to look at the nuts and bolts of implementing a promotion. This chapter looks at five components of implementation: budget, timing, communication, logistics and legalities. It then sets out a simple cycle to take you from initial idea to completed promotion.

BUDGET

In many cases, particularly if you are working in an agency, the budget is given and you simply have to work within it. Will you be able to achieve all you want within the available budget? Are you sure? If not, go back to the beginning and start again. It is best not to try to cut corners as it is usually more expensive in the long run.

What, though, if you have the freedom to set the budget? Money for promotions comes from the same budget as money for every other part of the promotional mix. Money for price promotions may be accounted differently (this is discussed in Chapter 12). There are five ways in which companies set their promotional budgets. They set the figure as:

- what they spent last year, plus a little bit more for inflation and any expected market growth;
- a fixed percentage of turnover, established over time for the company and industry;
- the same as, or in ratio to, what major competitors spend;
- the amount needed to achieve the defined marketing objectives – that is, what is needed, no more no less;
- in these cost-cutting days, if you have not – through marketing accountability – shown value for money from all your marketing, then expect to be given the same as last year or expect to be cut!

Marketing academics recommend the precise amount required is what should govern the budget. Commercial concerns override. Unfortunately unless you know what works, its precise cost and that it gave value for money, you are stymied. In principle, budgeting exactly what you need is the right way to do it. The only justification for spending money on promotional activity is that it will achieve marketing objectives that contribute to long-term growth in profits. Relying on what your competitors are doing or on budgets fixed by someone else in the past are excuses for not thinking through the business objectives that face you today. The WKS survey showed few firms changed their budget year in year out, that is reducing in real terms, and they did not change what they spent it on either. They ignored anything new – the new media, direct marketing, accountability, advertising other than press, TV or posters.

Starting with a blank piece of paper each year is a difficult task and, in practice, companies use one of the first three methods, a combination of them, or the last. However, for sales promotion, there is a particular reason for using the precise – the academic – method. Promotions can be costed as a separate and specific intervention in the market. The cost of making the offer and the margin it generates can be compared to the margin you would expect to make if you did not make the offer.

There is a simple piece of arithmetic that is basic to sales promotion and deals with the relationship between promotional packs, proofs of purchase, opportunities to apply (OTA), redemption rate and cost. In this example, assume you are offering consumers the opportunity to mail in for a free model car on a packaged grocery product. The sequence is as follows:

1. Your first decision is how many labels to print the offer onto. Assume you want the promotion to last for a month. Take a month's volume, add 10 per cent for extra uptake, and you can calculate the number of promotional packs required as being, say, 250,000.
2. Next, you decide how many proofs of purchase you will ask consumers to send in. Set it too low and your regular consumers have no incentive to buy more. Set it too high and your less regular consumers have no chance of participating. A good rule of thumb is to set it at the average level of purchase of the category (not your brand) in the promotional period – in this case, a month. Assume, on this basis, you decide on five proofs of purchase.
3. Now you can calculate the opportunities to apply (OTA). This is the number of promotional packs divided by the proofs of purchase. It is impossible for there to be more redemptions than this. In this case the OTA is 250,000 ÷ 5 = 50,000.
4. Now you must estimate the likely redemption level. This depends on the attractiveness of the premium, the ratio between proofs of purchase and purchase frequency, the amount of support you give to the offer, the strength of your brand and a host of other factors. Assume in this case a 6 per cent redemption rate. The calculation is then the OTA multiplied by the redemption rate. In this case it is 50,000 × 6 per cent = 3,000.
5. Now you can bring in the cost of providing the model car and receiving and handling applications. In the discussion on handling houses in Chapter 6, there was an estimate for handling a model car of 90p. Assume the car costs you £1.10. The total cost per redemption is thus £2.
6. Now you know the cost of this part of the promotion. It is redemptions multiplied by the cost per redemption, in this case 3,000 × £2 = £6,000. You can add to this the cost of artwork, special printing and other support for the promotion. Assume this is a further £6,000, giving a total of £12,000.
7. Finally, you can express this figure as a cost per promoted pack by dividing it by the number of promoted packs. In this case it is £12,000 ÷ 250,000 = 4.8p.

This last is a very useful figure. You can use it to compare the costs of different promotions on a like-for-like basis. You can use it to calculate how many extra packs you need to sell for the promotion to break even. If the cost is too high, you can also use it to go back to your calculations and try to find savings – for example, by asking consumers to contribute to the cost of postage, finding a cheaper model car, or increasing the number of proofs of purchase.

If you are running a coupon (see Chapter 12 for details), the same calculation applies. Remember that the OTA are not calculated on the readership of a newspaper, but on its circulation. Those with a higher number of readers per copy may have a higher redemption rate, but a coupon can only be cut out once.

You will also need to keep a careful watch on VAT. Customs and Excise produces a series of booklets dealing specifically with promotions, business gifts and retail promotional schemes. They are, of course, subject to change, so you should make sure you have up-to-date copies to hand.

TIMING

Sales promotions are often run to meet short-term market needs. They must also work with the lead times of intermediaries and suppliers. This makes timing a critical issue, and one about which there is often conflict. It is important to be clear from the beginning about the following time constraints:

- when the promotion is needed to impact on the consumer;
- how long it will last;
- how that relates to the purchase frequency of your product or service;
- what lead times intermediaries require;
- how long you have for print and merchandise delivery;
- when you need your promotional concepts ready.

The time available at each stage strongly affects what can and cannot be achieved. Managing this can be significantly helped by the use of simple project management charts.

COMMUNICATION

Every promotion is communicated in or on material of some kind. The options include:

- the wrapping of the product;
- leaflets in or with the product or service;
- leaflets separate from the product or service;
- advertisements in press, on radio, TV or posters;
- sponsored shows or events;
- posters, stickers and other support material;
- sales aids;
- mailshots.

At an early stage, you need to identify ballpark costs for what you want to do. You can firm them up later, but you need to know that the promotion is, in principle, affordable. To do this you need to:

- select the appropriate communication media;
- estimate the quantities needed;
- estimate the specifications (colour, weight, frequency and so on);
- estimate artwork, photography and other design requirements, and obtain ballpark costs at first, detailed costs later.

This can involve a great deal of phoning to print, media and other suppliers. A useful shortcut is to obtain one of the published guides to print and media prices, and base your estimates on that. Another is to keep a file of all promotions that you have costed, and cannibalize the prices. Sales promotion agencies tend to be particularly good and quick at this, as they have a wealth of experience to draw on.

While the nuts and bolts are being developed, time can be spent drafting the words that will be used to communicate the promotion. There are always two parts to the verbal presentation of any promotion: the up-front claim and the technical details, rules, instructions and other essential, but secondary, information.

It is common for agencies to present concepts showing what the printed material and advertisements will look like. This has one major danger: until the copy or scripts are written it is impossible to know how big the printed material will need to be. Often the concepts are presented and the budgets agreed but later someone has to ask for an increase in budget because the leaflet needs an extra page.

Write the copy or script first, even if only roughly. This will guide the designers and enable them to create a far better visual concept. Experience shows that the tighter the brief given to designers and copywriters, the better the results and the greater control you have over costs.

Use the Web sites of the ISP and DMA to obtain examples of the wording needed for coupons, etc. The Royal Mail on its Web site gives updated examples of direct mail costs for different sizes of mailings.

Keep the creative approach simple. You have very little time to communicate your concept to the consumer. It is better to have a 'Win a holiday' headline than 'Bloggins summer spectacular'. The first communicates the benefits, the second nothing to those not directly associated with Bloggins.

You'll also need to consider how the offer will be presented graphically. Whether it is communicated by leaflets, advertisements or in a small space on a pack, some form of graphics is needed. Even if you are doing the promotion yourself, some help will be needed here. It is important to reflect the style and feel of the offer in your graphic design and (if possible) enhance the underlying values of your product or service.

LOGISTICS

Every promotion requires something to be given away – whether it is a prize, a coupon, a free mail-in premium or a charity donation. Having isolated what the offer consists of (win a holiday, send in for a kitchen knife, redeem a 25p coupon) it is possible to do the following:

- draw up a specification for the items involved;
- estimate the quantity needed;
- obtain at least ballpark costs.

Again, it is helpful to have reference books to hand to short-cut the process of phoning or writing for samples and prices. Do use the Web sites for examples. You can then turn to the operational characteristics of the promotion – how the promotion will actually work:

- Who will do what?
- Where will items be stored?
- How will they be distributed?
- What resources are needed at each stage?

What comes into this depends very much on the scale of the promotion and on your own resources. For a simple retail promotion, it may be no more complicated than arranging the printing and distribution of POP material. Other promotions can be very much more complicated, and can involve marshalling half a dozen different organizations, a dozen types of printed material and offer materials of many kinds.

You'll need to ask yourself how feasible your promotion is. A brand manager once bought some excellent deck chairs at an extraordinarily good price for use as a dealer loader (these are gifts given to retailers – see Chapter 13). It meant that his dealer loader offer would be far better than usual and far superior to those of his competitors. Unfortunately he forgot that most of the sales representatives were on the road for three days at a time making 15 calls a day. The brand manager had forgotten to consider how to fit 45 deck chairs into a Ford Escort. However, before you decide it is not feasible, ask yourself how it can be done rather than accept that it cannot. Be positive. Only when every option has proved impossible should you give up. After all, your great idea deserves to see the light of day.

LEGALITIES

The legal and self-regulatory controls on sales promotion are discussed in Chapter 8, but it is worth discussing the subject briefly here.

It's best to start with the positive values that exist in your brand and in your relationship with your customers. Creative promotions have their origins in the values of a brand, in a shaft of lateral thinking that captures the imagination and fits the brief like a glove. However, sometimes, you can get carried away with enthusiasm.

Ask yourself, does the activity conform to the various codes of practice and the law? If it does not, then the worst thing you can do is to try to bend the promotion to fit. This usually ends up by emasculating the promotion and making it too complicated.

Remember also to check how the activity will reflect on the promoter. Short-term gains that are achieved by an unfulfilled expectation on the part of the consumer will damage the company's reputation in the longer term. If something looks too good to be true, it probably is: remember how the Hoover flights promotion (see Case study 24) almost killed the company.

A very simple rule to follow is to put yourself in the position of the consumer and think how you would feel about being made this offer. If you would be unhappy, then so will your targets. You may also think again of your imaginary village and see how its inhabitants would react. 'Do unto others as you would be done to' is as applicable to promotions as the rest of life. Think highly of consumers – they are neither stupid nor gullible.

A STRUCTURED PROCESS

Managing the implementation of a promotion is no easy task. It helps if you divide the work into three stages from brief to implementation, each separated by evaluation and decision phases, and resist the temptation to go straight to the detailed development of the first concept that comes to mind:

- Stage 1. Think through the possible solutions to the promotional brief. Define success. What KPI will you use to measure it? Reserve some budget to measure the KPI.
- Stage 2. Develop your leading concepts in outline form.
- Stage 3. Develop the top concept into an operational plan. Recheck the KPI.

Below, we will look at each of these three stages in turn, focusing on the work to be done at each stage – possible solutions, outline development and detailed development. Keep the stages separate but remember it is all one process. Think of the stages as a series of loops.

Stage 1. Possible solutions

Bear in mind the promotional objective and the promotional brief. Define success and set the KPI you propose to use to measure success. List possible concepts. Each concept will be described in a dozen or so words, often with further possibilities in brackets. A concept could be described as 'Competition – spot the ball (try a variant?) – holiday prize (Tenerife? Florida?) – plus vouchers for everyone who enters (if they cost less than £500)'. Another may be even less specific about mechanics, but focus more on a theme: 'Win a holiday – competition or free draw – total prize pot £5,000'.

Now you have to apply a rough filter to the ideas you have developed. Figure 7.1 shows how it looks in flow chart form. This stage is the top part of the figure.

In the short-listing phase, you will need to go back to the marketing objective and promotional objective and see whether or not your brilliant idea is likely to achieve the objectives. Keep the promotional brief to hand and remember how you defined success. To continue with the lager example from Chapter 5, will promoting it in tennis clubs really achieve a sufficient increase in sales? If it won't, you'll have to start again. Be particularly careful of the promotion that grips the customer, but not the objective. Sales promotion is there to meet a marketing objective, not simply to engage the customer.

Depending on the brief, you will end up with as few as one or two possible solutions or as many as half a dozen. You can take these forward to outline development. Typically, a sales promotion agency brings these items together on a 'concept board'. This is a rough illustration with the key message on it that instantly communicates the offer, backed up by one or two sheets of A4 on which is set out how the promotion will work and what it will cost. If you are doing it yourself, you will still need to see what the offer will look like and note down its key costs and operational characteristics.

Stage 2. Outline development

The task now is to flesh out the details of your short-listed concepts and to establish whether or not they will actually work in practice. This process is shown in the middle part of Figure 7.1 (page 98).

Working up the short-listed concepts is not a matter of doing different things to the first stage – it is doing the same things in more detail. So, for example, you will work out the detailed print specification and start writing the body copy. This process will narrow down the candidate concepts. You know that the concepts you are left with will work, and how they will work. These are the concepts to choose from. Now is the time to go back to the promotional brief, and critically examine each candidate concept against it. Which really fits the best? Which has strengths in one area, but loses out in another? Which really meets the promotional objective? Which gives the most added value? And which will turn on your target audience the most?

For a big promotion, formal research is often advisable at this point, but research of some kind can be done for every promotion – simply by asking people you know. Friends, colleagues at work, customers – all can be subjected to what is often (unfairly) called 'the idiot test'. Simply line up the concept boards, ask them to think themselves into the position of the target audience and rate your concepts on three criteria: clarity, attractiveness and accessibility.

It is surprising (and mortifying) how often your favourite concept will leave other people cold. You are too close to it to be objective yourself. And even if the concept is clear enough, there will be points where it can be improved and ideas for these tweaks will come from the most unlikely sources.

At the end of this process, you are in a position to select the top concept. If it fits the brief like a glove and excites the people you show it to, you know you have a winner on your hands. At the very least, you will have a sound, workable promotion that meets the brief you set. Now it must be turned into physical items, such as leaflets, posters and the like.

Stage 3. Operational plan

This stage takes your top concept through to implementation. The elements of this stage are shown in the lower part of Figure 7.1 (page 98).

This is the stage at which to check the criterion for success, set the KPI to measure and the budget to carry out the measurement, to finalize and check all the secondary copy for the promotion – entry instructions, rules, descriptions of the prizes and so forth. It is imperative to follow the Code of Sales Promotion Practice in doing so. Use the Web sites to check. The rough visual also needs to be turned into artwork for all the various printed items for the promotion. Outside help will almost always be needed here.

The materials necessary to the promotion can now be obtained. It is normally possible at this stage to beat the ballpark prices obtained earlier because you now have a firm intention to proceed, so it is worth shopping around for better prices.

It is particularly important to pay attention to the operational plan. Many promotions fail despite excellent concepts, superb designs and exciting offers because a simple error has been made in the administration system. It is vital to go through this in the finest detail, and to ensure that every aspect of delivery, handling and distribution is fully organized. Handling houses, and other suppliers described in Chapter 6, are crucial at this stage. A detailed operational plan sets out exactly what will happen when, by whom and how. A really tight plan leaves no room for error or misunderstanding, and saves a great deal of time in the long run. After a while, the framework of a good promotional operational plan for your own company will become established, and so the process of drawing it up will become quicker as time goes on.

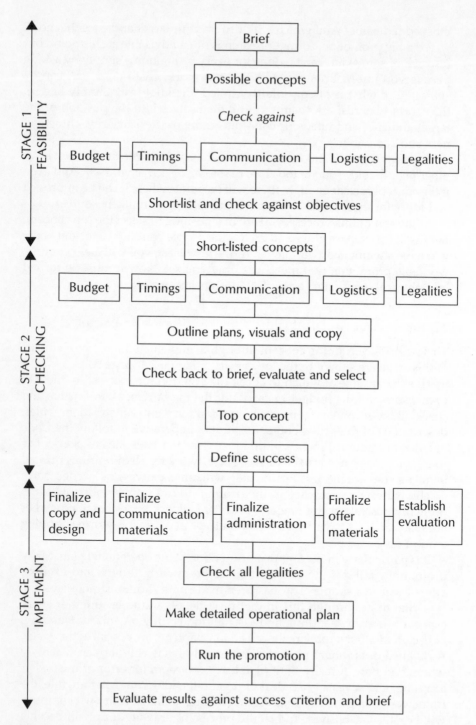

Figure 7.1 The brief to the result

The operational plan must include contracts with third parties. They are of particular importance where the operation of a promotion depends critically on another company performing functions delegated to it. Contracts should always be drawn up for the following:

- *Joint promotions.* These are a disaster if the relationship turns sour, and one of the most effective ways of promoting if the relationship flourishes. A contract not only establishes the ground rules, but also obliges each party to think through all the eventualities before committing to a promotion.
- *Agency relationships.* A relationship with a sales promotion agency should always be governed by a contract setting out mutual responsibilities.
- *Premium supply.* Contracts beyond normal purchasing conditions are not generally necessary if you are making a one-off purchase of premium items. They are necessary if, for example, you are seeking to call off items for a promotion in the future or if a special item is being made.
- *Support services.* Contracts are advisable with handling houses, auxiliary sales forces, telesales operators and other specialists.

The formats of contracts vary enormously. Some companies write special contracts, others use long and complicated standard contracts. Many find that an exchange of letters backed by a set of standard conditions of trade provides the best balance. As promotional redemption rates are not always predictable, it is important to allow for changes in requirements in your contracts, and to know on what basis the cost of any extra work is calculated.

Finally, you should establish responsibility for the marketing accountability accounting and evaluation systems. You decided what success would be, you set a KPI, and you need to make someone responsible for measuring the KPI. When you have the KPI results collected you will be able to evaluate the actual results against your definition of success. It is too late to think about how to evaluate a promotion after it has been run, when you have missed the opportunity to record much of the information. The time to do this is beforehand. There are various key measures that will flow from your objective (discussed further in Chapter 9).

IMPLEMENTATION

Now it is time to run the promotion. A promotion set up along the lines of the processes described here should run without a hitch, but it is always important to monitor its progress and be prepared to react to unforeseen developments. Redemption rates, in particular, should always be monitored closely against the expected rate. Remember, too, a promotion ends when you have analysed all the available information to establish whether or not it achieved the objective set and your definition of success, and to draw out whatever lessons can be learnt. This is the subject of Chapter 9.

SUMMARY

Implementing a promotion is a logical three-stage looping process. It is a mistake to try to take short cuts. The process can take a short time – just a week if necessary. The benefit of a system is that it takes you logically through all the stages and avoids costly mistakes. Following the system will not guarantee world-beating promotions, but it will ensure practical, workable promotions that achieve your objectives. It is vitally important to attend to issues defining success and setting the means of measurement – the KPI, budget, timing, communication, logistics and legalities in turning a promotional idea into a fully fledged promotion then evaluating it so that lessons can be learnt before repeating the cycle. Look again at Figure 4.1 on page 46 as a reminder.

8

Self-regulation and the Law

Promotional activity has long operated within the dual context of self-regulation and legal constraint. As early as 1890, the leading poster companies set up a Joint Censorship Committee to exclude objectionable posters. In 1907, Parliament passed the first of the modern pieces of advertising legislation, the Advertising Regulations Act, which gave local authorities power to control poster hoardings Both these developments concerned posters – the most publicly intrusive form of advertising. Both derived from an active public campaign. They are a measure of the close relationship between self-regulation and law and the impetus that public and political opinion gives to both.

The balance between self-regulation and law has varied over time, and varies considerably between countries. Within the EU, Germany has tended towards law, the UK towards self-regulation. However, the picture is not black and white – all countries have a mixture of both. Since the 1986 Single European Act, it has been an open question as to whether or not EU practice would tend towards one or the other. That balance is moving steadily towards greater protection of the consumer from unsupported claims. In the Introduction we discussed the importance of building long-term customer relationships, the foolishness of campaigns that undermine relationships, and increasing public concern about the ethical status of the company behind the brand. Promoters who understand that will have little trouble with either the codes of practice or the laws. However, both the codes and the laws include details that are not obvious at first sight. You need to take account of them in the letter as well as the spirit.

UK CODES OF PRACTICE

The British Code of Sales Promotion is a self-regulatory code written by people in the business in their own long-term self-interest. It is based on the view that self-regulation is preferable to laws for promoter and consumer alike. It is supported by the Code of Advertising Practice (CAP) Committee, and is under the supervision of the Advertising Standards Authority (ASA). All the codes are available on various Web sites (ISP, ASA, CAP and DMA). The fundamental requirements are that all promotions should be:

- legal, decent, honest and truthful;
- conducted equitably, promptly and efficiently;
- seen to deal fairly and honourably with consumers;
- in line with accepted principles of fair competition;
- in line with the spirit, as well as the letter, of the rules, and not bringing the industry into disrepute.

The Code is not a substitute for the legal protection of the consumer, producer or distributor against fraudulent practice, but a complement to the law. Promoters are expected to stay within both. Implementation of the Code is in the hands of individual sales promoters, whether they be companies or agencies. As with the law, ignorance of the Code is no defence for not following it. If you have not already obtained a copy, phone the ASA for one now (see under 'Trade associations' in the further information chapter at the back of the book) or better still download a copy now from the ASA Web site. Also download the ISP legal checklist.

The implementation of the Code is monitored by the ASA. The 300 complaints typically upheld by the ASA each year represent a fraction of the total number of promotions, but they involve some big names and some consistent failings. Every month, the ASA publishes a monthly report that details the complaints it has upheld, and some of those it hasn't. A sample of complaints upheld over the last few years highlights the issues at stake and forms the case study in this chapter.

The ASA Council decisions can be (and are) criticized from two directions – as being overly fussy and as being toothless. Injunctions have only been taken out three times in more than 20 years, but many other companies (notably tabloids) appear year after year for the same or similar infringements. In the final analysis, companies have to decide if they support a self-regulatory system or not. If they do, they need to take what the ASA says seriously, even if they think it is overly fussy and toothless (which it can be).

There are several regulars in the ASA's reports. Many relate to availability, participation and administration. Promoters are expected to have sufficient quantities of their promotional products to meet likely demand. Phrases such as 'subject to availability' do not relieve you of your responsibilities.

Demand should be estimated in advance, and you should also have plans to meet unexpected demand. If all else fails, an item of equivalent value must be offered. If there are limitations on participation, or any costs that consumers may incur in taking part, they must be clearly stated. Also, arrangements must be made to dispatch goods within 30 days.

Promotions directed at young children are an area of particular sensitivity – not least because children are such keen participators in promotions. The Code requires that they should be for products that are suitable for them. They should not take unfair advantage of children's lack of experience, encourage them to make excessive purchases, or cause conflict between them and their parents. Obtaining parental permission for a child's participation is often a good idea.

The word 'free' is one of the most powerful available to promoters, and its use is closely governed. If the consumer has to pay for anything other than postage, it may be a fine promotional offer, but it is not 'free'. This applies to a contribution towards a mail-in item, the cost of premium rate telephone lines as much as the requirement to make a purchase before taking up the offer.

The most unnecessary area of complaint relates to the rules of promotions – unnecessary because it is not difficult to get the rules right. The Code provides a list of rules that should be included in competitions, free draws and instant win offers. Keep them simple if possible, but always include entry conditions, the closing date, a description of the prizes, the criteria for judging entries and the availability of a winners list.

Complementary to the Advertising and Sales Promotion Codes, the CAP has produced specific rules for the advertising and promotion of alcoholic drinks, cigarettes, financial services, vitamins, health products, slimming products, cosmetics and medicines. There are also specific rules about environmental claims, distance selling, employment and business opportunities.

How do you make sure you stay within the Code? The CAP, which writes the Code, operates a fast, free and confidential Copy Advice Service, dealing with over 10,000 enquiries a year (for the telephone and fax numbers for this service, see the Advertising Standards Authority, under 'Trade associations' in the further information chapter at the back of the book). However, there is a downside to this: if you fail to follow the advice of the CAP because you disagree with it, you will not have a leg to stand on if there is a subsequent complaint. For this reason, members of the ISP often prefer to use the ISP's Legal Advice Service. Going to the CAP is a bit like going to a policeman to ask whether or not what you want to do is within the law. There are also various legal practices offering advice on sales promotion law.

Producing codes of practice has become a growth industry. Many of them are turgid, repetitive and entirely without teeth. Just as clubs think they need ties, so trade associations think they need codes. You should make your own judgement about what codes matter in your business. There are references to sales promotion in codes produced by the Consumers Association for business sponsorship of educational materials, for financial services promotion produced by the various financial regulators, by the pharmaceutical industry and by many other industry associations. The following codes can be particularly relevant to sales promotion:

- British Promotional Merchandise Association Code of Practice
- Direct Marketing Association Code of Practice
- DTI Code of Practice for Traders on Price Indications
- International Code of Sales Promotion Practice
- Institute of Purchasing and Supply Code of Practice
- Mail Order Traders' Association Code of Practice
- Promotional Sourcing Association Code of Practice
- Promotional Handling Association Code of Practice
- Independent Committee for the Supervision of Standards of Telephone Services Code of Practice

John Williams reprints many of these codes in his *Manual of Sales Promotion* – and they extend to more than 80 closely printed A4 pages. They frequently change, but as the downloads are free, it makes sense not to reprint them here. However, I suggest that you get hold of up-to-date copies of those that affect you, using the further information chapter at the back of the book.

UK LAW

More than a hundred UK laws affect the conduct of sales promotion, along with a growing number of EU directives. Some types of promotion – particularly involving packaging, product safety and statements at point of sale – are subject to Local Authority Trading Standards Officers. Legislative teeth have been given to the ASA by the 1988 Control of Misleading Advertisements Regulations, which gives the Director General of Fair Trading the power to take out a court injunction against an advertiser or promoter who continues to use an ad or promotion that the ASA has ruled against.

These regulations are some of the very few that were actually designed to control sales promotional activity. Most of the other acts and regulations were designed to control consumer credit, gambling, trade descriptions and so forth. It is not surprising, therefore, that the legal framework for sales promotion derives from small sections of a large number of acts, and that it is sometimes contradictory.

The Scottish legal system and some of the relevant legislation differs in details from that pertaining to England. However, for all practical purposes, the UK can be considered a single unit for sales promotion.

EU AND INTERNATIONAL LAW

Promoters thinking of running promotions in other countries – including the Republic of Ireland – must take account of the very different legal frameworks that apply in these countries.

Only in Greece, Spain and Portugal (among EU countries) are all the many UK techniques allowed. Germany is a graveyard for sales promotion: free draws, share-outs, collector promotions and next purchase coupons are among the techniques that are disallowed. The Benelux countries are fairly restrictive as well.

A rough guide to what is allowable in different EU countries is given in a table prepared and regularly updated by ISP (see Table 8.1). It is only a guide and promoters should always seek advice before applying a UK technique elsewhere.

Table 8.1 What can I do in Europe?

Promotion technique	UK	NL	B	SP	IR	IT	F	G	DK
On-pack promotions	✓	✓	?	✓	✓	✓	?	✓	✓
Banded offers	✓	?	?	✓	✓	✓	?	✓	✓
In-pack premiums	✓	?	?	✓	✓	✓	?	?	?
Multi-purchase offers	✓	?	?	✓	✓	✓	?	✓	✓
Extra product	✓	✓	✓	✓	✓	✓	?	✗	✓
Free product	✓	?	✓	✓	✓	✓	✓	✗	?
Reusable/other use packs	✓	✓	✓	✓	✓	✓	✓	?	✓
Free mail-ins	✓	✓	?	✓	✓	✓	?	✓	✓
With purchase premiums	✓	?	✓	✓	✓	✓	?	✗	?
Cross product offers	✓	✓	✗	✓	✓	✓	?	✓	✓
Collector devices	✓	✓	✓	✓	✓	✓	✓	✓	✓
Competitions	✓	?	?	✓	✓	?	✓	✓	?
Self-liquidating premiums	✓	✓	✓	✓	✓	✓	✓	✓	✓
Free draws	✓	✗	?	✓	✓	✓	✓	✓	✓
Share outs	✓	✓	?	✓	✓	?	?	✓	?
Sweepstake/lottery	?	✗	?	✓	✗	?	?	✓	✗
Money off vouchers	✓	✓	✓	✓	✓	✓	✓	?	✓
Money off next purchase	✓	✓	✓	✓	✓	✓	✓	✗	✓
Cash backs	✓	✓	✓	✓	✓	✗	✓	✗	✓
In-store demos	✓	✓	✓	✓	✓	✓	✓	✓	✓

Key ✓ = permitted ✗= not permitted ? = may be permitted
Source: ISP

CASE STUDIES

The following five case studies, taken from ASA reports, deal with typical infringements of the Code. Some are obvious, some less so. In answering the questions that follow each example, bear in mind that the ASA Council is not infallible – it may make judgements that you or others want to dispute.

CASE STUDY 16. COCA-COLA

Coca-Cola ran a promotion in January 1990 headlined 'Free music – 10,000 music vouchers to be won'. To take part, consumers had to phone a premium rate telephone number, at that time charging 38p per minute at peak times. People complained that this meant it was not 'free', that consumers effectively paid to enter and Coca-Cola benefited from that payment.

The ASA upheld the complaint. Although there was an option to participate by post, it was only possible to do so after 30 April – three months after the promotion began (ASA Report 184, August 1990).

What steps could Coca-Cola have taken to keep this promotion within the Code if it still wanted to use the word 'free'?
If it didn't use the word 'free', how else could it have described the promotion?

CASE STUDY 17. VAUXHALL MOTORS

The company offered '£1,500 cash back' on its Astra GTE and £1,000 or £500 on other Astra and Nova models in a series of press ads in 1991. People complained that when they went to the showroom, they found that the £1,500 cash back didn't apply to the GTE Convertible, and that some of the other models featured in the ads were not available.

The ASA criticized Vauxhall for not making it clear that different cash back arrangements applied to the GTE Convertible than to other GTE models. It also criticized the company for not extending the cash back offer when it ran out of stock during the promotion, particularly as it was continuing to run ads for it (ASA Report 9, February 1992).

How could Vauxhall have ensured that the consumer offer on the GTE Convertible was clear within the meaning of the Code?
Assuming all the ads were booked, what steps could Vauxhall have taken to ensure that it stayed within the Code when stocks ran out?

CASE STUDY 18. *THE EXPRESS*

The paper ran an offer in 1993 headlined on the front page, 'Free ice-cream for every reader'. In fact, the voucher inside the paper entitled them to a double scoop of Thornton's ice cream for the price of a single scoop, as long as one scoop was a specified flavour.

The ASA upheld the complaint (ASA Report 31, December 1993).

What words could The Express have used in its front-page headline to keep within the Code?
Would it have been acceptable within the Code for the restriction to specified flavours to have been in small print on the inside?

CASE STUDY 19. *THE SUN*

In 1996 *The Sun* ran an offer headlined on the front page 'This paper gives you a FREE go in tonight's £30m lottery... YOUR FREE National Lottery Syndicate ticket is inside *The Sun* today... and it could win you a share of tonight's £30m roll-over jackpot. That's right, it could be you!' On page three, the paper continued, 'Play SYNDICATES for £30m tonight'.

In fact, *The Sun* had not bought its readers a 'free go' in the Lottery. It had bought 40,000 tickets, one for every hundred copies of the paper sold. Readers could, at best, expect one-hundredth of any prize. Also, the forecast jackpot was not £30 million, but £23.8 million.

The ASA said the promotion was misleading (ASA Report 61, June 1996).

How do you think this promotion differs from the Sellotape promotion (Case study 27), which was not criticized by the ASA?
How could The Sun have rephrased its promotion to keep within the Code?

CASE STUDY 20. BALKAN HOLIDAYS

The company ran a brochure ad in 1996 claiming, 'Free up to age 12! All two-week beach holidays and two-centre beach/mountain holidays to Bulgaria'. Unfortunately, it was not true. People complained that some holidays did not have free child places.

The ASA upheld the complaint (ASA Report 67, December 1996).

Would consumers have a case in law for holding Balkan Holidays to its offer of a free child place on all holidays?
How effective do you think the ASA has been in persuading advertisers not to make misleading offers of this kind?

SUMMARY

Sales promotion is a practical, nuts and bolts affair and there are a lot of detailed rules to follow in both the Codes and in legislation. There are also some broad principles that reflect good business practice. The collective need of promoters to avoid intrusive legislation makes it important to follow both the spirit and the letter of the Code. Following the Code is not difficult if you use one of the copy-checking services available to help you. If in any doubt, contact the ISP (if you are a member) or a specialist legal practice. Each country has different laws governing sales promotion, and you need to take them into account.

Marketing Accountability and Research

DOING MARKET ACCOUNTABILITY AND RESEARCH

Marketing accountability is best carried out by a marketer defining the sales promotion success and setting the KPI, with someone else carrying out measuring/recording of the KPI. The marketer then compares the figures with the success definition, and an evaluation is produced.

Whichever way you go, it is important to be clear that marketing accountability and research is designed to produce actionable answers to specific questions that significantly affect the decisions you have to make. If the answers are not actionable, or their impact is insignificant, nothing will have been achieved. This applies to all types of marketing accountability and research discussed in this chapter.

MARKETING ACCOUNTABILITY: HOW TO DEFINE SUCCESS, SET KPIS, MEASURE AND EVALUATE PROMOTIONS

Sales promotions are undertaken to achieve specific promotional objectives, which are normally part of a campaign to achieve a marketing objective.

They are undertaken in preference to other marketing activities because they are thought to be the most effective way to achieve the task in hand. To be effective, they must offer real benefits, and that normally costs money. So, it is absolutely critical that you ensure your promotions prove to be value for money by defining the success criterion of your promotion, setting KPIs by which to measure, measuring and finally evaluating to see if you have achieved success, otherwise they will not be as effective as they possibly can be. The lessons learnt can be borne in mind for the next cycle of promotion (see Figure 4.1, page 46).

Far less accountability is undertaken in sales promotion than in other fields of marketing. The reasons for this are various:

- individual promotions seldom have the budgets that justify an additional amount for marketing accountability;
- promotions can, in many respects, be measured by sales results;
- there is often not the time to define success, set a KPI, measure and evaluate market accountability before the next promotion is due.

The point is made in the book, *Value for Money Marketing* (by Roddy Mullin, published by Kogan Page, 2001) that marketing accountability has to become part of company culture before it is routinely applied.

However, those who do evaluate their promotions after defining success, setting KPIs and measuring, know the benefits it brings – and there is every reason to undertake evaluation. This chapter looks at the ways in which you can define success, set KPIs, measure and evaluate your promotions, both in what you have to do before and after undertaking any particular piece of activity.

THE PURPOSE OF MARKETING ACCOUNTABILITY

Like a lamppost, marketing accountability should be used to shed light, not to lean on. It cannot make decisions for you, but it can narrow the areas of uncertainty and limit the possibility of error. Once a culture of marketing accountability is part of a company's culture then there will be records of what works and what does not. Marketing accountability is an iterative process that will very rapidly save you money. There are three main stages of promotional marketing accountability:

1. *Thinking accountability.* Define success. Set KPIs. Make someone responsible for measuring the KPIs. Thinking accountability and planning for marketing accountability is an excellent input into strategic questions such as how to split your marketing budget between advertising, sales promotion, direct marketing and publicity. It has the added benefit of

providing evidence and facts to put in front of finance directors to demonstrate the effectiveness of marketing and show value-for-money marketing. It does assume that a culture of marketing accountability exists and all other marketing activities are also accountable in order to make the budget allocations. Sales promotion will, of course, be onto a real winner if it is the only accountable activity.

2. *Measure.* You can do this in a test stage to identify the particular promotional concepts that will meet the objectives you have, or monitor throughout a promotion or just collate the collected measurements at the end. Be aware if you are measuring a change in behaviour or attitude that you may have to measure the KPIs before your promotional activity so you can record the change resulting.

3. *Evaluate.* Compare the effect and impact of promotions you have undertaken with your definition of success and feed this evaluation into the planning of future promotions. A good evaluation system is used by all those in the organization who run promotions, is consistently applied and makes the results available to everyone who needs to know now and in the future. It is a key to collective learning in any company or agency and, over time, becomes a valuable asset.

KEEPING EVALUATION KNOWLEDGE

The challenge in setting up an in-house evaluation knowledge system is knowing what you need to record and what you can reasonably discard. The challenge in operating it is finding the time to do the recording while the evidence is still available, and knowing what to circulate, what to put on your database and what to keep in manual files. Make the system too complicated and you run the risk that it will not be used. Make it too simple, and you will not have the information you need next time round.

In sales promotion, this challenge is tougher than it is in many other areas of business because promotions are so varied and so often conducted by staff who move on to other jobs. Many agencies have built a spreadsheet of response rates to different coupons, free mail-ins and other offers. These are invaluable, but are at the pinnacle of a good system. The place to start is recording the basic data for each promotion you run.

How an evaluation knowledge system works

The most practical approach is to produce a document wallet containing all the key information about a promotion. You can organize your data under the following four headings. Under the first three, you can either write an appropriate paragraph or include a piece of paper in your file. The last one requires you to stand back from the evidence and think.

Background and objectives

List here the products on which the promotion ran, the quantities involved and the name of the promotion. Also record the three key points that led you to undertake the promotion: the marketing objective, the promotional objectives and the answer you gave to the question, 'Who do I want to do what?' Including the reason why the objective was set ('we faced a major challenge from a new competitor') locates the promotion in a context that may be forgotten in a year's time.

Description

This is a detailed description of what the promotion involved. You may be able to include your operational marketing plan – but, before you file it, make sure you update it to show what actually happened, not what you planned to happen. Make sure you include:

- the offer made to the consumer;
- mechanic (including detailed rules and entry requirements);
- operational structure (who did what, agencies and suppliers used);
- communication materials (type and quantity);
- media support;
- timings;
- trade/intermediary support;
- sales force activity (if relevant);
- copies of all relevant printed or video material;
- suppliers and contacts.

What happened

There are three primary measures of the results of a promotion, and they relate, respectively, to promotional response, sales and finance. In many cases, it is simplest to include the evidence in your document wallet rather than to spend time entering it into another document. For example, if your handling house gives you an analysis of applications for a free mail-in, simply include that piece of paper. Make sure you cover:

- *Marketing accountability:* how success of the sales promotion was defined, what KPI was set, and a record of the KPI measurement, evaluation and analysis of the result against the success criterion. You should note whether the result met, nearly met or did not meet the success criterion you set.
- *Promotional response:* consumer uptake of the promotion, trade participation, the results of any market research or surveys undertaken, a note of any consumer, trade or sale force comments.

- *Sales:* sales figures for the periods before, during and after the promotion, the results of any continuous surveys of market share, distribution and penetration, relevant figures for competitors' products.
- *Finance:* the cost of all material produced for the promotion, any trade discounts, fees and other costs, and any calculations that you make about the profit contribution the promotion made.

Sales and finance data will, in most cases, be information generated by other parts of the company. Make sure you include information that helps in promotional evaluation, not just because it is there.

Analysis

Did the promotion work? How you answer this question depends on the culture of the company. To listen to some brand managers and agency personnel, there's never been a promotion that didn't transform the fortunes of the promoted product. For the analysis to be useful, however, you must be as honest as possible. You should refer back to the promotional objective, the brief and the success criterion and the KPI you set.

You should include *statistics* – how the promotion performed against quantitative objectives set for participation, sales, penetration and market share; how it performed against the operational marketing plan you set, the budget and timings. You should also include *comments* – an assessment of the lessons learnt from it, particularly what you would do differently next time, and the experience it has given you of suppliers, trade partners and internal departments.

The analysis section is not just a matter of reporting that sales increased by 11 per cent against a target of 10 per cent. If a major competitor suffered a production blip at the same time, you need to record it. Analysis is about why a promotion performed as it did. The answers are not always easy to find, but repeated and honest analysis makes the process easier.

What to look out for

Putting a promotion finally to bed with a document wallet containing the information and analysis listed above is the basic building block of a marketing accountability system. Before you put it away, though, you need to make sure that:

- the wallet is indexed and accessible so others can find it;
- any basic data that can be held on a central database – for example, response levels – are transferred;
- there is a debrief meeting so that experience is shared.

The enemy of good evaluation is the next job, but resist the temptation to switch to it. Taking these steps would, in most companies, transform the quality of promotional evaluation. It would even give you the information you need to enter your promotions for, and maybe win, an ISP award.

For sales promotion, marketing accountability can be used to address the following type of questions:

- Did the sales promotion achieve the objective?
- What was the cost to achieve the objective of that sales promotion?
- Was the sales promotion value for money?
- How did the sales promotion compare in value-for-money terms with other marketing activities or sales promotions we have used to achieve the same objective?
- Was the KPI used the most appropriate and was it effective?

The answers enable better planning next time.

RESEARCH

Research is useful to support decisions on the use of sales promotions in general and choosing one in particular.

Questions market research answers about attitudes to sales promotions in general

- How do particular groups of intermediaries and potential customers respond to sales promotional offers?
- What kind of promotional offer do they find most compelling?
- What other products and services would they link your own product or service to for the purposes of joint promotions?
- How do they react to different kinds of charity offer?
- What frequency of purchase is it sensible to aim at in constructing proof of purchase requirements?
- What was the impact of a promotion on brand values and on the reaction to the promotion by those who did and those who did not take up your offer?

It is dangerous to rely on a hunch. Do the research.

There are various ways in which you can go about doing promotional research:

- *Doing it yourself.* This is the only way to undertake factual desk research on sales patterns and evaluate it yourself, as only you will have access to the data. Because resources are normally limited, the more you can do the other types of research yourself, the more likely it is to be done.
- *Using specialist researchers.* Most market research companies will undertake promotional research, and a number have developed specialist methodologies in the field.
- *Including it in an agency brief.* Sales promotion agencies now have longer-term relationships with clients, and often have in-house resources in market research. It can make sense to build both a marketing accountability and a research element into every brief if you use an agency.

The greatest advances in this area have been made in promotions to children and young people, where changing fashions have made it critical to understand the issues that motivate them. On a larger scale, it is too much for one brand. There is immense scope for it in alliances such as that between Cadbury Schweppes, Bass, Kimberly-Clark and Unilever to pool research and database information.

These questions are answered by a mix of field research (where you actually ask people or pay market researchers to ask the questions) and desk research (where you find out and use the field research of others).

Questions market research answers to decide which sales promotion to use

The following have a bearing on the selection of a particular sales promotional concept over others:

- the level of response you can expect from a particular offer with particular entry requirements;
- the effect on response rates of changing a particular element in the promotion; for example, the number of proofs of purchase required or the nature of the premium item;
- the clarity of communication in the particular way the offer is themed and expressed;
- the effect on the image and value of your product or service made by a particular promotional offer;
- the level of spontaneous interest in, and therefore the attractiveness of, different promotional concepts.

The most sensitive issue is always the response rate. For a free mail-in this can vary from 3 to 15 per cent or more. On-pack coupons can be redeemed at rates of anything between 5 and 25 per cent. This variance has enormous implications for your budget, so reducing the area of uncertainty is crucial.

It is important to be clear about which of these questions actually have a bearing on your choice between a number of competing promotional concepts. In many cases, all the concepts will have a similar effect on the image and value of your product or service and it will be pointless to explore the matter further.

The questions are best answered by desk research for data held by you from previous sales promotions or from studying the data of others.

Evaluative research

The straightforward in-house part of evaluative research is collecting together all the factual data on response rates, sales patterns, consumer complaints and other readily measurable variables. This type of evaluation should be standard operating practice and is covered in the final section of this chapter.

All mail-in promotions produce a list of people who took up the offer. These form an excellent list for running a simple postal questionnaire. Getting to those who did not take up your offer requires rather more effort in list building, but it is important to obtain proper comparisons. More in-depth research into consumer reaction to promotions can be obtained via group discussions.

Desk research

Desk research has the major advantage that it can be done by yourself, at your desk and at nil or low cost. If you can answer the questions – or at least narrow the amount of uncertainty – by means of desk research, it is always best to do so.

There are three main data sources for desk research, and they can be built up over time to provide you with the material you need to evaluate competing promotional concepts.

Your own promotions

Details of your own past promotions are the best and the first form of research data. An evaluation system is recommended on pages 111–114, which should be used after every promotion.

Using these data for research purposes means identifying similarities and differences between past promotions and your promotional concepts, and intelligently estimating from there. The data can also be used to identify the promotions that will work with particular target groups and to achieve particular objectives.

Competitors' promotions

It is possible to build up a fair amount of market intelligence about the promotions run by your competitors, their likely cost and their likely effectiveness.

It should be standard practice to buy every promotional pack and collect every promotional leaflet issued by your main competitors. From these you can list the nature of the offer, the entry requirements and the theme used.

Rather more detective work is required to gain an estimate of costs, response rates and effectiveness:

- For a prize promotion, simply cost the prizes on offer. For a premium promotion, obtain and cost the premium on offer. Make an estimate of the quantity of leaflets and other support material, and cost these, too. This should give a rough indication of budget.
- Use your own sales data, and continuous market research data if you subscribe to them, to establish whether or not any discernible sales effect has been achieved by your competitors' promotions. Other tracking studies can measure their impact on awareness, distribution and other variables.
- Make your own subjective assessment of the clarity of communication of the offer, and its impact on brand values, awareness and other less quantifiable measures.

None of this is an exact science, but the information will provide you with the best available guide to what your competitors have found effective.

Wider promotional activity

There are various sources of information about sales promotions in a wider sense. These include:

- the trade magazines *Incentive Today, Promotions & Incentives* and *Sales Promotion*;
- regular features on sales promotions carried in the weekly advertising and marketing press, in particular *Marketing, Marketing Week* and *Campaign*;
- publications from the ISP and, in particular, the annual brochure describing winning promotions entered for the ISP awards;
- occasional research reports published by a variety of business information and research organizations, including Euromonitor and Mintel;
- conferences on sales promotional issues, normally in London, at which leading practitioners describe and discuss promotions they have undertaken and trends in the industry.

Those few companies that employ an in-house sales promotion manager benefit from the build-up of expertise in this area, and it is also a particular strength of sales promotion agencies. However, anyone spending any significant sum on sales promotion should make it their business to monitor and evaluate wider sales promotional activity and learn from it.

Field research

Field research involves collecting information directly from the market by way of a sample designed to be representative of your target market. There are four main methods that can be used for promotional research:

1. *Street interviews,* which provide quantitative responses to a relatively simple set of questions. As a means of testing the response to promotions immediately after purchase, interviews outside superstores can be particularly effective.
2. *Hall tests* (where consumers are invited into a nearby church hall or similar venue), which also provide quantitative responses, but allow more opportunity for detail. This can extend to creating a simulated buying situation and comparing consumer behaviour.
3. *Group discussions or focus groups,* which provide considerable qualitative information on consumer attitudes, and are often used before quantitative testing. Of all the methods, these are most likely to provide individual and social feedback on promotional ideas.
4. *Postal and telephone questionnaires,* which have major cost savings over face-to-face interviews. Because of the need to see promotional offers, their use in promotional research is really restricted to planning and evaluative research.

The use of all these types of field research is a science in itself and, as such, is outside the scope of this book. However, there is a view that field research should be treated with more caution in promotion than in other areas of marketing.

The reason for this relates to the gap between what people say they do and what they actually do. It is well known that consumers understate their expenditure on socially disapproved activities such as smoking and drinking. In the same way, they understate their enthusiasm for sales promotional offers. Field research can be misleading if it takes at face value what people say rather than what they do.

MARKET TESTING

Market testing overcomes the gap between what people say they do and what they actually do: it measures actual behaviours in the marketplace.

This technique is prohibitively expensive for most applications of market research because it involves placing a product or service out in the market and producing it in uneconomic production runs. However, for sales promotional research, it is much more feasible. It is often quite possible to sticker a small quantity of a production run with a particular offer and use it as a door-drop sample. In the retail food trade, it is no longer possible to test a promotional offer in a particular store or area and measure the response, but it remains possible to do so in the leisure trade. For service companies, the exercise is even simpler – just produce a short run of the leaflets or other material communicating the offer and try it out in one part of your market.

Clearly, there are logistical and planning aspects to take into account, of which the most important is the time required to organize and evaluate the test. Some promoters believe that the danger of good ideas being seen and adopted by competitors makes field testing impossible. Others believe that lack of field testing means that really innovative ideas are held back, as promoters do not have the faith to take a risk. Back in the 1960s, it was standard practice for Procter & Gamble to field test promotions and develop innovative concepts (see Case study 33). One of the major advantages of a strategic approach to sales promotions is that the time for proper market testing can be built in.

SUMMARY

Proper marketing accountability, defining success, setting KPIs, measuring and evaluation make sure that you are getting your money's worth from your promotional expenditure, and that you are spending it on the right things. There is no excuse for failing to evaluate every promotion, or for failing to do the basic desk research beforehand. This should be planned into every piece of promotional activity.

Use of field research and market testing depends on your budgets, but can only help to reduce uncertainty. In the end, research cannot make the decisions for you, particularly in such a fluid and fast-moving field as sales promotion. However, in order to help plan in the future and compete for budget with your finance director, marketing accountability is essential. Marketing no longer has the luxury of not delivering value for money.

Part II

Sales Promotion Techniques

10

Off-the-shelf Offers

For all the variety of promotional objectives, there are some offers that come up again and again – because they work again and again. An industry has grown up that creates and supplies these offers to promoters. Many of them revolve around travel, hotels, theme parks, films and insurance. They often offer a benefit out of all proportion to the cost to the promoter – such as something worth £50 to your customers that only costs you £1.

Of course, the £49 has to come from somewhere. An immense amount of ingenuity is put into devising offers of this kind and most of them are largely funded by a third party. There are some very good offers as well as some distinctly dodgy ones. Before using any of them, it is essential to understand how they work, what the people supplying them are getting out of them, and what conditions apply to their use.

This chapter describes the leading off-the-shelf offers that businesses can use, what to look out for and the questions to ask anyone selling you the latest unmissable offer. By following the rules, you can snap up excellent deals and avoid leaving behind you a trail of disappointed and angry customers.

Remember, sales promotion is constantly changing, so you should make your own enquiries before using any particular offer. (The addresses of leading suppliers are given in the further information chapter at the back of the book.)

FREE ACCOMMODATION

The offer

Free hotel room offers date back to 1971, and have been going strong ever since. The concept is simple: you purchase a number of free room vouchers from a specialist operator, which can be used by your customers to obtain free accommodation at a specified range of hotels. The stipulations vary. During the 1980s, the standard requirement was that consumers bought their meals (breakfast and dinner) at the hotel. This would cost them £10–£20 per person per night. Over time, people became wary of over-priced hotel meals. The offer now tends to be 'two nights for the price of one'.

How it works

The logic of this offer is strong. Hotels have a high level of fixed costs. However high or low their occupancy rate, they still have to pay their capital costs and most of their staff. An empty room is revenue lost forever. The 'free room' concept meets the needs of hotels to fill rooms rather than leave them empty. Satisfied guests can also be expected to return at a later date, paying the full rate.

Hotels participating in such offers are generally privately owned and smaller: the big chains are able to devise and advertise their own 'bargain break' discounted weekends, which (in terms of the discount being offered) can come to the same thing.

Of course, if a hotel offered deals of this kind to everyone, it would soon go out of business. So the offer must be restricted to people who would not otherwise come, those who genuinely are 'extra customers'. Free room deals are therefore communicated by companies that put together a list of hotels on a national basis, and make the offer available as a promotional tool.

What to look out for

A large number of companies supply free room offers. Some are better than others, and the concept is still getting a bad name as a result of some cowboy operators. Customers can ring a hotel to book a room and find that it no longer participates or that rooms are only available in the middle of February. Sometimes they will find that the requirement to buy meals or pay for one of the two nights has not been made clear, that prices are different from those quoted, that they are accommodated in a second-rate annexe instead of in the main building or that the price of the night they have to pay for is the same as the cost of a weekend break.

All this rubs off on the companies that use such a promotion as a sales tool. They are blamed – and rightly so. Giving your customers a duff promotion is bad business and ignorance is no excuse. Sadly, some very big companies (and very big advertising agencies) are still making this mistake.

The answer is to select a reputable company that has been operating free rooms for some years, has a well-controlled and regularly inspected hotel network and adopts a long-term and professional approach. There are several of these companies; they are not much more expensive than the cowboys, but they are infinitely better.

The characteristics that distinguish a good operator from a bad one are straightforward. You can use these questions to sort out the professionals from the cowboys:

- Do they operate a central reservations system?
- Do they ensure that bargain breaks offered by their hotels outside the free room service do not devalue that offer?
- Do they recommend (and insist on) a description of your promotion that accords with the Code of Sales Promotion Practice?
- Do they provide evidence that the list of hotels is regularly inspected and updated?

You can expect to pay around £3 to offer your customers three nights' free accommodation for two, £6.50 for seven nights and £10 for 14 nights. Three-night offers are typically valid in 150 hotels, longer breaks in 300 hotels. Some operators also offer a 'club membership', which costs around £20 for any number of three-night breaks in a 12-month period. Others offer a 'holiday bond' which gives £500- or £1,000-worth of accommodation costs and amounts to much the same over an extended period. Costs to the promoter for all these offers are substantially discounted for large quantities.

Free rooms have deservedly been working successfully for a quarter of a century and have been used to enormous effect by companies from banks to motor manufacturers. Barclaycard, for example, issued 500,000 over a two-year period to new users of the Visa card, with a very high level of customer satisfaction. Usage of the vouchers is often as high as 30 per cent, which indicates the high regard consumers have for them. There's no harm in running an offer that's been used 10,000 times before – after all, straight cash discounts have been used millions of times. The secret of successfully using this offer, and most of the others in this chapter, is an accurate match to promotional objectives.

HOLIDAY VOUCHERS

The offer

Holiday vouchers give customers a saving of around 8 per cent when they book almost any package holiday, but with some operators the saving can be as high as 11 per cent. The saving can be given in a variety of ways – as a cash discount, traveller's cheques, a duty-free shopping voucher, free luggage or any other item of equivalent value. The most popular are foreign currency and cash discounts.

The size of the saving is also variable. It can be geared to the price of the holiday booked. For example, £20 off a holiday costing £200–£300, £30 off a holiday costing £300–£400. It can be a flat sum (typically £50, £100 or £200) with certain conditions, for example that the holiday booked be for two adults for a minimum of two weeks or, on higher-value savings, that it is spent on long-haul flights and holidays.

How it works

Customers achieve the savings by mailing their holiday vouchers to a nominated specialist travel agent, together with the completed booking form from the back of a tour company's brochure. The travel agent deducts the value of the vouchers from the cost of the holiday – or gives it in traveller's cheques, duty-free vouchers or any other product of equivalent value.

The price you pay to offer this deal varies enormously. In reasonable volume, you could expect to pay around 75p for a £50 saving on a European holiday, and around £1 for a £100 saving on a long-haul holiday.

The key to this offer is the discount allowed by package tour companies to travel agents. This is normally 10 per cent, though some companies also offer overriding volume discounts of 2 to 3 per cent. This discount more than covers the cost of making the booking and processing the travel documents. It is needed, however, to cover the high overhead costs of running a high street shop, staffing it through the week and providing the advice that some customers require prior to booking.

If the job of a travel agency can be reduced simply to making the booking and processing the travel documents, the cost of handling each booking falls radically. This is what the specialists who provide holiday voucher offers have done, and it is what enables them to offer savings of around £50 on a standard family holiday.

What to look out for

There are very few drawbacks to this offer. Most people are quite capable of collecting their holiday brochures, making their choice of holiday and completing the operator's form at the back. Perhaps unfairly, they can even seek their local travel agent's advice first!

More than a dozen firms now offer holiday vouchers. Travel agent chains offer them, too. Using a high street chain makes booking easy for customers, but the savings tend to be lower than when using a firm that operates by post. There are six main things to look out for in these firms:

1. Are they ABTA, IATA and ATOL bonded to act as travel agents?
2. Have they experience of running this offer? It is very easy for an inexperienced firm to get its margins wrong and end up going out of business, leaving your customers high and dry.
3. Is it the best deal available? Working this out requires some simple calculations to establish the level of discount being offered. If it is not a very good deal, it is not likely to motivate your customers.
4. Are the conditions realistic? Some operators insist on at least two adults booking. This may be restrictive if you are selling to single people. Others insist that people take out holiday insurance; you should check that their price for insurance is reasonable.
5. What up-front price are you paying to participate? This varies greatly and should be in proportion to the value of the saving to your customer. The nearer a holiday voucher operator gets to rebating the whole discount, the more it is reasonable to charge you. Some will, of course, try to charge you at a high level as well as hanging on to a large chunk of the discount.
6. Are all the relevant operators' brochures included? Almost everyone includes the main brochures, but if your market is young people, for example, you should check that specialist brochures directed at them are also included.

DISCOUNT COUPONS

The offer

Several firms create and promote books of coupons that give savings on a range of theme parks, family days out, restaurants, cinemas and services such as dry cleaning and film processing. Some of them are off-the-shelf. For example, Entertainment International publishes 165 different 'city books' for cities around the world. They also produce a 'premier dining' directory, complete with membership card, offering savings at 400 UK restaurants. You would expect to pay £17 per book for quantities of fewer than 1,000, and £6 for quantities over 10,000 (1998 rates). It becomes economic to overprint a standard product with your own brand name and message in quantities of over 1,000.

The form of the saving varies greatly within each book. The main variants are a 10 per cent discount, a £3 cash saving, children free with adults, one admission free with a full-price admission, or one free course in a meal for two people. They vary as widely as this because each participating outlet determines the deal it wants to offer.

Most of these discount books or cards are themed on entertainment and leisure. For large quantities, specials can be constructed. For example, in 1996 Barclays Bank wanted a reward for 16–18-year olds opening a bank account. Entitled 'Student cash code', it offered savings with Red or Dead, Fosters, WH Smith, the Youth Hostel Association, Pilot Fashion, Sony Music, Deep Pan Pizza, Warner Bros cinemas and others. A 24-voucher version of this cost £1.72 for 10,000 and just 47p for quantities of over 250,000. On the theme of 'get together with your mates', Ruddles inserted a 12-voucher book offering over £200 in savings in four-packs sold in the off-licence trade. The vouchers were redeemable in places including the SnowDome, London Dungeon and the American Adventure Theme Park. The unit cost to the promoter was about 20p.

At a different end of the market, the *Financial Times* ran a promotion early in 1994 offering 'lunch for a fiver' and featuring a range of leading restaurants. It followed it up with a 'gourmet breaks in France' offer. This required readers to collect 12 tokens published in the paper over a fortnight and send in £10. In return, they received a directory of French hotels and a further offer for P&O ferries. Altogether, 8.7 per cent of *Financial Times* readers responded, and sales increased by 6 per cent on weekdays and 4.5 per cent on Saturday. Fundamentally the same offer, targeted at totally different lifestyles, is as effective at the top and the bottom of the market. This type of promotion has continued since that time. In April 2002, the *Daily Telegraph* was offering meals for a fiver after collecting sufficient vouchers.

How it works

These are very much two-way promotional tools. Participation is sold to those offering the discounts on the basis that it will bring in extra custom from those to whom you have given the vouchers.

If a holiday-maker seeks out a restaurant or museum on the basis of possessing a discount voucher, then that is certainly true. Everyone is happy – the participating outlet that gets the extra business, the customer who makes the saving and you (the promoter) who have paid very little to give the books of coupons in the first place.

What to look out for

The drawbacks arise in the small print. A big directory can turn out to include only a few restaurants or parks near where any single customer lives; there may be limitations on the days of the week when the offer is valid; the location may offer its own superior offers, which make yours look second-rate; and there may be tiresome restrictions, such as on the use of credit cards. And, of course, not everyone wants to plan their leisure time round a set of discount offers.

Consumers can see these offers as a substantial and attractive bargain, but they can also be devalued by offers that seem too good to be true and end up being a con. An offer of '£100 of savings' that turns out to be £90 off a £1,000 cruise plus a host of 10p coupons would certainly be misleading. It is important to ensure that any discount coupon really does offer genuine savings, and that it is not talked up beyond what it really delivers.

TWO-FOR-ONE FLIGHTS

The offer

These offers work on the simple proposition that one flight is free when a second flight is paid for at the normal rate. There are numerous variants on the theme. In 1996, Guinness offered instant win prizes of free flights on its draught bitter, plus the opportunity for all purchasers to obtain half-price flights with British Midland to Paris, Amsterdam and Brussels in return for four ring tabs. Barclays Bank offered the chance to 'Fly free with Virgin Atlantic' to those opening new savings accounts.

How it works

Airlines face the same situation as hotels: an empty seat is revenue lost forever. They thus make blocks of seats available at less popular travelling times for use in sales promotions. On a typical London to Paris flight, the return flight may cost £120. The consumer buys one return flight for £120, and gets the other free. A travel promotion specialist, such as P&MM Services, would pay the airline about £65 for each seat. The balance of the cost – perhaps £10 – is the cost the promoter pays for the voucher.

What to look out for

The same considerations apply to your choice of operator as to free accommodation offers. However, there are some additional points to check.

Air fares are highly varied and there are many ways in which airlines offload surplus seats. It is important to make sure that your offer is at least as good as the standard discounts offered in the travel sections of the weekend newspapers. Be warned by the experience of Hoover (Case study 24): its flight promotion was so attractive that people bought the product simply to obtain the offer – and nearly destroyed the company.

Be aware of the boom in Internet flight bookings – Ryanair, Easyjet, Buzz and Go. A recent sales promotion based on Virgin flights sounded good but a check on the Web site showed that you could buy flights over the Internet that were cheaper than those offered in the sales promotion.

HIGH STREET VOUCHERS

The offer

More than 160 retailers and other suppliers produce vouchers for gift and promotional use. The concept started in 1932 with the launch of book tokens, swiftly followed by record tokens. Since the 1970s, it has become a branded business: books and gardens are the only remaining generic vouchers. According to the Voucher Association, voucher use is worth £1.15 billion a year, and is growing twice as fast as retail sales as a whole.

Discounts for vouchers are very low – nil on small quantities, and up to 5 per cent on quantities of over £50,000. The choice is between a single-store voucher (Marks & Spencer and Boots are the most popular) and one that can be used in a wide variety of stores (the Bonusbond, produced since 1971, can be used in 25,000 stores, including many leading chains).

How it works

Vouchers are off-the-shelf products, but cost the promoter their face value or close to it. In this they differ radically from the other promotions discussed in this chapter. So why use them? The reason is that they carry with them the brand values of the retailer. If £10 in cash were given, it may be used to pay a bill. However, a £10 voucher redeemable at a leading store brings with it the anticipation of a pleasurable shopping trip and a purchase that might not otherwise be made.

What to look out for

Vouchers are cash alternatives. The main point to watch is that they need careful administration. They can be bought direct from suppliers, from producers such as Bonusbreaks, or from firms that act as clearing houses for a wide range of retailers' vouchers.

Be aware that many department stores now offer promotional evenings to their store card or account card holders. Debenhams typically gives 20 per cent off everything for an evening open only to those on their mailing lists.

INSURANCE OFFERS

The offer

Every car owner or mortgage holder is obliged to hold relevant insurance. Take-up of other insurance products – for house contents, legal expenses, personal accident, travel and so on – varies enormously and is very much lower. Every type of insurance can be used as a promotional premium, but the less widespread products are particularly attractive.

An insurance principle also lies behind assistance and helpline telephone services, whether for legal advice, pet care, travel or household maintenance. In all these cases, the cost of providing the advice (normally by means of a dedicated telephone line) depends on the proportion of those entitled to use the advice line who actually do so. Advice lines can be offered in exactly the same way as insurance. A breakfast cereal, for example, may want to offer a benefit that is attractive to pet owners. Free pet health insurance or a free advice line on caring for your pet could both be provided on an insurance principle.

How it works

Specialist brokers – among whom PIMS/SCA is the market leader – have put together insurance products in a number of areas that (in volume) are far cheaper than the policies that consumers can buy from their brokers or insurance companies, thus offering consumers high perceived value.

For example, insurance for a £1,000 camcorder could cost the consumer £80 if bought from a broker. Its cost to a promoter is much less, and reflects five areas of cost-saving that the promoter can offer the insurer:

1. Take out the selling costs of the broker and the administration and marketing costs of the insurance company, and the actual insurance cost is just £30.
2. Part of the cost of insurance reflects the fact that it is often only taken out by those with a higher than average risk. Offer an insurance to everyone, and the average cost reduces to reflect low- as well as high-risk customers.
3. You could also give the insurer the opportunity of a bounce-back offer – a second offer sent to those who respond to the first offer. The bounce-back offer will give the insurer the potential for new business.
4. Offer publicity for the insurance firm on your product or in your advertising and it may subsidize the offer from its own advertising budget.
5. Write the policy in such a way that claims are settled with a new camcorder and not cash, and you reduce the level of fraudulent claims.

All these measures can mean that, in bulk, an insurance worth £80 to the consumer can cost the promoter less than £10. It's then a real possibility to offer 'free insurance' as an attractive and low-cost incentive.

Sometimes, a trial period of insurance can be offered without cost to the promoter. In 1990, the *Daily Mail* offered three months' free pet health insurance in return for a number of proofs of purchase. About 30,000 people responded – and the insurer took the cost of the claims that resulted. It also converted 7,500 people into regular customers, clawing back its costs and making a profit over time.

Insurance products can be varied to suit a range of products and services. Lloyds Bank offered insurance-based benefits free to those who took out loans for cars and house improvements. For cars, the benefit included road assistance; for house improvements, it included home repair assistance.

What to look out for

Like any insurance policy, these specialist policies need to be examined closely for exclusions that limit their real effectiveness. It is essential to use a specialist broker that understands both insurance and marketing, and to make sure that there is a genuine consumer benefit in the offer. The best of them are as good as any policy bought in the normal way, and very much cheaper. This is because they pass on real economies:

- There are economies of scale for an insurance company in providing 10,000 policies in one go, especially for low-cost policies.
- Those who have received free insurance make a good mailing list for insurance companies to sell the same or related products to, and insurance companies make an allowance for this.
- One-off policies with fairly low insurance ceilings distributed widely across the population tend not to be abused by customers making false claims, and the insurance cost can be averaged across high- and low-risk consumers.
- Insurance companies like to achieve retail visibility and be associated with leading brand names.

Because insurance companies are looking for volume, this promotion is more suited to larger than to smaller businesses, although there is no reason small businesses should not get together to make the offer. Insurance promotions have been used extensively with electrical goods, in the motor trade, with mobile phones, credit cards and leisure products, such as bicycles. They could be used more widely.

Be aware of the recent interest shown by *Which?*, the consumer magazine, in electrical goods insurance. *Which?* researched and found that very few electrical 'white' goods such as washing machines failed in the first six years of their use. The customer was being sold a warranty that extended beyond the first year's warranty required by law. *Which?* considered this was a scam and customers were being taken for a ride.

PACKAGED SCHEMES

The offer

Take free accommodation, two-for-one flights, discounts on cinema tickets, half-price entrance to theme parks, a restaurant privilege card, 50 per cent off household insurance and £200 off selected holidays and what do you get? You get the kind of package that is offered by Safeway as part of its ABC loyalty card, by Barclays Bank as part of its Barclayloan Lifestyles scheme and by Toyota as part of its Club Toyota owners' incentive.

These particular packages were put together by P&MM Services, one of the leaders in the customer loyalty market, and there are several other suppliers. A promoter could also construct them individually, but there are evident savings in using schemes that have already been negotiated.

How it works

A packaged scheme marks the point at which sales promotional devices become part of a long-term loyalty scheme. The emphasis shifts from providing a short-term reason for buying to providing a basis for building relationships over the long term. The contents of the package can be accurately targeted by selecting the particular balance of offers that suits the lifestyle and aspirations of the customers you want to attract. And the benefits to the hotels, airlines, theme parks and restaurants included in the package can correspondingly become more long term. The lifestyle package becomes a platform on which different companies can reach each other's customers and strengthen their identification with them to their mutual benefit.

A particular packaged scheme in wide distribution is Air Miles. It currently claims 1.5 million collectors and an 89 per cent awareness level. Its basic offer is flights, but Air Miles can also be used for cruises, ferry crossings, action weekends, theme parks and cinemas. Providers in 2002 included Tesco after Sainsbury's stopped (1 point for every £1 spent: 250 points convert to 40 miles); NatWest credit cards (1 mile for every £10 spent); and Vodafone (1 mile for every £10 spent). Consumer rewards can be claimed from as little as 100 miles, though most flights require very many more.

Air Miles are used for consumer promotions, trade promotions and staff incentives. Smaller companies, and those wanting to use them in low volumes, can buy them at 20p each for a minimum quantity of 25,000 miles for employee and sometimes business-to-business use. In moderate quantities, the price drops to 15p each, and downwards from there for large-scale sector-exclusive offers.

What to look out for

Building a long-term incentive scheme is a significant investment. A major scheme may cost as much as 3 per cent of turnover. It is not worth doing unless you are clear that your target audience is going to be more substantially attracted by it than by the lower prices your competitors may offer. The issues involved are discussed in Chapter 7, and Case study 26 shows the different approaches to the petrol market taken by Shell and Esso.

FREE FILM PROMOTIONS

The offer

A long-running off-the-shelf promotion is the offer of free film processing. These offers are normally made available to promoters for a fixed fee that includes handling and redemption.

How it works

A typical free film promotion would offer a colour film worth £3.50 in the shops in return for five proofs of purchase of a 60p product and 20p for postage. This promotion would run on a million packs and would be supplied to you for a fixed fee of just £12,000 by a specialist film processing company. Across the million packs, the fixed fee would amount to just 1.2p per pack. This enables you to compare the cost to other offers (see under 'Budget', Chapter 7, for how to do this). There are four distinct stages involved in the processing company's ability to arrive at this cost (the figures are illustrative and the latest figures should be obtained):

1. The OTA figure is calculated. This is arrived at by dividing the number of packs on which the offer is communicated by the number of proofs of purchase required to participate. In this example, there are a million packs and five proofs of purchase. So, a maximum of 200,000 films worth £700,000 at retail price could be redeemed.
2. The predicted redemption rate is calculated. This is the estimate of the number of people who will actually take up the offer. It varies widely, but, in the absence of specific information, it is fair to assume 5 per cent. This reduces the likely number of films that will be redeemed to 10,000 with a retail value of £35,000.
3. The offer is linked in with a 'bounce-back' offer – a second offer is made to those who respond to the first offer. Those who receive their film will also receive a letter from the processing company offering discount mail-order film processing. The money made on the film processing allows the company to subsidize the first offer of the free film.

4. The processing company will add in its administrative and handling costs to arrive at a fixed cost for providing the promotion as a whole. This will be expressed to the promoter in pence per OTA. In this case, the offer will be quoted at £12,000 or 6p per OTA on 200,000 OTAs. This can in turn be expressed as a cost per promoted pack – in this case 1.2p per pack (all 1998 rates).

Once the promoter has accepted this quotation, there is nothing more to worry about. The processing company will supply the film, receive the applications, send out the films and take care of all related handling issues. The company will also bear any fluctuations in redemption. Whether 500 or 15,000 people send in for films, the price to the promoter remains the same.

What to look out for

This is a promotion that gives a fixed, all-in cost and brings to bear the interest that film processing companies have in recruiting new users to reduce the cost to the promoter. It is a promotional evergreen because film processing is a large and varied market.

This example has focused on free film as a fixed-price promotion. Some companies also offer free processing, free cameras, free sunglasses, free tights, free model vans, or any other item, on the same principle. The common factor in all cases is the bounce-back letter – in the case of model vans, it is often an opportunity to collect more model vans.

When both the offer and the bounce-back are film-related, it is easy to see the commercial benefit for the film processing company and how this enables it to subsidize the promotional cost. The same applies to collectibles, such as model vans. The picture is rather different when the commercial benefit in the bounce-back becomes tenuous – for example, when a film processing bounce-back is included with a pair of sunglasses.

Fixed-fee promotions then become a version of promotional risk insurance, which was discussed in Chapter 6. It can be very useful for a promoter to insure a promotion against an unexpectedly high redemption rate. There can also be good arguments for paying a company to take on the whole promotion for a fixed fee, particularly if you lack the time to organize the premiums and handling yourself. Fixed-fee operators offer that service. However, it may cost more than if you organize the premium and the handling yourself and take out promotional risk insurance. The commercial logic of fixed-fee promotions depends on the degree of subsidy the operator can give the promotion on the strength of the bounce-back.

CASE STUDIES

The case studies that follow offer two successful examples of the use of travel and activity promotions, and a disastrous one. They provide a graphic illustration of the issues discussed in this chapter. As you are reading them, ask yourself the questions that follow each case study.

CASE STUDY 21. TANGO

In the last 10 years, Tango has grown to be the most successful, imaginative and stylish youth-focused soft drink. It dominates the fruit carbonates market, not least as a result of a radical approach to advertising, packaging and PR.

The brand sets serious objectives for its promotional work. In 1994, these included increasing the frequency of purchase, encouraging purchase of larger sizes, appealing to all trade sectors and creating ownership of a unique event.

This led to Tequila Option One's two-stage promotion. The first asked consumers to collect 16 points from Tango packs to claim a 'free go's' directory. This offered a free go at three of 30 activities that included bungee-jumping, windsurfing, music workshops and go-karting. It featured on all pack formats, with varying points being required to obtain the directory depending on the size of the pack. Sales increased by 20 per cent during the promotion.

The second stage was a series of three one-day events in August in Scotland, Nottingham and London. Named the 'Tango Bash', each of these was held in conjunction with a local radio station, with tickets available at HMV stores for £6 plus one proof of purchase. Proceeds were donated to the Prince's Trust. They featured high-profile groups and fashion gurus, music and activities, and attracted more than 30,000 participants.

This promotion involved thinking big and building partnerships. The 'free go's' directory is a version of the event and activity booklets featured in this chapter. The 'Tango Bash' events were organized in conjunction with local radio stations, giving substantial free coverage. Donating proceeds to the Prince's Trust opened doors to celebrities and media coverage. Tango created something unique to itself, but it did so by orchestrating existing networks and resources.

In communications terms, every possible media type was used: regional TV, press advertorials, point-of-sale material, PR, in-store videos in a sports chain, radio, advertising on the tube in London, a road show. The events also provided a setting for trade and press hospitality. It is a good example of sales promotion creating brand properties, and doing a job well beyond traditional definitions of sales promotion.

Why was a package of activity events particularly appropriate for Tango? What logic can you see in Tango's decision to have a two-tier promotion, with both an activity directory and a series of outdoor events?

CASE STUDY 22. *THE SUN*

January is a key time for switching newspapers or switching off them altogether. It is also a key time for booking holidays. *The Sun* addressed the challenge of locking in existing readers in January 1995 with a promotion that succeeded on a colossal scale.

The paper optioned all low- and mid-season capacity in 140 UK holiday parks. It produced a 12-page pull-out brochure in the paper and backed it up with a £220,000 TV campaign. Readers were asked to collect six tokens on six consecutive days and mail them in with £8.50 per person per four-day holiday.

Around 1.1 million passenger holidays were redeemed – making *The Sun* the country's biggest UK tour operator. The paper sold 180,000 (3 per cent) more copies during the promotional week. It won an ISP Gold Award and an award for an outstanding contribution to UK tourism. Unsurprisingly, the promotion has been repeated in subsequent years.

This is sales promotion on a massive scale – an option not open to many brands. However, at the heart of it is a simple deal. It sold off-season breaks for the holiday camps and newspapers for *The Sun* by virtue of a compelling customer benefit that also benefited all concerned.

What package of activities other than discounted UK breaks would have been suitable for The Sun's *readers?*
If you ran a holiday park, what steps would you take to gain the maximum benefit from The Sun's *promotion?*

CASE STUDY 23. PASSPORT TO THE MILLENNIUM

Brief

Bt.spree.com, BT's online shopping site, required a powerful 'online' promotion to drive site registration and encourage return visits. Working in partnership with brandsynergy.com, P&MM's remit was to package and fulfil the promotion, which had to have a high perceived value and appeal to the broadest customer base possible. The ultimate objective was to achieve 50,000 'online' registrations by the end of the promotional period and to create a database of registered shoppers that would enable bt.spree.com to communicate on a regular basis with future targeted promotions.

Solution

Online vouchers to the value of £2,000 to be awarded to the first 50,000 customers to register on the bt.spree.com site. The first 50,000 visitors who registered received an electronic booklet of 14 vouchers offering discounts to the value of £2,000 against products and services including:

- £150 off theme park tickets;
- £25 off a one-week holiday for two from any ABTA/ATOL tour operator brochure;
- two nights for the price of one at Moat House Hotels;
- £60 worth of UCI cinema vouchers.

Vouchers could be redeemed immediately 'online' after registration or up until the final redemption date of 21 December 2001.

Communications

Communications included a high profile launch with an appearance by TV celebrity Carol Smylie, targeted direct mail, national radio and press ads, and banner ads on the Web. In addition, fulfilment was supported by P&MM with a dedicated 'online' queries service and customers also benefited from a secure credit card payment system.

Comment

We wanted something that would appeal to a wide range of people; this promotion worked by attracting the right people to the right site. The advantage of an online promotion is that it takes down all barriers to entry you get with a mailed response. A visitor can register, claim their vouchers and them redeem instantly online with no human interaction!

CASE STUDY 24. HOOVER

In autumn 1992, Hoover needed a promotion to pull itself out of the doldrums. Hoover Europe, owned by the American Maytag Corporation, had made a £10 million loss in the first nine months of the year. It launched an offer of two free flights to America for £100 or more spent on any Hoover product. The promotion was to dog the company for the next five years.

Within weeks, retailers were reporting that Hoover products were walking out of the door. People were buying two vacuum cleaners at a time to take advantage of the offer. The travel agency handling the promotion reported 100,000 responses by the end of 1992, twice what they had expected. The downside of the promotion was also becoming clear. Consumers were reporting unexpected delays and difficulties in obtaining flights. Industry experts were asking how Hoover could possibly fund two free flights to America from the profit on a £100 sale.

In March 1993, an investigator for BBC TV's *Watchdog* programme took a job in the travel agency's telesales department. The trick, it appeared, was to use the small print of the offer to put off those who wanted to book their free flights – unless they also booked accommodation, car hire and insurance worth at least £300. Some consumers persisted in trying to take up the offer, and took Hoover to court. In 1997, Hoover was still paying out to those who took their cases against Hoover to the county courts.

Meanwhile, Maytag had sold the company and provided £20 million for the cost of picking up the pieces of an offer that should never have been made. It was foolish in many ways. The economics of the promotion never made sense. The estimates of redemption were unrealistically low. The procedures for handling were inadequate. Also, when the scale of the disaster became apparent, Hoover did too little, too late to put it right.

What would you do to avoid getting into the mess that Hoover did?
What effect do you think the Hoover experience has had on public confidence in sales promotion?

SUMMARY

The offers featured in this chapter can strike consumers and promoters alike in two ways: it can seem a piece of magic that something worth £50 can only cost £1; it can also seem a sleight-of-hand in which someone must be losing out somewhere. The truth is more ordinary. Offers that sound great but cost little work on the basis of a number of related factors:

- They bring to bear the commercial interests of a third party – whether this is a hotelier seeking to fill empty rooms or a film processing company wanting new customers.
- They use the discount structure available in certain industries (particularly travel and insurance) to create savings opportunities that customers could not otherwise obtain.
- They are created and marketed by specialist companies with immense experience in the field that are constantly seeking to devise new offers; the best of them have been around for 25 years or more.

Avoiding the dodgy schemes and securing the opportunities that the good schemes create depends on promoters keeping their eyes open, asking hard business questions and not being mesmerized by seemingly unmissable offers. It is simply not worth degrading your business reputation by using a dubious offer any more than it is worth tarring all these offers with the same brush. If any of the offers in this chapter strike you as unmissable, be cautious. Remember not to take an offer and find a use for it; always start with your promotional objectives.

11

Joint Promotions

Most promotions involve giving away some of your margin in the form of discounts, cheap interest rates, competition prizes or premiums. Extra business should more than pay for this, but there's no getting around the initial investment. Joint promotions involve sharing that cost with someone else. No company or charity wants to do this for you without getting something in return. The secret of joint promotions is establishing a mutually beneficial partnership.

Joint promotions are defined by two fundamental factors: they bring together organizations in different markets that share a common set of customers, and they give participants a real commercial benefit that each side is anxious to realize for the other.

This chapter shows how businesses should go about setting up and running joint promotions. Any business can do it, and it is one of the fastest-growing and most beneficial forms of promotion. This chapter looks first at the planning principles and then at four main types of joint promotion – sampling, referral coupons, charities and loyalty schemes. Finally there is the phantom partnership – using an event in the public domain without a formal partnership agreement.

PLANNING PRINCIPLES

Most companies spend time thinking about their own market and their own customers. Naturally enough, they think about them from their own business viewpoint, and in relation to their own competitors. So, for example, a pub will think about the drinkers in the area, what they look for from pubs, what interest they have in food and related services and how the market splits between young and old, male and female, and lunch and evening trade. Equally, a detergent manufacturer will think about customers as people with clothes that need washing, their expectations, the washing machines they use, the family units they belong to and so forth.

Identifying a joint market involves thinking about your customers in broader terms, both in relation to other people who are trying to sell to them and in relation to people you are trying to reach who are already customers of someone else. The key to planning a joint promotion is an accurate profile of your existing customers. The key elements in this profile are:

- demographic data – age, sex, social class, geographical distribution;
- their relationship to you – how often they buy, at what price level, with what degree of loyalty;
- their needs, interests and aspirations – other things they buy, what they want from life.

The third level is increasingly the key determinant for joint promotions. Credit card companies were among the first to spot it with the development of affinity cards in the 1980s. Now virtually every major charity and interest group from the Royal British Legion to the Liberal Democrats has its branded credit card, typically rebating the organization concerned 1 per cent of the value of credit card spending.

What, though, of those who have no such affinity or only a weak one? Barclaycard offers the equivalent of the rebate in the form of points that can be collected for catalogue items in its Profiles scheme. That is fine as far as it goes, but the benefits are limited to the items in the catalogue. HFC Bank took this thinking a step further in 1997 with the launch of the Goldfish card. This works on the basis of a partnership with British Gas (which offers up to £75 off certain gas bills), Asda (which offers discounts on shopping) and Boots (which offers discounts at Boots and its other outlets, including Do It All and Halfords).

What distinguishes those attracted by a British Legion card, Barclaycard and Goldfish card? The fundamental product is the same, though interest rates and conditions vary, and they can be used interchangeably in almost any outlet that accepts credit cards. The distinction is the affinity that their possession indicates – to a particular charity, to assembling catalogue points or to mid-market shopping discounts. There is only a limited correlation between demographics and affinity: the critical point is that people have different affinities.

Many joint promotions are short term, designed to achieve trial or sampling objectives. Others are developed on the basis that there is a long-term customer overlap between non-competing brands. They reflect the development of the idea of 'tribal marketing'. The idea is that we are forming modern tribes, characterized by our purchasing habits. Those who belong to English Heritage, support charities and go to bookshops form a different tribe to those who do DIY, enjoy home entertainment and join discount clubs. It is possible to conduct research to define these tribes, but they prove difficult to pin down. It is more effective to develop promotional offerings that enable people to define their own tribal affiliations, and to use the increasingly extensive lifestyle databases to attract more of the same.

The process has also developed in business-to-business markets. It is important to profile the size and type of industry, the number of employees and the level of person you deal with. But that is only the start. People in business belong to different tribes as much as consumers. Some feel an affinity to golf, some to charitable work, some to business benefits. Identifying these affinities enables you to seek out partners who are not competitive to you with whom you can run a joint promotion.

Once you have created this profile, the next stage is to establish which other companies share the same customer profile. The more thoroughly this profiling is done, the more likely it is that a joint promotion will be successful: the closer the fit, the better it is for both sides.

The biggest obstacles to successful joint promotions lie in the process of making them work. The major culprits are greed, misunderstanding and suspicion. However well the customer profiles fit, if your intended partner is not prepared to talk to you openly about their own customers, and is determined to get the maximum out of it without putting anything back in return, the result will be as disastrous as any other partnership erected on false foundations.

When you have identified likely partners with whom you have customer profiles in common, look for those with whom it is possible to establish agreement about each other's objectives and honesty about tackling present and possible difficulties. Even when there appears to be initial enthusiasm on both sides, a number of factors can emerge that can scupper the best-laid joint promotions. It is therefore vital to ensure the following:

- *Involve everyone.* If the deal involves other people in your company communicating details of another manufacturer's products, they will only actually do so if the promotion is fully explained to them and they share your determination to make it work. Involvement of senior management in joint promotions is particularly important.
- *Make realistic promises.* Everyone is inclined to talk up the number of customers and contacts they have. This can lead to considerable suspicion when it turns out not to be the case. It is best to be realistic at the start about what you can guarantee to deliver.
- *Avoid unplanned changes.* Circumstances can change in a company for all kinds of reasons, which lead to a particular promotion being played down. This can be hard for partners to understand, particularly if they

are fulfilling their side of the bargain. Management must undertake at the start to minimize this risk.

- *Build in good liaison.* Once a deal is set up, it is tempting to get on with the next job. Good liaison is essential to successful joint promotions, and it must involve people at every level of the company throughout the life of the promotion. It is essential to set up the machinery for both liaison and resolving disputes.
- *Bargain realistically.* Everyone wants to get the best deal, and negotiates accordingly. However, because joint promotions depend so heavily on goodwill, it is a mistake to bargain simply to minimize your costs and maximize your returns. Bargaining should be directed at maximizing mutual benefit at an agreed cost to both sides, and both sides must agree to this in their negotiations.
- *Be proactive.* There is a tendency for the company that made the initial approach to be expected to make all the running and contribute most. This is a mistake. Once the promotion is conceived, it becomes a third entity, shared equally, in which both sides should be proactive.

The only way to establish whether or not likely partners will have the qualities needed for joint promotions is to talk to them. This can often be done via an intermediary, such as a sales promotion agency. The agency can oil the wheels to a considerable extent, and is likely to have met similar circumstances before. Alternatively, membership of the same Chamber of Commerce or business club can provide the basis for a fruitful business relationship. Whichever route is adopted, it is essential to keep your eyes open. If the goodwill and honesty are not there, it is a waste of time proceeding any further.

Once you have found a likely partner – one with a customer profile like yours and that you believe you can work with – it is possible to hammer out the needs you each have that can be met by a joint promotion. Normally, you will have this in mind at the beginning of the process of looking for a joint promotion partner.

The needs joint promotions can meet include the following:

- to gain trial for your product or service from among the customers of another product or service;
- to associate your product or service with someone else's in the mind of your target audience;
- to make a promotional offer that will attract your customers at low cost to yourself;
- to explain to your customers new ways in which your product or service can be used;
- to place your product in an environment where potential customers are likely to see it;
- to reduce the cost of a planned activity by sharing it with someone else.

Each side must be able to see the promotion fulfilling one or more of these needs. Normally, they are not identical. For example, company A will be seeking to generate trial, while company B will be seeking a low-cost promotional offer. This can lead to the partners in a joint promotion being categorized as the carrier (the product on which the offer is carried) and the carried (the benefit that is carried).

Building partnerships is no easy matter. A natural evolution of participants is normal. It may also be that, in some cases, partnership principles have not been thought through as well as they could have been.

SAMPLE PROMOTIONS

The offer

When people buy product A, they obtain a sample of product B. This is often something that they need to buy on a continuous basis to use product A or where there is a clear connection between the usage of the two products.

How they work

A long-established example of sample promotions is a free packet of washing powder in new washing machines. It carries with it the actual or implied approval of the washing machine manufacturer for the particular brand of detergent. The free sample is of real and significant value. Other examples include the banding of packs of Nescafé with packs of Hobnob biscuits – creating a clear link between the brands in a common usage occasion.

What to look out for

This is one of the most effective ways of gaining trial and, if the partner is selected well, it can be highly cost-effective too compared, for example, to a door-drop sample. However, the cost of giving away full samples is high, and it is normally necessary to include some repeat purchase incentive as well. Both the cost and the potential of this promotion make it one to test very carefully in advance.

REFERRAL COUPON PROMOTIONS

The offer

When people buy product A, they receive a coupon they can redeem against purchases of product B. These promotions are often called 'cross-ruff, or cross-rough, coupons' – a name that implies that they are a hit or miss affair. The name has stuck although there is nothing rough about them, and they are particularly common between non-competing brands owned by the same company.

How they work

An example is the book of holiday-related coupons given with purchases of Thomas Cook's traveller's cheques. Another is a 'kids eat free' promotion, first developed by Persil and Little Chef in the mid-1980s and now widely used by child-related household brands in partnership with family eating and leisure operations.

What to look out for

Referral coupons have the advantage of being far cheaper to run than sample promotions, but lack their level of trial-gaining impact. They have important benefits in that you can measure how many people have been enticed across, and that they do not require special packs. Run as a partnership between half a dozen or more companies selling complementary products, they can be particularly effective.

CHARITY PROMOTIONS

The offer

Charity promotions – or cause-related marketing – take many forms. At the heart of it is evidence that customers are more likely to buy from firms that are seen to contribute to social and environmental needs. Many of the UK's best-known charities go out of their way to meet both their own fundraising needs and the requirements of the firms they team up with. It is a commercial relationship, and all the better for it. Charities need funds, new supporters and wider publicity. Businesses need promotions that show their worth in extra profit and also link them to issues that matter to consumers.

NCH, the National Children's Home, one of the biggest partners in sales promotion, is very clear about this: 'Each promotion with a manufacturer or service company is tailor-made for maximum commercial effectiveness'. So runs the introduction to its publicity leaflet, aptly entitled, 'Selling almost anything with NCH is kidstuff'.

Every non-commercial organization has a market it appeals to. It may be national and across the board, such as a major children's charity, or it may be local and quite specific, say, a local arts theatre or a regional sports organization. There needs to be a close fit between the image and values of the non-commercial organization and those you are seeking to put across for your company. There also needs to be a close fit between your target market and the market from which the non-commercial organization gains its support. Selecting the market thus involves a degree of lateral thinking about your customers:

- What sorts of charities and voluntary organizations appeal to them?
- What kinds of project would they like to be associated with?
- What sorts of charities and voluntary organizations connect with the usage area of your product or service?
- What are the charitable and voluntary concerns that are likely to have the highest public exposure over the coming months?

From answering these questions, it is possible to draw up a list of areas – sport, arts, children and so on – that look suitable. It is then best to look through one of the charity reference books to find out which organizations operate in the areas you have chosen. The Charities Aid Foundation can be a good starting point for this.

How they work

There are various types of charity promotion. Among the longest established are collector promotions, which require consumers to mail in wrappers or coupons that are designated as being worth a certain amount to the charity. The promoter counts the wrappers mailed in and hands over the equivalent sum. Very often, charities will ask for a guaranteed minimum to justify the use of their name and to reflect the difficulty of estimating redemption levels. Collector promotions run with charities can generate a huge response, particularly if schools and youth organizations can be encouraged to collect the wrappers or coupons.

For example, opticians Dollond & Aitchison teamed up with Barnardo's in the run up to Christmas 1996, a traditionally quiet time for optical sales. Dollond & Aitchison pledged £5 for every pair of spectacles sold, and raised £229,000. The offer was featured in 430 Dollond & Aitchison branches, 315 Barnardo's branches, in a London media launch with Anthea Turner, and in regional media events with celebrities from local pantomimes.

Charity links can be used effectively to achieve defined purposes. BT wanted to remove the old, pre-microchip phone cards from circulation during 1996. To do so, it offered a donation to Shelter when the old phone cards were handed in, which both collected a large number of phone cards and £100,000 for Shelter.

They can be equally effective as a long-term differentiator. HP Foods re-launched its ketchup brand in November 1995 with a licence to print the NSPCC 'Happy Kids' logo on the front of its bottles in return for 1p for every bottle sold. On Fathers' Day in 1996, it offered an 'I Love My Daddy' mug as a self-liquidator, triggering a further 25p to the NSPCC. Van den Burgh supported its London marathon sponsorship by offering a sports bag as a free mail-in item on Flora and promising £1 to the British Heart Foundation for every bag claimed. The link between the Marathon, Flora and the prevention of heart disease was reinforced in the minds of consumers as a result of this promotional activity being used again in 2002.

Charity promotional events have taken a wide variety of forms, from the Oxo/Barnardo's Champion Children of the Year to the Jaguar/NCH Royal Gala Evening at the Albert Hall. These events are pegs on which to hang a host of other promotional activities. They can be particularly good for business entertaining and can give rise to free draws, mail-ins and other promotional activities. Events depend critically on your imagination in devising something that will stand out and then attaching the promotional mechanics to it.

What to look out for

The criteria that apply to charity promotions also apply to promotions with voluntary or community organizations, such as sports and arts associations, and are similar to those that apply to joint commercial promotions. There is the same need to be clear about what each party is in for, and to identify a common set of customers. There is the same need to ensure commitment on both sides, keep everyone involved and secure good liaison; and to be wary of the pitfalls of over-promising, being reactive, of over-bargaining and of unplanned changes on either side.

There are four additional factors that are particular to non-profit organizations, and which need to be taken into account in finding out what they want. Some of them do not apply to the very big national charities, which have their own sales promotion departments, but they are all-important in dealing with smaller organizations. They are:

1. *Locate the priority objectives.* Most non-profit organizations have an almost limitless set of needs and wishes. Finding out the priority objectives that are within your means to realize takes time, patience and understanding.
2. *Identify the decision makers.* Non-profit organizations tend to be run by committees and have complicated internal processes. It is essential to understand these processes, to know where the real decisions are made and under what constraints and influences the decision makers are working.
3. *Establish trust.* The ways of thinking in profit and non-profit organizations are not identical, and an element of initial suspicion and distrust is understandable. It is essential to think yourself into the values and aspirations that motivate those involved in a non-profit organization – whether they are helping the young or the old, organizing sports events

or putting on plays. These are invariably centred far more on the thing itself than on the money that makes it possible. To establish trust, you must associate with these values.

4. *Have respect.* The implementation of any non-profit organization promotion must ensure respect for the recipients of the money raised. For example, people with disabilities find it offensive to be called 'the disabled' or to be described as 'sufferers' from a 'disease'. Considerable sensitivity is required to ensure that raising money is not done at the expense of self-respect.

Approached in this open way, it is possible for companies to sit down with charities and other non-profit organizations and hammer out a deal that meets the needs of both sides. However, remember that your commercial needs are fairly clear to the outside world; the onus is on you to find out the needs of your prospective non-profit partner.

LOYALTY SCHEMES

The offer

From petrol stations to airlines to supermarkets, loyalty schemes are near universal. Large-scale schemes invariably involve joint promotions – there simply is not enough in any one company's product range to cover all the lifestyle needs that a loyalty scheme tries to meet. The offer to the consumer is both simple and endlessly varied: sign up for the scheme, provide purchasing and demographic data, obtain a card and start collecting. From the management viewpoint the concept is equally simple. Develop the version that suits your business, and you have a loyalty scheme. Or do you?

How they work

There is considerable dispute about how loyalty schemes work. Are they really about loyalty or are they just old-fashioned 'points mean prizes' collector schemes dressed up with electronic cards and relationship language? Alternatively, are they a means of delivering highly sophisticated database marketing on a mass scale?

Supporters of loyalty schemes point to the substantial increase in market share enjoyed by Tesco since it launched its Clubcard in 1995. There is an expectation, fostered by promoters of schemes such as Air Miles, that the present 140 schemes will coalesce into a series of consortia, each comprising a bank, supermarket, airline and utility, telecoms and leisure business. On this reading, the operation of loyalty schemes becomes central to a firm's market positioning.

Doubters accept that loyalty cannot be bought, but believe it is possible to use card-based schemes to target particular types of buyers and increase the amount and frequency of their purchases. Effective management of data is critical to this, and the measure is whether or not the particular incentives you give create additional sales. Managers can cite examples of this happening and not happening – it is far from automatic.

There are three radically different views among marketing people. The strongest critics of the schemes point to evidence that the more someone buys of a particular product category, the more products they will buy within it. Thus, the more you travel by air, the more airlines you will use. The more supermarket shopping you do, the more supermarkets you will use. If there are loyalty schemes available, and you like participating in them, you will participate in them all. Of course, market share can change, but that comes about because of an increase in both frequent and infrequent users. What does not change is the ratio between the frequent and infrequent users of your products or services. In fact, across dozens of markets, that ratio is found to be constant. Loyalty schemes are, according to this argument, a complete misnomer. Read also page 14 about bonding with a brand.

So, the question remains open: what part did Tesco's loyalty scheme play in the bundle of characteristics (price, convenience, store layout, checkout speed and so on) that influence the consumer to choose one supermarket over another for a particular shopping trip? Proponents of loyalty schemes often neglect to recognize the progress made by Asda in the 1990s despite its lack of a loyalty card, and the continuing loss of market share by Sainsbury's both before and after its loyalty card launch.

What to look out for

It is essential to recognize that 'loyalty' schemes are not about loyalty, but about providing repeated reasons for customers to use your product or service. They are a bundle of sales promotional techniques, of which the principle one is a long-term collector scheme. On the back of that, they can be used to convey short-term incentives of every kind and to engage the consumer in competitions and special events. The downside of these schemes is their cost and complexity, and the danger that they can become a substitute for attending to product and service quality. It is best to measure them on a disaggregated basis – not the scheme as a whole, but each mailer, each subsidiary offer. The scheme works to the extent that its separate elements work.

The expectation is that loyalty schemes will come to an end in their present form in due course, just as Green Shield stamps did in the late 1970s. Their demise was predicted in the sales promotional press within months of the take-off of UK supermarket schemes. It has not happened yet, but there is a cycle in sales promotion, well-illustrated in Case study 28 on Tesco's experience over the last 20 years, and Case study 33 on a classic Procter & Gamble promotion of the 1960s.

In the meantime, promoters should focus on the detail: if the individual elements are answering the question 'Who do I want to do what?', it does not matter whether they are dressed up as a loyalty scheme or not. If the individual elements are not persuasive reasons for the consumer to act, no 'loyalty' framework will make them effective. Long after the present wave of loyalty schemes have gone, these individual elements – 'buy one, get one free' (BOGOF) offers, special evenings, items to collect and the like – will still be going strong under another name.

PHANTOM PARTNERSHIPS

The offer

Not everyone can sign up the joint promotional partners they would like. When McDonald's signed up as official Euro '96 sponsors, its competitors Burger King were left without a direct link to a theme dominating the public imagination – and smaller fast food outlets were left completely in the cold. The 'phantom partnership' can come to your rescue in such circumstances.

How they work

Phantom partnerships are about making a connection with an event in the news without breaking copyright law. In summer 1996, McDonald's ran a 'game of two halves' promotion, offering football merchandise and match tickets. Burger King built on its sponsorship of the England, Scotland, Wales and Northern Ireland teams with an instant win promotion offering football merchandise and match tickets.

However, what if you don't have any agreement in the relevant field? Flymo didn't, and it gave away free branded footballs with selected mowers, produced POP material showing the cherub from its TV ad kicking it, and offered £50 cash back in the event of Scotland or England winning (which seemed more possible as the event progressed than it did at the beginning). Case study 27 in this chapter describes a similar phantom partnership between Sellotape and the National Lottery.

What to look out for

Cross the line into implying a partnership and you will have the full weight of copyright lawyers on your head, and rightly so. Imply a partnership with a charity that you do not have, and the public reaction will be damaging.

However, make a legal connection that does not infringe copyright with an event like Euro '96 and most people will applaud your imagination. It is an ideal field for enterprising and careful promoters looking to hook their brands onto whatever is uppermost in the public mind.

CASE STUDIES

The three case studies chosen here reflect three different types of joint promotions: a business-to-business promotion, a long-term loyalty scheme and a phantom joint promotion. Other case studies in this book that are relevant here are the Bovril sampling campaign (Case study 4), the Sainsbury's 'Schoolbags' collector promotion (Case study 5) and the Jacob's Club and Co-op 'Music for Schools' promotion (Case study 8).

CASE STUDY 25. NATWEST/BT

New small businesses are formed all the time. How do banks attract them as customers? In autumn 1993, The Communications Agency hit on a simple mechanic that picked up on a key concern of the start-up business: how to be connected to telephone and fax at the lowest cost.

NatWest teamed up with BT to offer three concrete telecommunications benefits. In return for opening a small business account, customers could obtain a free business telephone, £35 off a fax machine and 15 per cent off an answering machine.

Against its primary objective of driving recruitment of new accounts, the promotion worked well – new account openings were 52 per cent ahead of target. It also worked against its secondary objectives – showing that NatWest understood the needs of small business, and gave its sales force a simple, clear offer to focus on. The promotion won an ISP Gold Award. It couldn't be simpler or more direct in concept and execution, and offered reciprocal benefits for BT.

What other partners could NatWest have sought who would have appealed to the start-up business?
What mechanisms for communicating this offer would you have recommended to NatWest?

CASE STUDY 26. SHELL

Petrol purchasers in 1997 were faced with a complicated choice. From the supermarkets, claiming a 21 per cent market share, there were low prices, but often inconvenient locations. From Esso, there was 'Price watch' – the claim of petrol at supermarket prices right on main driving routes. From Shell, and most of the other forecourt businesses, there were various heavily promoted card-based schemes.

Shell's 'Smart card' was launched in 1994 as a five-year programme to take it to the millennium. The background to the promotion devised by Tequila Option One was clear: Shell was the market leader, but losing share in the absence of a long-term loyalty programme. It needed to build sales while maintaining premium pricing, and embrace all motorists while targeting high-mileage users. It needed a long-term scheme that still gave the opportunity for tactical promotions.

Shell's Smart card was set up with the participation of Air Miles, HMV record shops, UCI cinemas, TicketMaster and other third parties. It offered a choice of instant redemption and long-term saving, third-party purchases and catalogue purchases, charity donations and personal benefits. It was promoted via TV advertising, door-to-door, promotional assistants and POP on forecourts, local radio promotions, direct mail and inserts in charity magazines. The structure of the card offers both security for points and the capacity for detailed analysis of transaction history. Within a year, Shell had achieved the figure of 3 million cardholders.

Shell's Smart card won an ISP Gold Award and exceeded all its early targets. It has continued to develop, with partners changing to include Dixons, Curry's and Victoria Wine. How will it look at the end of its life – particularly in relation to Esso's very different price promotion? That promotion is estimated to have increased Esso's market share to rival that of the supermarkets, at colossal cost to its margins. There are real questions about its sustainability.

The trade-off between market share and margins is a critical decision for any company. Petrol retailers face a particular challenge in relation to supermarkets: they have high fixed costs in refining and oil exploration, while supermarkets can buy on the 'spot market' without any such investment. Margin calculations are thus very different for supermarkets and petrol retailers.

Sales promoters can do very little about that. They can help target those for whom price is not the critical factor – and they tend to be mainly high-mileage drivers, often buying petrol at their company's expense. Shell's persistence with its Smart card and Esso's persistence with 'Price watch' suggest that it is possible for collector and price promotions to run side by side in the petrol market, appealing to people with different priorities.

Looking at the current range of Shell's partners, what do you think they have in common?

Look around at the current range of petrol forecourt promotions. What do they say about each company's answer to the 'Who do I want to do what?' question?

CASE STUDY 27. SELLOTAPE

Sellotape is both the generic name in the sticky tape market and the premium-priced brand leader. It's not an exciting product, and the person buying it for office use is often not an end-user. How could Sellotape underline its brand leadership to these buyers?

Tequila Option One saw that an answer was offered in 1994 by the launch of the National Lottery. Sellotape formed a syndicate to buy 10,000 £1 tickets for an early Lottery draw on behalf of office users who submitted a proof of purchase. Entrants needed company permission and could devote their winnings to charity. This ensured the promotion was within Code guidelines. It also encouraged buyers to discuss with their managers the reason for preferring Sellotape to cheaper brands.

There was no major prize for the syndicate, but the promotion increased sales by 40 per cent in the six-month period of its run. Could it be repeated? Perhaps not with the Lottery, but with any other major event that offers the opportunity for a low-cost promotional piggyback.

What current and forthcoming events do you think could provide the opportunity of a phantom partnership such as Sellotape's with the National Lottery (now Lotto)?

Look at Case study 19 in Chapter 8, which covers a Lottery-related promotion run by The Sun. What did Sellotape have to do to ensure that the syndicate arrangement did not promise customers more than it could deliver?

SUMMARY

Joint promotions are the staple promotional vehicle of companies such as Procter & Gamble, Lever Brothers and Kellogg. There is every reason for companies of every size to emulate them. However, it is vital to remember that joint promotions are based on a mutual business-building partnership.

The best test of success is if both partners want to run it again. If you have identified your market and identified likely partners with the necessary thoroughness, and you enter into the process with integrity on both sides, they will work a treat. If not, you are best keeping away from them.

Promotions with charities and other non-commercial organizations can have enormous publicity benefits, excite tremendous response and associate you with values that are important to your customers. They must be undertaken responsibly and with respect for the needs and feelings of the people you are helping, but they are rightly a commercial operation.

Price Promotions

Price is the only element in the marketing mix that produces revenue. All the others involve you in costs. Fixing the price is one of the most difficult and sensitive parts of marketing strategy. It is also a feature of relatively developed markets: in many parts of the world, price still means the point at which buyer and seller are finally in agreement.

Economists have a model of 'perfect competition' in which many suppliers face many buyers in a market with very little product differentiation. Much of the purpose of marketing is to remove the firm from dependency on perfect competition. That is why so much effort is spent creating superior-quality products, developing brand identities, building distribution strengths and establishing unique customer relationships.

Why throw this away by getting involved in price promotion? That is the argument of those who regard price promotion as a destroyer of brand identities. This chapter sets out the different ways that companies think about price promotion and the many techniques available. So much discussion of price promotion is hindered by different ways of thinking about price that the first two sections look at the principles of price setting and price segmentation respectively.

HOW PRICES ARE SET

Some companies have made the absence of price promotion a key part of their positioning. Woolworth and Marks & Spencer did so in the last century when they pioneered the idea of 'one price for all'. Daewoo did so when it launched its manufacturer-owned retail showrooms in the UK in 1995. In distinction to the rest of the motor trade, there is simply no discounting in a Daewoo showroom.

Why can't everyone be like Daewoo? The first reason is competition. It only needs one company to discount its prices for others to feel the need to respond. Companies would, in general, prefer that this did not happen. That is why, in most countries, there are laws that prevent manufacturers fixing prices between them. Until 1962, resale price maintenance (the ability of manufacturers to fix retail prices) was the norm in the UK. When the book market was opened to price competition in 1996, it was the fall of one of its last bastions.

The second reason is that companies have different costs of supply. By reducing cost by means of superior productivity, firms can achieve the profits they seek and still charge lower prices than their competitors. Being the lowest-cost supplier is one of the main strategies for achieving competitive differentiation.

The third reason is the variation in demand. Some people are more sensitive to price than others. Most people travelling between Leeds and London may prefer to take an early morning train. Rail companies have long recognized that over-full morning trains and empty mid-morning trains neither satisfy customers nor maximize revenue. It therefore costs more than twice as much to travel before 9 am than it does after 9 am. That divides travellers into those who are prepared to put time before cost, and those who are not or cannot.

These three elements – competition, supply and demand – contribute to an individual firm's pricing decisions. Setting the price of a product or service is not a primary concern of sales promotion. The normal selling price to final users and intermediaries will be a factor to take into account in planning a promotion, as are the product's packaging and distribution. Sales promoters are not normally asked to review pricing strategy, any more than they are asked to review brand positioning. However, just as sales promotion alters the product, packaging and distribution in the interests of short-term advantage, so it gets involved in altering the price.

The approach your company takes to pricing strategy determines, to a large extent, how price promotion can be used and how the firm accounts for the difference between normal and promotion prices. Much of the disagreement about the use of price promotion arises from people not understanding the difference between two fundamental pricing strategies.

The first is the 'target mark-up'. In this process, the company decides the margin or profit it wants to make, and adds that to the product or service cost. Sometimes this margin is calculated from the return on capital the company wants to make, sometimes it is the standard level of return in the industry. For many years, advertising agencies marked-up goods and services by 1.1765 to give a return of 15 per cent. The professional body for architects recommends a scale of fees for marking-up building costs. This method starts with supply as the primary factor in setting the price.

The second simple method is the 'going rate'. This starts with competition rather than costs. The price is set by reference to what other people are charging. Builders, printers and designers will all look at the going rate for particular jobs at particular times. They then work back to the costs that they will incur, and see how much margin they can make. They start with competition rather than costs because they know that if they don't get the job, there's no margin anyway. This method is often used alongside a target mark-up, at least as a point of reference. If they did not have a mark-up in mind, they would not be able to tell whether a particular job would be profitable or not.

These two simple methods lead to very different views of promotional pricing. Those who work on the basis of target mark-up will always think that a discount equals money given away, but does it? Only if they would have been given the order at the higher price. Those who work on a going rate basis are always engaged in promotional pricing, but it tends to be unstructured. Every quotation is its own price promotion. It is difficult to make sure that they are not giving money away unnecessarily.

How do you resolve this dilemma? More sophisticated companies balance a concern with competition and cost with an emphasis on the third element in pricing strategy – demand. This leads to three different pricing policies:

1. *Psychological pricing* – works on the basis that we often think a high-priced product must be better than one costing less. Firms will set a high price and defend it. Perfume companies try to stop discounters selling their products because the cost of perfume is part of its specialness. Those who go for psychological pricing will often aim at a small section of the market that is looking for the very best and is not sensitive to price. They will regard price promotions as totally unsuitable for them – and they will be right. This is consistent with the quality of life now sought be customers, enhanced by marketing copy such as, 'You're worth it' and, 'Spoil yourself'.
2. *Value pricing* – based on the idea that top quality and low prices can go together. This works for a company if it can achieve a volume big enough to give it the lowest production costs in the market. The aim is to set a consistently low price and maximize volume. Among retailers this strategy is reflected in the 'everyday low prices' (EDLP) claim made by Wal-Mart in the United States and Asda in the UK. Price promotions can be part of this, but not a central part.
3. *Segment pricing* – the pricing strategy in which price promotions really come into their own. It starts with the idea that people are different. Some are sensitive to price and some are not. Some will shop around and others will not. Some will wait to enjoy a service or receive a product and others

will not. The argument is that prices should be determined in accordance with the demands of each segment of the market.

Until chains of shops began setting 'one price for all' in the 19th century, the price was always negotiated between buyer and seller. In some markets (for example, the price of shares on the Stock Exchange or commodities on commodity exchanges) it still is. Segment pricing is a sophisticated and modern way of managing individual negotiation on a mass scale. The next section looks at this approach in more detail.

SEGMENT PRICING

What makes a segment? Marketing people talk about segments of the market in a variety of ways. There are occupation and income classifications that enable them to distinguish ABs from C1s and C2s. They also talk about them in lifestyle terms. Aspiring young professionals may be of similar age and income to lager and football fans, but spend their time and money very differently. People can also be segmented by their stage in the lifecycle, from dependency to pre-family and post-family.

Segmentation is a delightful game, and marketing magazines are full of new ways of doing it. The practical problem comes when you try to design versions of a product to meet the needs of the segments you have identified. This is the process of 'versioning' a product. The theory is that for each segment of the market there should be a version of your product that fits it like a glove. Unfortunately, this is very difficult to do.

When Midland Bank (now HSBC) launched a series of bank accounts for different segments of the market in 1987, it did so in these terms. Its 'Orchard' account was aimed at older, more settled people, the 'Vector' at the young and mobile. Unfortunately, these segments did not exist in the way they thought. Customers became confused about the segment they were supposed to be in, and unsure why different charging and service arrangements applied to them. In 1996, Orchard and Vector were replaced with the Midland Bank Account – a single product that could be varied in its details to suit individual needs, but was not versioned by segment.

If you peel an orange, the segments are immediately obvious. If you peel an apple, they are not. You can chop it up into segments if you want to, but they are your creation – they are not inherent in the apple. Midland's Vector and Orchard accounts failed because the bank did not understand that difference.

For promotional pricing to be effective, segments have to be real. Business travellers will pay more to travel at a convenient hour than leisure travellers. That is a real segment for ticket sales. However, do business travellers want something different to leisure travellers from the catering facilities at a station? One study suggests that for catering services there are two rather different segments: those in a hurry and those not in a hurry. These cut right across the business and leisure segmentation.

There are three rules of thumb for telling whether or not a segment is real enough for segmented pricing to work:

1. People in each segment must have different sensitivities to price – that is, they must be prepared to pay different amounts for the same service or product.
2. There must be some physical, structural or time separation between the higher and lower priced segments, preventing those in the higher priced segment deciding to buy at the lower price.
3. The segments must be real enough for consumers not to feel dissatisfied and resentful, and for the cost of operating segmented pricing to be worthwhile.

The most common segments are formed on these principles as follows:

- *Time.* Travelling or telephoning at busy times of the day costs more than at quiet times. Buying toys before Christmas costs more than after Christmas. A video costs more when it is first released than later on.
- *Location.* Conveniently located shops, hotels and restaurants charge more than less conveniently located ones. Products and services brought to you cost more than those you have to fetch.
- *Conditions.* Buying in volume costs less than buying in small units. A year's subscription costs less than an individual theatre ticket or copy of a magazine. Tickets bought in advance will cost less than tickets bought on the day.
- *Version.* Superior service costs more than the standard. Peace of mind can be bought, but at a price. Fundamentally, the same product or service can be versioned or packaged at different price points.

The sales promoter is primarily concerned with promotions that last for a particular time period, take place in particular locations, have conditions attached to the deal and apply to some but not all versions of a product. This is what differentiates intelligent price promotion from wholesale, self-destructive discounting.

IMMEDIATE DISCOUNTS

These are discounts off the normal price that are available immediately at the time of purchase. They take six main forms, from seasonal discounts to extra-fill packs. These very different forms can obscure the thing they all have in common: the consumer can buy a given amount of a product for less.

Immediate discounts have a number of important strengths. Everyone likes a bargain: the queues at the January sales in Oxford Street are living proof that people will go out of their way to seize a bargain. Immediate discounts are a tremendous sales clincher and a powerful and immediate incentive to buy in consumer markets where 70 per cent or more of purchase decisions are made in the shop.

Their weaknesses, however, are very serious. Discounting can rapidly degenerate into price wars. Your competitors can readily copy it. It often does not distinguish between those who would have bought without the discount and those who need it. It is also extremely expensive. An immediate discount tends to cost you exactly what it saves the customer. Discounting can also downgrade the value of your product or service and lead to a situation where no sales take place at normal price. Very rarely do the sales gains achieved by price reductions lead to a sustained increase in market share. Immediate discounts are powerful but, like a powerful drug, they can quickly take over and destroy your business. Companies must also be aware of the substantial legislation governing the making of bargain offers that properly constrain the making of unreasonable price comparisons.

Seasonal discounts

The offer

These are price reductions designed to boost sales in off-peak seasons, move outdated lines or heavy stocks, bring forward purchases or improve cash flow.

How they work

In their familiar form of retail 'sales', they are now highly formalized, and have become a seasonal sales promotion far removed from their original purpose of moving end-of-season stocks. Some retailers have run 'closing down sales' (typically oriental carpet shops!) continuously for several years, a practice that stretches the bounds of legality. Leisure companies use seasonal discounts very widely, charging different prices in their low, mid and high seasons.

What to look out for

The critical issue is the logic of the season. UK families who give presents on the feast of the Epiphany (6 January) rather than on Christmas Day can use the post-Christmas sales to buy their presents. That's not a problem while only a minority do so. Holiday companies found their margins severely squeezed in the early 1990s when consumers found that holidays could be bought cheap in a late-booking sale. Excessive use of sales ends up with consumers deferring purchase to the next sale.

Multi-buys

The offer

These are a particular form of quantity discount offered by retailers (and funded by manufacturers) for multiple purchases of the same item. Consumers are offered a discount for buying two or more packs of the same brand. A long-established variant is the BOGOF – 'buy one, get one free' – that is flashed on-pack, on the shelf or in newspaper advertisements.

How they work

Multi-buys normally work by means of barcodes. The shop's EPOS system counts up the number of items with a particular barcode and applies the discount automatically. Multi-buys have become hugely significant. A study of the laundry detergent market by the London Business School found that multi-buy promotions in the top multiples had nearly tripled in number between 1994 and 1996. Average discounts had risen from 18 to 25 per cent. Since 1990, the leading detergent firms had increased the proportion of their consumer promotional spending on multi-buys from 20 per cent to 65 per cent.

What to look out for

Multi-buys are easy promotions to set up and give quick and measurable results. They can be very effective for a manufacturer needing to combat competitor action. However, there are significant costs. Multi-buys have become the standard mode of purchase for some consumers. The London Business School study found that 95 per cent of multi-buys are bought by just 27 per cent of households – mainly larger families who are, in general, better off. The level of sales increase a brand enjoys when a multi-buy is offered can be between 50 and 200 per cent. The hangover after the party comes later – when the same consumers switch to your competitor's multi-buy.

Used sparingly, multi-buys are an effective way of stock-building in the consumer's home, and can encourage greater usage simply by virtue of greater volume. They also block purchases of competitors' products until stocks of yours are exhausted. However, they have become a millstone around the neck of manufacturers, blocking other forms of sales promotion.

Also, the manufacturer often doesn't get the credit: 56 per cent of consumers think the retailers fund them.

Outside retail markets, multi-buys exist in the form of quantity discounts. For example, magazines offer discounts for signing up for longer subscriptions. Here it is far easier to calculate the cash and loyalty benefit of signing people up for quantity and getting the money up front. The traditional BOGOF is an effective promotion when not over-used.

Banded packs

The offer

There are several options for banded pack offers, but they come to the same thing: two or more of the same product are banded together or placed in an additional outer wrap so that the consumer buys them together.

How they work

Drink and confectionery brands are regularly sold in a variety of banded packs, whether of 12, 24 or more individual units. The price normally falls as the quantity increases.

What to look out for

Unlike with multi-buys, there are packaging costs associated with banded packs. There is also a need to negotiate additional line listings, and to hold stocks of the additional packaging variants. The benefits are that banded packs are clearly a manufacturer's initiative and tend to be less under the control of retailers. They can increase the amount of space available to the product in the shops and can encourage stock-building by the consumer. A banded pack can be a powerful incentive to volume purchase.

Reduced shelf price

The offer

This is the commonest form of price promotion. A standard product is on sale with a shelf sticker or poster showing a reduced price.

How they work

If a £1 item is discounted by 25p, it can be shown in a variety of ways: 'normally £1, now 75p'; 'only 75p'; '25p off'; 'our price, 75p'; 'save 25p'.

Signs of this kind are commonplace in clothes shops, consumer durable retailers, food stores and pharmacies. They can be funded by the retailer seeking to shift stock or establish a price advantage on goods that consumers use to make comparisons between retailers. They can also be funded by the manufacturer via display allowances. Often they are jointly funded.

What to look out for

The important point is the credibility of the standard price. Since the demise of resale price maintenance, it has become ineffective (and now illegal) to claim price reductions against a recommended price that is not actually charged. The DTI's code on bargain offers must be followed in justifying shelf price reductions.

More generally, shelf price reductions are simple and effective to operate, but give discounts indiscriminately. They can serve to reduce the willingness of the consumer to pay the full price.

Reduced price offers

The offer

Reduced price offers (RPOs) are flashed on-pack, offering a saving ('10p off') or a price slashed through and a lower price given. They differ from shelf price reductions by being printed on-pack.

How they work

It is one thing for the manufacturer to print a reduced price on-pack, and quite another to ensure that the reduced price makes sense in all retail outlets. They require an additional line listing and separate stocks and packaging. Many retailers now refuse to take them, and will increasingly require that they receive the same margin as if the full price were charged.

What to look out for

For the consumer, RPOs are an attractive offer – volumes of sales certainly rise when an attractive reduction is made. It also gives the manufacturer control over the price charged to the consumer. However, it is an expensive promotion in terms of margins and packaging and, increasingly, difficult to run with major multiples. Used too often, it can devalue the standard price. It can also lead to rapid copying, resulting in almost all products in a sector being reduced in price.

Extra-fill packs

The offer

These are packs flashed '25% extra free' or '550ml for the price of 440ml'. They differ from RPOs in that the price remains the same, but the quantity of the product sold for that price goes up.

How they work

Extra-fill appeals to existing users of your product, who can get more for the same price. They can also be useful in trading consumers up to larger sizes. The costs for the manufacturer include packaging origination and carrying additional stock. There can also be difficulties with some retailers in obtaining new listings and shelf space.

What to look out for

The major advantage of extra-fill packs over price reductions is that the perceived value to the consumer is more than the cost to the manufacturer. Once the packaging has been paid for, the cost of additional ingredients is often low. Extra-fill does not devalue the product in the way that price reductions do. However, they are readily copied: in off-licences it often seems as if every major lager brand is an extra-fill product.

DELAYED DISCOUNTS

These are forms of discount that are not immediately available at the point of purchase. The purchaser will normally have to do something after purchase in order to benefit from the saving. The crucial feature of delayed discounts is that not everyone who thinks they are going to take up an offer actually does so. Everyone is familiar with buying a product on the strength of a '20p off next purchase' coupon, sincerely intending to make use of that coupon and finding it in the kitchen drawer some months later – normally after its expiry date. This is the principle behind delayed discounts.

Delayed discounts enable savings to be targeted at people who fulfil the range of conditions that you wish to impose. The non-redemption level means that the size of the saving offered can be higher, and therefore more attractive. They also allow an opportunity for creativity that is not normally available with immediate discounts.

The weaknesses of delayed discounts include their lack of immediacy: a bird in the hand can be worth two in the bush. They also involve additional handling and postage costs for both the consumer and the supplier. A £10 voucher could well have added on costs of around 80p: postage for both you and the consumer, plus the costs of envelopes, handling and voucher redemption. These costs are great news for the postal service, but can detract from the value of the offer you are making. There is also the danger that an excess of complexity can turn off participants: if a saving is being offered, it should be apparent that that is the case.

The major form of delayed discount is a coupon that can be used against a future purchase. These are discussed in the next section. Other common forms are cash rebates, cash share-outs and repurchase offers.

Cash rebates

The offer

In a cash rebate, the customer is invited to collect tokens from a number of packs and mail them in to receive a cash voucher. This promotion can also be used as a variant of the BOGOF, where a coupon is mailed for the full cost of another product. The value of the cash rebate can also be varied, as can the conditions of entry; for example, buy a complete set, and we'll rebate you £10.

How they work

Cash rebates require postage from consumer to mailing house, and from mailing house to consumer, which adds significantly to their costs. They have been overtaken in consumer goods markets by multi-buys, but are effective in sectors where goods are more expensive and where EPOS systems have yet to make their mark. They are particularly popular in financial services – '£500 cash back when you take out a mortgage' is a typical example.

What to look out for

If the offer is less substantial than £500 (which everyone will take up), the cost to the manufacturer of a cash rebate will depend on the number of people who actually take up the offer. As there is always slippage between the numbers of people who are attracted by an offer and those who take it up, this enables a more attractive offer to be made. The size of the rebate must justify the postage and handling involved. In financial services markets, cash rebates are a highly effective way of incentivizing people with their own money.

Cash share-outs

The offer

In this offer, a sum of money is divided among all those returning the requisite number of proofs of purchase from a product or service. It is typically communicated as 'send in five proofs of purchase for your share of our £100,000 share-out'. Variants can include the option of sending in an unlimited number of POPs.

How they work

The predicted redemption rate is carefully calculated to ensure that participants will receive a reasonable sum of money, normally equating to that which they would receive on a cash rebate scheme.

What to look out for

The main advantage of the cash share-out is the scale of the sum that can be offered. This can be attractive. However, it involves a substantial amount of postage and handling and can cost more to administer than the benefit given to the consumer.

Repurchase offers

The offer

Purchasers of consumer durables, such as fridges or hi-fis, are offered a commitment by the manufacturer to buy back the product at a specified point in the future (often five years) for the same amount as they paid for it. A variant is to offer a lower guaranteed trade-in price.

How they work

This offer at first seems like a guarantee of bankruptcy for the manufacturer. It relies on three considerations:

1. a great many people will forget to apply for repurchase in five years' time;
2. inflation will have eaten into the value;
3. those who do ask for repurchase form a good market for repeat purchase.

What to look out for

Offers of this kind need to be carefully calculated and insured, and low inflation levels are making them less attractive than they were. They can also seem too good to be true – certainly in the full repurchase form. However, as a means of making an offer with a higher perceived value than cost, they have their advantages in markets with repurchase cycles of five years or so.

COUPONS

The offer

Coupons are used to provide an immediate or delayed discount on a product or service to end-users or intermediaries. They can be distributed in a wide variety of ways, all of which have different redemption rates and vary considerably in popularity over time. They are used so extensively that they form a subject in their own right. As with delayed discounts, the critical factor is the level of redemption and the slippage between being attracted by the offer and taking it up.

How they work

A coupon is, in principle, a straightforward thing to organize: you print your coupons giving a specified saving on next purchase; you distribute them; retailers or other intermediaries accept them in part-payment for your product or service; and you reimburse the intermediary. If there is no intermediary involved, it is even simpler: you simply accept your own coupons in part payment.

Coupons are the nearest most of us get to printing money, and we do so in huge volume. It is critical to think through questions of distribution, redemption and format.

There are seven main ways of distributing coupons:

1. on or in your product or service;
2. door-to-door;
3. in newspapers;
4. in magazines;
5. by direct mail;
6. in store;
7. via a Web site – printing off the coupon.

These different ways of distributing coupons are described by the coupon industry as different 'media'. They have different shares of the total number of coupons distributed. Figure 12.1 shows coupon distribution by year. Figure 12.2 shows redemption.

The difference is the radically different levels of the redemption rates of the various media, which range from less than 1 per cent to over 20 per cent. The different redemption rates by media are shown in Figure 12.3. Note that

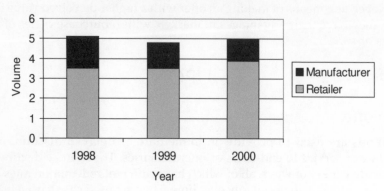

Figure 12.1 The share of distribution of coupons by media

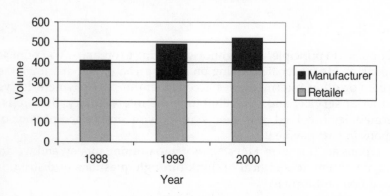

Figure 12.2 The share of redemption of coupons by media

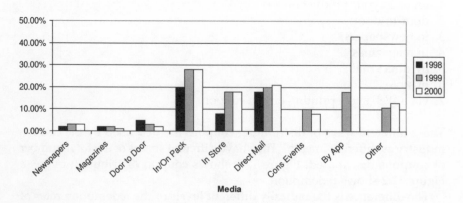

Figure 12.3 Average redemption rate

there is also considerable change year-on-year. Although the general differences between different forms of media are clear enough, there is considerable variation over time.

So how do you decide which way to distribute your coupons? It depends what you are trying to achieve. Different coupon 'media' have very different uses and characteristics:

- Coupons in or on a product or service are primarily a generator of repeat purchases and a reward for loyalty; they are not effective for new users. Despite this, Oddbins offered a 12.5 per cent discount off a case for new registrants to its online service; it has never followed up the registrants. Web site recruitment of new customers can expand your business.
- Door-to-door couponing is most effective for targeting a particular geographical area – for example, near a shop. It has relatively high distribution costs, but is effective in gaining new users, particularly when used in conjunction with a sample.
- Newspaper couponing is apparently wasteful (up to 99 per cent non-redemption), but the figures need to be related to the huge size of newspaper circulations. Whether it works on your product or service as a trial generator or as a reward to regular users can only be determined by experience.
- Magazine couponing is similar to newspaper couponing, but can be more carefully targeted. Magazines also allow Tip On Coupons stuck onto the page.
- Direct mail is the most expensive and also the most targeted form of couponing, and has the highest redemption levels after in-store couponing.
- In-store couponing has the highest redemption levels of all categories. Its usefulness must be tested to establish whether or not it really does generate extra business for your product or service or simply provides a convenient discount to those who would have bought anyway.

Getting the format of a coupon right is vital for something that can be used as money. Clear guidelines have been drawn up for the grocery trade for the design, structure and organization of coupons. These are available from the ISP, and you should ensure you have an up-to-date copy – download one now from its Web site.

Any couponing activity requires a redemption system. If you are going to redeem your coupons yourself, the redemption systems are a matter for your own internal accountancy. If they are to be redeemed by intermediaries, you need to ensure that all likely intermediaries will accept them and that they will be duly recompensed for their trouble in so doing. The best answer is to use one of the handling houses that specializes in coupon redemption and discuss your requirements fully with them. The leader in this field is NCH Promotional Services. NCH's experience is considerable, and has saved many a promoter from expensive error.

What to look out for

There are three major problems that can arise with any couponing activity:

1. *Estimating redemption.* The ranges given above are only averages and the cost difference between a high and low redemption can be huge. It is always best to test couponing on a small scale before you use it widely.
2. *Malredemption.* Malredemption is large-scale fraudulent redemption. It arises, for example, from a batch of newspapers being systematically cut for all their coupons and redeemed at a friendly retailer. There are ways of coping with it, and handling houses are best able to advise on this.
3. *Misredemption.* This differs from malredemption in that it is the result of individuals redeeming individual coupons against products or services they have not bought. It is almost impossible to act against without the support of retailers. For many years, major multiples accepted coupons irrespective of the products bought. In the mid-1990s, they agreed to check that the products on the coupon had been bought, but this is not something that is easy to police. An allowance must be made for a proportion of coupons (which cannot be accurately determined) to be misredeemed. If you are redeeming your coupons yourself, this will only arise as a result of human error on the part of your own staff.

Despite these difficulties, coupons are a promotional evergreen. They are a good way to provide a price benefit without making it available on every pack sold. The secret is to use coupons in a creative and carefully targeted manner, and to calculate in detail the redemption costs against the extra business you gain.

FINANCE DEALS

The offer

Consumer credit has grown by leaps and bounds in the last 20 years. It accelerated dramatically during the 1990s as credit controls loosened and financial innovation increased. Popular resistance to buying on credit (if it ever existed except as a nostalgic memory) is certainly a thing of the past. For these reasons, every business needs to understand how enabling customers to buy now and pay later can be used to its advantage. Fundamentally, this is a sales promotion operation.

If a customer pays by cash or cheque, it does not matter where that money comes from. Our interest as sales promoters is where the customer looks to us to help with the credit arrangements. This section is designed to tell you how to do it and how to evaluate the options.

Finance arrangements are one of the oldest sales promotional tools. It was commonplace until the 1960s for grocers, butchers and other tradesmen to run credit accounts for their customers. Popularly referred to as buying 'on tick', it had the benefit of any credit offer. Of course, credit arrangements of this kind never registered in the Treasury's money supply figures. It is one of the reasons that the view that we live in a uniquely credit-based society today should be taken with a pinch of salt.

Zero per cent finance is one of the great sales-clinching offers of all time in 'high ticket' markets – those in which the consumer needs to lay out a substantial sum to make a purchase. It has been widely applied in the motor, furniture and consumer durables sectors. Like most creative finance offers, its application is potentially far wider.

Zero per cent is the pinnacle of a range of reduced interest offers. If bank loans are averaging 10 per cent and credit card interest is averaging 26 per cent, an offer of 6 or 8 per cent interest is also attractive, and very much cheaper to offer.

These offers share in common the fact that, at any one moment, money has a certain price. The price depends on who you are, how much you want, and over what period. The price of money can be found in the financial pages of the newspapers, and takes its lead from the rate set by the Bank of England. This is the benchmark against which, at any one time, reduced or 0 per cent interest offers can be set.

How they work

If a company lends money at less than the rate that it pays to borrow it, it has to make up the difference from somewhere.

For example, an electrical retailer offering an interest rate of 4 per cent on a £199 product, and paying interest at 9 per cent to the bank, must bear the difference of 5 per cent. What this amounts to requires fairly complicated calculations, which are best left to finance professionals. (It should be noted that here and elsewhere in this chapter interest rates are quoted at their flat or nominal rate, which is simpler for our purposes. The Consumer Credit Act requires, among other things, that the annual percentage rate (APR) is quoted for all interest rates.)

Having done the calculations, it is possible for the electrical retailer not only to put a figure on it, but also to compare the cost to that of any other promotional offer. Let us assume that the offer we have described will cost the retailer £25. It is directly comparable to a £25 discount, insurance with a cost of £25 or a premium costing £25. Which works best? Different offers appeal to different people, and the finance offer will appeal most to those who have need of finance to make the purchase. For this reason, consumer durables retailers tend to ring the changes on the offers they make.

While the principle of subsidized finance is fairly simple, the forms it can take are immensely varied. There are four key forms of subsidized finance.

1. Manufacturer and finance house deals

These deals are normally set up by major manufacturers that sell through dealers – they most commonly occur in the motor trade. For example, Rover Group concluded a deal with Lombard to borrow on behalf of its customers a large slice of money at 8 per cent. It then constructed a range of interest rate options for its customers. These ranged from 4.1 per cent (for repayment in 12 months and a 50 per cent deposit) to 6.5 per cent (for repayment in 48 months and a 20 per cent deposit). Dealer and customer would agree the actual price of the car in the usual way. The net amount owing would then be repaid by the customer at the interest rate selected.

Rover Group, meanwhile, would pay Lombard the difference between 8 per cent and what the customer was actually paying. The calculations involved would not directly concern either the motor dealer or the customer, both of whom were benefiting from Rover Group's deal with Lombard.

2. Intermediary and finance house deals

Finance companies such as Lombard generally dislike concluding deals of this kind with companies other than major manufacturers. If you want to persuade them to do so, it is helpful to understand their criteria. These are the main ones:

- The item should be durable, identifiable and movable (DIM). This covers products that last, which have serial numbers on them and can be removed if the debt is not paid. Cars, boats and machinery obviously fit the bill.
- The debt outstanding should be less than the resale value of the item should they be forced to repossess it. The answer to that is to have relatively high deposits and relatively short repayment periods.
- You must be an honest, trustworthy, credible business.

Given that you can satisfy these criteria – and others of a more technical nature – there is no reason for not approaching a finance house to construct a finance deal that you can subsidize.

3. Personal loan deals

Items that are not durable, identifiable and movable – for example, furniture and carpets – cannot be financed by a finance house. The reason is that the item itself cannot provide adequate security against non-payment. One answer is for customers to take out a personal loan, normally secured against their house. The manufacturer or retailer can then subsidize the interest rate in the same way as with a finance house deal. There are many credit providers with whom these deals can be negotiated.

4. Unsecured finance

The final major form of subsidized finance involves the manufacturer or retailer providing the credit without direct recourse to any external source of money. Furniture retailers commonly use it.

Let us assume that a furniture retailer sells a three-piece suite on a no deposit, 0 per cent interest deal. The cash price is £1,040, and the credit price is £10 per week for two years. Applying discounted cash flow calculations to the repayments, the furniture retailer can calculate the value of the sale on the day it is made. Two of the crucial elements in this calculation will be the company's view of the movement of interest rates and inflation over the two-year period and the expected level of bad debts. Assuming these estimates are correct, it can identify the true value of the sale in profit and loss terms. The repayments then become a matter of cash flow.

Calculated incorrectly or with an over-optimistic assessment of likely bad debts, this method of providing subsidized finance is a sure-fire way of going bankrupt. It is a route that only the most hardened, experienced and cash-rich businesses should even think of.

What to look out for

Most marketing people do not need to be experts in consumer finance. Getting involved in 0 per cent finance deals or other subsidized interest rate offers calls for a fairly sophisticated knowledge of the potential, the pitfalls and the economics of our financial system. If you are willing to master the arithmetic and study the systems, the rewards can be considerable. However, even so, it is best to appoint a professional to do the job for you or at least to check your calculations. It is also vital to follow closely the requirements of the Consumer Credit Act and other legislation.

TRADE PRICE PROMOTIONS

In Chapter 1, we identified a critical feature of promoting via intermediaries such as retailers. A promotion that attracts the retailer but not the consumer may still work; a promotion that attracts the consumer but not the retailer is unlikely to get off the starting blocks.

The distinction is often made between 'push promotions' (aimed at pushing products via the retailer to the consumer) and 'pull promotions' (aimed at the consumer, pulling products via the retailer). The distinction is not an absolute one – most promotions need both pull and push if stock is not going to sit on the shelves (not enough pull) or not reach them in the first place (not enough push). This section looks at the push element in the mix – the use of price to give retailers reasons to support the promotion of your product or do the promotion themselves. There are five main forms of trade price promotion.

1. Overriders

The offer

An overriding discount is agreed at the beginning of a year between a supplier and a purchaser, and is payable by the supplier at the end of the year if the purchaser has achieved agreed targets.

How they work

Overriders normally relate to the volume taken over the year, but can also cover display, distribution and other business targets. If the targets are not reached, the overrider is not paid. They are heavily used by food and motor manufacturers and holiday companies supplying via retailers. Some motor dealers derive most of their profit from overriders, discounting the normal trade margin to their own customers.

What to look out for

Some purchasing professionals dislike overriders on the grounds that the cost to the supplier is simply built back into the price. Suppliers also dislike them because, over time, the targets can become ritualized and purchasers can expect their overrider as a right. Nevertheless, they are widely used, and in some markets cannot be avoided – they become a cost of doing business. The trick is to make sure that the targets set for the overrider in annual negotiations give some benefit to both parties over what would otherwise have been achieved.

2. Display and advertising allowances

The offer

These are allowances for a retailer to conduct some piece of promotion for the manufacturer. The allowances can pay for media support, stack ends, leaflets, coupons, window bills, display and any other form of retail support.

How they work

Most retailers have a tariff for almost every form of promotional support – from a stack end to a window bill. Increasingly, allowances are charged for listing a product, and investment in the retailer's in-house magazine or advertising is a required cost of doing business. Allowances that used to be at the discretion of manufacturers are increasingly at the command of the retailer. The growth of EPOS systems has enabled even medium-sized retailers to know exactly how much of a product can be sold from a given position in the store, and to charge manufacturers accordingly.

What to look out for

Manufacturers need to look closely at the total profitability of each product line in each retailer. Take away the total of all allowances, overriders, volume discounts and other trade discounts from the selling price to the retailer and you have the net selling price. Take your manufacturing and promotional costs away from that and you know the contribution to overheads you are achieving from that retailer on that product line. If possible – and it often is – allowances should be targeted to achieve particular results, such as extra display and advertising. In many cases, allowances have become part of an increasingly complicated calculation of the cost of doing business with a particular retailer. You need an equally complicated financial system to work out if it is worthwhile.

If you are a small or medium-sized retailer, there is massive opportunity for increasing your margins by claiming allowances. The major multiples all have sophisticated EPOS systems that give them the power of knowledge. It is knowledge that gives the retailer power, and small retailers still have a long way to go in acquiring it.

3. Volume and case bonuses

The offer

These are short-term bonuses given by manufacturers to retailers. A case bonus is an amount of additional discount given per case bought. A volume bonus is an amount of additional discount given for buying a certain volume of product – more than would normally be bought at that time. Sometimes these take particular forms; for example, a baker's dozen is the practice of charging for 12 cases while supplying 13.

How they work

Volume and case bonuses are used by manufacturers to fill a pipeline into the trade, to make life difficult for a competitor by filling stockrooms or to encourage a retailer to offer shelf price reductions. They also work in some trade sectors as a means of encouraging display and support for promotional activity. The hugely successful 'Bass Nights' developed by Bass in pubs across the country relied on this mechanism. Pubs were offered a kit comprising posters, quiz games, merchandise prizes and other items to run a themed fun night in the pub. These were good news for the consumer. What appealed to the landlords was the offer of a free keg of beer. This put extra margin behind the bar – and encouraged them to run Bass Nights as often as they could.

What to look out for

Nothing is easier than giving the trade additional discounts in the hope that it will increase sales of your product, but it is a slippery slope that leads to increased expectations of discounts and a steady lowering in your average selling price. It is essential to use volume and case bonuses intermittently and only in return for defined benefits. As retailer power grows in most sectors, this is easier said than done. It is one of the main reasons promoters seek alternative promotional mechanisms that do not devalue the brand's price to the trade or consumer.

4. Count and recount

The offer

The name 'count and recount' derives from days when salespeople would habitually go into customers' stockrooms to count the stock. Count and recount gave the retailer a bonus on the difference between the count and the recount – in other words, on the amount that had been sold. In most sectors, it can now be done by EPOS counting the quantity sold through the till, but the principle is the same.

How they work

Count and recount puts the focus of the manufacturer's discount on what is sold to the consumer. It provides a good reason for the retailer to ensure that products are not just taken in, but sold on to the customers.

What to look out for

In major multiples, this technique has largely been replaced by mechanics such as the multi-buy, which have a similar effect. In other trade sectors, count and recount is a way of giving trade discounts that do not simply end up increasing retailer margins. It gives an incentive to consumer sales.

5. Credit offers

The offer

The provision of credit is as important to the retailer as it is to the consumer. Providing the trade with enhanced credit terms can encourage earlier and deeper stocking of your range.

How they work

Multiple retailers derive a significant part of their profits and their positive cash flow by taking payment from their customers two months or more before they pay their suppliers. In these markets, the manufacturer is a key source of capital. In other sectors, trade payments can be faster, and the manufacturer can vary the payment period. This is particularly important in seasonal businesses, such as garden centres.

What to look out for

The cost of credit can be calculated for trade promotions in the same way as for consumer promotions. It is important to be aware of the risk of bad debts and to be clear that you have the financial resources to carry the delayed payment. If you can do so, using credit is a powerful means of trade promotion.

CASE STUDIES

The first of the three case studies in this chapter illustrates the long-range alternation of price and value promotions in Tesco's promotional strategy. The other two are examples of price promotion taking a far more focused form in the case of two particular brands than it is often assumed to do.

CASE STUDY 28. TESCO

During the mid-1970s, Tesco became the largest grocery user of Green Shield Stamps. These were stamps produced by a third-party operator, rather like a low-tech version of Air Miles. Consumers collected them at the checkout, stuck them into books and exchanged the books for merchandise at the equivalent of Argos catalogue shops. They were widely available at petrol stations and other retailers as well as at Tesco. Green Shield Stamps were a central element in Tesco's strategy for customer loyalty. They were also costing 2 per cent of turnover, and were spiralling out of control. Double, even quadruple stamps were becoming commonplace.

On 9 June 1977, Tesco signalled the end of Green Shield Stamps and plunged the grocery trade into a bitter price war with the launch of 'Operation checkout'. Shops were closed on a Saturday night, windows were covered and the Sunday press predicted a major development. When they opened the next day, they revealed deep, long-term price cuts in every department. Other retailers were forced to respond in kind. The price war continued into the early 1980s, radically increasing the major multiples' market share, depressing their profits and forcing a wave of closures, mergers and rationalizations. Tesco's own market share shot up from 8.5 to 12 per cent.

The recession of the early 1990s brought a new spate of price wars, with retailers competing with discount shops and the expected development of warehouse clubs by developing a secondary range of low-priced own-label 'value' lines. As the economy improved from 1993 onwards, so the threat of the discounters proved to be less serious than commentators had expected.

Tesco again rocked the grocery world with the launch of Clubcard in February 1995. It initially offered a 1 per cent saving on spends of over £10, plus a range of product offers. Clubcard quickly attracted over 5 million customers and was credited with driving Tesco's market share up to 18.5 per cent and producing a 16 per cent rise in sales in the first year. Competitors, including Safeway's ABC card and Sainsbury's Saver Card, also quickly followed it. In 1997, Boots took loyalty cards a stage further with the launch of an electronic card offering a 4 per cent discount. A number of cooperative retailers, which had originated rebates to consumers in the form of the 'dividend' in the 1840s, also experimented with new electronic forms of dividend.

When in 2002 Sainsbury's dropped Air Miles, Tesco immediately took them up – some would say returning full circle to its Green Shield Stamp days. The delight of sales promotion is that everything changes, but over a 20-year period, some things look much the same.

The huge investment made by Tesco in shopping online has at last proved successful. It matches customers' requirements in terms of time and quality of life. Studies show that 43 per cent of Tesco's top (high value) customers are 100 per cent bonded to the Tesco brand – choosing not to even think of buying anywhere else. A bonding to the brand is a new concept in 'loyalty'.

Where does Tesco go next? There are two safe predictions: that it is unlikely to retain the same formula forever and that it is unlikely to let its competitors be the first to make the change. What is less clear is the direction of the change. It is still offering price competition. Through its online operation it can monitor precisely what customers purchase. Clearly it has an advantage that could be exploited in a new form of sales promotion tuned to individual customers.

What would you expect those consumers most attracted by the promotional policy adopted by Tesco in 1978 to do today?
How has Tesco organized its total product and promotional mix to keep them on board?

CASE STUDY 29. GALE'S HONEY

In 1994, Nestlé's long-established honey brand, Gale's, faced a classic brand squeeze. It was 15 per cent more expensive than own-label honeys, and there was a price increase in the offing. Consumers viewed honey as. . . honey! Sales were slipping, brand loyalty was diminishing, a major multiple was threatening to delist, and there was little money in the budget. Cutting the price may have worked in the short term, but would have made the premium charged over own-label versions, ultimately, unsustainable. So, what could Gale's do?

The Nestlé brand manager set its sales promotion agency SMP a long list of objectives – reduce the rate of sales decline, avoid delisting, create impact on-pack, increase distribution, encourage multiple purchase, build loyalty – and keep the cost of the promotion under control. There's virtually everything in that list of objectives, but they boil down to one thing: provide an interesting reason for Gale's buyers to buy more. Also, one major constraint: keep the cost under control.

Getting to the heart of a long brief is a major challenge in sales promotion, and that was the first part of the agency's job. The agency built on the idea of buying more by opting for a 20p off next purchase coupon as the basic offer. It is a tried and tested mechanic for repeat purchase, but hardly exciting. It can also be expensive. So, the agency devised a novel multiple choice.

The 20p on-pack coupon was printed on latex. It could be scratched away and, if you were lucky, reveal a prize of £10. The consumer was then faced with an interesting choice: the chance of £10 or the guarantee of 20p. Once scratched off, the 20p coupon became invalid. The problem then was what to offer the majority of consumers who opted to win £10 but didn't win it. Instead of nothing, they found a beehive logo, which could be collected, for a range of Gale's pottery items.

The promotion worked. Distribution increased from 80 to 85 per cent, delisting was avoided, sales increased by 15 per cent, and coupon redemption was kept to less than 2 per cent. Also, the database of Gale's collectors was dramatically increased.

When you're in a tight corner, promotions need particularly careful thought. This could so easily have been a standard '20p off next purchase'. By asking consumers to have a bet on a £10 prize and not leaving them with nothing if they lost, Gale's hit every part of the brief.

The promotion also illustrates the difference between a marketing and a promotional brief. Nestlé's list of objectives was a wish list. The promotion was a very well-targeted answer to the question 'Who do I want to do what?'

If Gale's Honey put out a brief with the target of attracting new users, what promotional mechanics would be appropriate?

When you look at the list of promotional offers allowed in different parts of the EU in Chapter 11, what parts of this promotion would you have to change if you wanted to run it across the EU?

CASE STUDY 30. WORCESTERSHIRE SAUCE

Lea & Perrins' Worcestershire Sauce is one of those products more likely to be found at the back of many people's cupboards than in everyday use. Yet, a wide range of daily dishes could be spiced up by a dash of Worcestershire Sauce if only it could be brought to the front of their minds.

The agency Lovell Vass Boddey sought to do this with a multi-layered campaign that won an ISP Award in 1995. Data from previous promotional responders was profiled against a lifestyle database to target 2 million households with a mini-pack. This contained a sample of the sauce, a 10p off next purchase coupon and a free mail-in offer for a recipe book.

The coupon usage rate was 10 per cent, and uptake for the recipe book 6 per cent. Responders also received an additional coupon against next purchase and a lifestyle questionnaire, which received a 25 per cent response. This fed into planning and profiling for further promotions.

Door-drop samples, money off next purchase coupons and mail-in offers of recipe books are all standard promotional mechanics. The characteristic of this promotion was their intelligent integration and the use of database profiling to increase targeting accuracy before and after the promotion.

What alternative means of coupon distribution were available to Worcestershire Sauce and what benefits/disadvantages would they have over the one chosen?

What factors would you take into account in calculating the proof of purchase requirement to make for the recipe book?

SUMMARY

Price promoting is playing with fire. All the surveys show that consumers prefer it to any other form of promotion. They also show that it devalues brands and leads to an expectation of even more price promotion. The same holds true for the trade.

Promoters are most likely to use price promotion effectively if they think in terms of segment pricing, look for concrete benefits from each discount they give and use price promotion intermittently. One of the key challenges of sales promotion is to find value promotions that work as well as (or nearly as well as) price promotions and add to, rather than devalue, brand values. However, price promotion continues to be a benchmark for promotional effectiveness and is often made unavoidable by trade pressures and competition.

13

Premium Promotions

Premium promotions are offers in which the benefit comes in the form of an item of merchandise. Why a 'premium'? The reason for the choice of name is lost in the mists of time. It can cover anything from a potted plant, through a virtual pet, to a magazine. It can be a standard item or uniquely created, branded by the promoter or off the shelf. Indeed, all merchandise and all products are potential premiums.

Sales promotion agencies and promotional suppliers are more frequently involved in this type of promotion than in price promotions because selecting and sourcing the premium, organizing handling and redemption and conveying the attractiveness of the merchandise is an industry in itself. Because of this, premium promotions play a big role in the sales promotions that are discussed in the marketing press.

Premium promotions are the most frequently used value offer. They are particularly good at giving the opportunity to enhance brand communication in a tangible way. There is considerable scope for originality, too, for creating something unique to your product or service that the competition cannot copy. There is scope for creating real consumer excitement and for placing in consumers' homes items that will be used for years to come. The relationship this can create with the brand is one of the longest-lasting effects of sales promotion.

There is a permanent tension in sales promotion between offering money off (price promotions) and offering a material, preferably brand-enhancing benefit (value promotions). Case study 33 at the end of this chapter details how Procter & Gamble moved from one to the other – and back again. The basis of premium promotions is competing without tampering with the price.

This chapter looks first at the four main premium promotion mechanics: on-pack offers, with-purchase premiums, free mail-ins and self-liquidators. It is important to understand the different characteristics of these mechanics, but, in practice, they are blurred by a fifth category – the brand extension promotion.

CASE STUDY 31. HAAGEN-DAZS

An example of this is the 'Dedicated to Pleasure' CD sponsored by Haagen-Dazs in 1996. Produced by EMI, the CD used the company's distinctive press advertising on the cover, and included the Sarah Vaughan track 'Make yourself comfortable', used in its TV advertising. It sold over 60,000 copies, gave the brand a presence in 3,500 music stores and reached the Top 20 for compilation albums (itself constituting over a third of total music sales).

What else could the CD be used for? It could be made available free for a large number of proofs of purchase (a free mail-in), sold at cost price (a self-liquidator) or offered in company ice cream parlours free with multiple purchases (a near-pack). For practical reasons it probably could not be attached to cartons of ice cream in the freezer (an on-pack), but it could certainly be given to trade customers (a business gift). In other words, the different types of premium promotion are self-contained, but can be combined with the right premium to carry the values and advertising images of the brand in a series of different contexts.

Thinking this way has its dangers: always remember that the premium must grip the promotional objective. Using a premium simply because you've got it to hand is a mistake – it must justify itself against each of your objectives.

ON-PACK OFFERS

The offer

This is a form of premium promotion in which the premium is physically attached to the product. If it is in the product, as with breakfast cereals, it is sometimes called an 'in-pack' promotion. If the premium surrounds the product, replacing its normal packaging, as with a storage jar for coffee, it is sometimes called a 'container' promotion. An example of a straight on-pack is a magazine covermount – a premium taped or bound to the magazine cover.

How it works

These promotions have similar characteristics to the immediate discounts discussed in Chapter 12: they have instant appeal, give an immediate benefit and do not divert resources into handling and postage; they are also quite expensive to run.

Whether it is appropriate to put a premium in, on or around the product depends very much on the nature and size of both the premium and the product, and the characteristics of your packing processes. It would be evidently impractical to include a paintbrush in a tin of paint and unnecessary to go to the trouble of taping a toy to the outside of a cornflakes packet. All things being equal, it is best to put the premium in the product; next best to attach it to it. These steps prevent consumers taking the premium but not buying the product. However, there can be considerable costs in creating new shipping containers and in disruption to high-speed packing lines. Retailers can also be resistant to non-standard pack sizes, particularly in the grocery trade. The use of on-pack offers is thus a matter of carefully weighing costs and benefits.

Covermounts are universal in the magazine market. There are periodic statements that they have gone too far, and that magazines will start competing on editorial quality instead, but the use of covermounts goes on increasing. As with much sales promotion, the value is two-way. In every sector of the magazine market, there are increasing numbers of interchangeable products and consumer loyalty is low. For manufacturers of certain products – notably book and music publishers – gaining exposure for the product on a magazine cover can be a very good means of sampling potential customers.

Ideal covermounts are flat, cheap, attractive and useful – which is why calendars, diaries and books are found on magazines as different as *FHM*, *Yachting Monthly* and *Options*. However, there is a limit to the use of paper. IPC claimed sales increases of 10 to 15 per cent from using confectionery as covermounts – a Chocolate Orange bar on *Essentials* and low-sugar Canderel on *Healthy Eating*. In both cases, the products were new to the market, so gave their manufacturers a targeted sampling opportunity. In the case of Canderel and *Healthy Eating*, the consumer match was particularly good.

Use of on-pack premiums in the child and teens markets include pens, make-up and badges on magazines and the extensive use of character merchandise on confectionery. Nestlé uses figurines of Disney characters from the *Lion King* to *Pocahontas* in the place of caps on larger Smarties tubes. Once the Smarties have been eaten, the figurine forms part of a collection of characters that the child can keep. This collector element in on-pack premiums is less developed in the magazine market, but could be applied there too.

The reusable container form of on-pack offer makes the premium the packaging and the packaging the premium. Familiar examples include glass storage jars with instant coffee. They offer high-perceived value, and can be made as a range that encourages repeat purchase. It is not a concept that would work in the service sector, but it is an excellent (and often quite cheap) promotion for any product that needs packaging.

What to look out for

Immediate free premiums suffer from the cost of giving away anything worthwhile on a low-priced product. They do not discriminate between those who would have bought without the incentive and those incentivized to buy, meaning that some of your promotional spending will be wasted. There is often an extra cost of new outer packaging and adjustments to packing processes to take into account, which is not of benefit to the customer. Used extensively, however, as with covermounts, they can simply become a cost of doing business rather than an additional offer.

On-pack offers are best compared with immediate price offers, and here the advantages really show. They do not devalue the product's price and they can develop and reinforce brand identity. If you have selected the right item, immediate free premiums can be a very powerful incentive to buy. The principal factors to look out for are that the premium should be right and the offer cost-effective in margin terms.

WITH-PURCHASE PREMIUMS

The offer

These are promotions in which the premium is not physically attached to the product, but is available at the point of purchase. They are sometimes called 'near-packs' as a result of the retailers' habit of locating the premium near to the pack or product being promoted, and sometimes 'gift with purchase' (GWP).

In the service and retail sectors, these promotions all roll into one: when you buy the service, you collect the premium. Examples include a free portable TV when you buy a car, a free personal filing system when you appoint an estate agent and a free carnation at the conclusion of a restaurant meal.

These promotions are very common in duty-free outlets and at cosmetics counters in department stores where vanity bags or other items are given away when a purchase of a particular brand is made. They also work well in the pub trade, so long as great care is taken not to overburden bar staff. Case study 33 at the end of this chapter describes a classic grocery near-pack promotion in the 1960s, and Case study 36 a near-pack used in the pub trade.

How it works

As with all premium promotions, a number of factors have to be brought into balance: the attractiveness of the premium for the target market, its relevance to the brand, its cost, and the practicality of handling it. With near-packs, handling is a critical issue because arrangements have to be made for the product to be available at the point of purchase without being taken by those who do not buy the product. For these reasons, near-packs work best in outlets where there is counter service (as in the case of cosmetics counters) or where it is possible and worthwhile to use field marketing staff (as in duty-free outlets – see Chapter 2 for details of field marketing). It is generally not possible to use near-packs in grocery multiples today.

The premium can simply be a one-hit reward, such as a vanity bag with a purchase of cosmetics. It is also possible to include in the bag samples of other products, and to include coupons to be used against the purchase of full-size packs. That way the gift with purchase feeds into subsequent sales.

What to look out for

Near-packs give a direct and immediate incentive to buy one brand in preference to another without devaluing the retail price. The right incentive – such as a cosmetics vanity bag – can add real value to the brand proposition, but they are expensive, involve careful arrangements at point of purchase and reward those who would have bought without the incentive. They are, in practice, restricted to high-margin products.

FREE MAIL-INS

The offer

Free mail-ins are premium promotions in which the customer collects one or more proofs of purchase and sends them in for the item on offer entirely free or at no cost beyond postage. The benefit is delayed and not immediate. It is also subject to action on the part of the consumer after purchasing the item. Unlike on-packs and with-purchase premiums, not everyone who is encouraged by the promotion to buy will send in for the premium.

How it works

The word 'free' is one of the most compelling and powerful in our vocabulary. Rightly, it is subject to stringent restrictions. An offer is 'free' only if the customer pays nothing to obtain the item other than collecting the requisite number of proofs of purchase or pays only for postage in one or both directions. It is fair enough to say 'free with 30p for postage' if that is the cost of the postage, but it is not allowable to say 'free with 50p for postage and packing'. Promotions that require a telephone entry can be 'free' only if a non-premium telephone line is used – in other words, if the promoter is not recouping some of the costs by making profits on the telephone service.

A critical question in the structuring of a free mail-in promotion is the number of proofs of purchase that your customers must collect in order to obtain the item. This is a rule of thumb exercise, and follows these criteria:

- The number must reflect the typical purchase frequency of your product category. Note that it is category frequency, not brand frequency: the purpose of a free mail-in is to encourage consumers to use your brand rather than your competitors' for more of their purchases of that type of product. If more than one was required for a free mail-in on a hi-fi or life assurance policy, that would be absurd, but for cat food or a visit to a pub, 10 or more would be wholly reasonable.
- The number must also be influenced by whether or not you are seeking to influence trialists, light users, medium users or heavy users of your product or service. The higher the number, the more you move along the spectrum towards heavy users. The lower the number, the less likely it is to make any difference to the purchase frequency of heavy users.
- The level of redemptions is directly proportional to the number of proofs of purchase required. Raise the number of proofs of purchase and you lower the redemption level, and vice versa. This has obvious budget implications. The decision on the proof of purchase level is often taken in response to the level of redemption that is affordable.

The level of consumer redemption is naturally affected by the attractiveness of the premium (which you will want to maximize) and the closing date for applications (which you should set so that no products will be on retail sale after the closing date).

Two further factors are more amenable to alteration. You must decide whether or not to make any charge for postage and whether or not to offer a Freepost facility for customers to mail in their proofs of purchase. Note that the lower the postage costs are in each direction, the higher the response rate will be. You must also decide whether or not to restrict the offer to one application per household: this can unfairly restrict the reward to heavy and loyal users, but it also cuts out people exploiting an attractive offer aimed at less regular purchasers.

Free mail-ins can be used as part of a bigger promotional package. Remember, Gale's offered branded collectibles as a consolation offer to those who failed to obtain a £10 instant win (Case study 29).

CASE STUDY 32. SMITHKLINE BEECHAM

SmithKline Beecham did the same with a promotion for Ribena in 1995, themed on the 'Casper' film. Consumers were invited to look under bottle ring pulls or inside cartons to see if Casper had 'spooked' their pack and given them a cash prize or a special Casper bubble watch. If not, they could collect tokens for the watch or, on the bottles, for a Casper beaker that revealed ghostly characters as it was filled.

Using free mail-ins in this way means that a promotion works at two levels: as an instant-win incentive for light users and as a collector offer for heavy users.

What to look out for

The operational planning of free mail-ins is critical. Things can go wrong with the handling, with the design of the premium, with delivery dates and so forth. Getting them right is a matter of sound organization and attention to detail.

The most difficult issue is organizing a supply of premiums to match your expected redemption level. It is embarrassing to be so optimistic that you have a warehouse full at the end, and equally embarrassing to be unable to meet demand. This leads many promoters to seek over-redemption insurance or to contract with a company prepared to supply all the premiums redeemed at a fixed fee (this aspect is covered in Chapter 6).

Unless you contract out the promotion for a fixed fee, you will need to develop a contingency plan to deal with the twin problems of over- and under-redemption. Make an estimate of the likely flow of redemptions over the promotional period, then monitor the flow over the first few weeks to give you early warning of what the final redemption level will be.

If a free mail-in redeems at less than its expected level, you may be left with surplus premiums. You have three options: agree a sale-or-return arrangement with your premium supplier at the beginning (difficult if the premium is specially branded); sell off the surplus to a company specializing in the disposal of unwanted premiums (normally at a significant loss); or keep them for another (but probably equally unsuccessful) promotion.

If a free mail-in redeems at above its expected level, you may be faced with difficulties in obtaining sufficient extra premiums in time. Clearly, your early warning system should help here. It is also advisable to make arrangements for rapid extra deliveries with your premium suppliers at the beginning. Section 35 of the Sales Promotion Code makes it clear that 'phrases such as "subject to availability" do not relieve promoters of the obligation to take all reasonable steps to avoid disappointing customers'. If you cannot supply the premium you promised, 'products of a similar or greater quality or a cash payment should normally be substituted'. The best option is to order slightly fewer items than your expected redemption level, and have good arrangements for rapid resupply with your suppliers.

Finally, you will need to organize the system for warehousing the premiums, receiving customer applications, sending out the premiums, banking the postage contributions (if any) and handling any subsequent customer complaints. There are specialist companies called 'handling houses' that can provide this service if you decide not to do it yourself, and these are discussed in Chapter 6.

SELF-LIQUIDATORS

The offer

A self-liquidator promotion (SLP) is one in which the customer pays for all (or almost all) of the cost of the premium and its associated handling and postage. Such an offer cannot be described as 'free'. At best, it can be described as a 'bargain' when the cost is still below what customers would pay in the shops. A typical example of a self-liquidator would be a 'Super kitchen knife – just £1.99, plus 50p postage and packing'.

How it works

A self-liquidator works in exactly the same way as a free mail-in, except that the customer pays for all or most of the cost of putting on the offer.

What to look out for

Self-liquidators were popular in the days of resale price maintenance, before the widespread development of retail discounting and mail order. In the 1970s, they fell out of favour. It became less and less possible to price a self-liquidator at a level that made it worthwhile for consumers to send in for it. Redemption levels of 1 per cent or less became common.

So why do companies go on using them? The reason is that there are some cases in which they can be valuable. Nestlé, for example, created a series of watches that it offered as an SLP in France, Spain and Portugal on its Nesquick and Chopaquick brands. Produced in bulk in Switzerland, they featured an N instead of pointers and a rabbit and a dog respectively, which lit up when a button was pressed at night. They sold at significantly less than comparable watches. Many book and CD products can work as SLPs because the retail margins remain very high. Collectibles such as branded merchandise can also be effective among regular users of a brand.

Self-liquidators work if one or more factors are present: you locate a premium at a radically lower price than that at which it is available anywhere else; you create an image for your premiums that makes it a desirable, full-price item; and if the margins in the category are very large. With these exceptions, self-liquidators are an attempt to run an extra benefit offer without actually giving an extra benefit. It is not surprising that customers give them the thumbs down.

BRAND EXTENSION PROMOTIONS

The offer

Forty years ago, businesses relied on resale price maintenance and branding was in its infancy. No one walked round in Brylcreem clothing, however much they put it on their hair. No one wore Burtons labels on the outsides of their shirts. Elvis Presley releases were not accompanied by a merchandise deal. The same change in the nature of business competition that has led to the decline of self-liquidators has led to the increase in brand extension promotions. The Haagen-Dazs promotion cited earlier in this chapter is a typical example. Many of these make a profit for the promoter.

An offer that makes a profit is a particularly attractive form of promotion. It adds to, rather than uses, your marketing budget, and turns the normal worry about redemption rates on its head. If each redemption makes you money, the more the merrier!

How it works

Brand extension promotions began when companies realized that people would pay high prices for merchandise carrying their brand names. Early entrants into this business were soft drinks brands (Coca-Cola), alcoholic drinks (Guinness) and cars (BMW). Items were sold by coupons on the product, mail-order catalogues and off-the-page advertising. During the 1980s, Coca-Cola extended the principle to retail shops selling only Coca-Cola-branded merchandise. They became a profit centre in their own right.

Confectionery companies have followed the same principle in a different way. Nestlé's Christmas stockings have long contained a tape, book or toy in addition to a selection of confectionery items. Once the premium exceeds the cost of the confectionery, it is questionable which is product and which is premium. The inclusion of collectible self-assembly plastic or other models is a permanent feature of Kinder Surprise eggs and several brands of yoghurt aimed at children. Cosmetics companies, such as Revlon, have created bags containing a complete nail-care kit, and sold them as a temporary special product.

Confectionery companies, notably Cadbury's, have also been successful in licensing their brand names for use on a range of items, including lunchboxes and rucksacks, in return for a royalty on each item sold. The line between the premium purchased by the company for promotional use, the product manufactured under licence by a third party and the brand extension jointly marketed by both in their mutual interest has become blurred. Film companies too license their film names and products used in films can benefit from such association.

Customer magazines are a form of premium. A 1996 Mintel survey identified 246 customer magazines in the UK, among which financial services with 43 magazines, travel with 34, IT with 26 and retailing with 25 were particularly well represented. Customer magazines are a promotional benefit in themselves, a platform for further promotional offers and a means of engaging other firms in joint promotion. Their scale is colossal – *Ford Magazine*, published in four variants, has a print run of 800,000 copies, putting it among the top 20 UK consumer titles.

Is this sales promotion? In the Introduction, sales promotion was defined as a range of price and value offers designed to achieve marketing objectives by changing any part of the marketing mix to influence the behaviour of end-users or intermediaries, normally for a defined time period. Changing the product by including things in it or creating new products by putting your brand name on them is a sales promotional activity. It requires the promoter to think laterally about the brand – not just as a bar of chocolate, but as a bundle of values that can be expressed equally well in clothing, bags, watches, albums and magazines.

What to look out for

The critical question to ask yourself if you are considering this type of promotion is, 'What business am I in?' The danger is that managers become overexcited about what are often marginal profit opportunities in branded merchandise and neglect the marketing of their core product.

Be aware of the point at which an activity ceases to be promotional and becomes a business in its own right. *The Guinness Book of Records* began as a promotional premium for Guinness. It has become an entirely self-standing product that many will not even associate with the dark liquid that gave it birth.

BUSINESS GIFTS

The offer

Business gifts are items given to trade customers to promote goodwill. In the grocery trade, they are often known as 'dealer loaders' – a reference to their historic use in persuading dealers to load up with stock beyond their requirements in return for an item of merchandise.

How they work

A survey by Mintel in 1997 of large and medium-sized companies showed that existing customers are the main focus of business gift activity – cited by 63 per cent of respondents. Branding of items was seen as essential by 70 per cent of respondents. Few companies spent more than £20,000 a year on business gifts and most were not wholly clear as to why they were doing it. Yet, judging by the level of advertising for clocks, calendars, ties and leather goods in the marketing press, business gifts are big business. Not knowing why you're doing it simply isn't good enough.

Some specialists in the industry draw a firm distinction between a premium and a business gift. A premium is seen as an item designed to persuade a consumer to buy one brand rather than another. A business gift is seen as something that has impact, attractiveness, usefulness and longevity, but has no such focused objective. This is a false distinction. Eversheds used a highly imaginative premium item to encourage firms to contact it about intellectual property law (Case study 14). Electrolux used a tape recorder in a special box to encourage buyers to list a new product (Case study 35). Chapter 5 described the use of a single wellington boot to encourage commercial property agents to visit a new development. These are examples of items of merchandise being used in imaginative ways to persuade business customers to do something. The key sales promotional question, 'Who do I want to do what?' therefore applies to business gifts as much as to any other area of sales promotion.

The public sector and many large organizations have rules preventing their staff receiving gifts of more than token value from suppliers, and these must be respected. However, 80 per cent of businesses are small operations run by their owners and there is no conflict of interest between owner and buyer. If this is your market, an item of merchandise can be a perfectly reasonable way of persuading them to buy one brand rather than another. When NatWest wanted to encourage start-up businesses to choose it rather than another bank, it teamed up with BT to offer what was, essentially, a consumer promotion (Case study 25).

Approaching business gifts in this way enables you to use them in a cost-effective and focused way. Avista has sometimes given well-made and distinctive soft toys with discreet branding to our clients at Christmas. They seldom cost more than £10, and have this objective: 'We want our clients to think of us as people who are imaginative, know about premiums and care about families'. Business gifts can be used to achieve other objectives, too:

● 'We want personnel managers to have our telephone number on their desk at all times.'

- 'We want leisure centre staff to carry their personal kit in one of our sports bags.'
- 'We want shipping managers to put a map of the world on their walls that shows our shipping routes.'
- 'We want marketing executives to come to our seminar on opportunities on the Internet rather than to those of our competitors.'
- 'We want chief executives to understand that we are at the leading edge of thinking in our business.'

Note that the promotional objectives in all these cases are specific and deliverable. If the objective in the first example is specified as 'we want personnel managers to telephone us every time they need temporary staff' it cannot be delivered by a business gift. Having your telephone number on their desk is helpful, but the objective is not then a foregone conclusion. You will need to use it as part of a promotional campaign, not as the campaign itself.

The objectives cited above could be delivered, respectively, by a branded desk clock, an up-to-the-minute sports bag, an overprinted map, a free book on the Internet and a reprint of an article discussing your firm that appeared in an industry magazine. None of these items is particularly expensive. Some, such as the magazine article reprint, demand imagination and effort, but cost almost nothing at all.

When you are looking for business gifts, there are three sources. The first is to go direct to the many companies that advertise in the marketing press or to your local *Yellow Pages*. This can take time, but is the cheapest way of doing it if you know exactly what you want. The second is to use a business gifts catalogue. There are very many of these, often syndicated to local agents. Burostat, for example, produces a 124-page annual catalogue of gifts that local agents overprint with their own name. The advantage of this is that you have a single source of supply, can order in small quantities and that many items are available from stock. The third approach is to use a premium sourcing house (discussed in Chapter 6), but they are only really interested in large quantities or wide ranges of items. The advantage of using them is that they know about the latest technologies and designs and can search out and design something original for your company.

What to look out for

There are rules governing VAT and income tax on business gifts, particularly those given internally. Make sure you have a copy of the latest Customs and Excise advice and are in touch with your Inland Revenue office if you have any doubt.

Make sure you have also understood the internal rules of the companies you do business with. Violating a rule that puts the recipient of a gift in an embarrassing position is bad business: no one can have as a promotional objective 'I want my customer to be embarrassed'.

That said, make sure you apply to business gifts the same rigorous thinking about promotional objectives that you use in other areas. Don't expect them to do more than they can do, but make sure they do that job well.

CASE STUDIES

The four promotions in this chapter specifically focus on near-packs, on-packs and business gifts. Other relevant case studies for premium promotions are Kleenex Facial Tissues (Case study 6), Eversheds (Case study 14) and NatWest/BT (Case study 25).

CASE STUDY 33. PROCTER & GAMBLE

Some promotions are remembered for years, if not decades. Test this out by asking someone over 50 if they remember the plastic roses promotions of the early 1960s. This is the story behind it.

In the late 1950s, Procter & Gamble and Lever Brothers were locked in trench warfare. Daz was an innovative synthetic detergent when it was launched by Procter & Gamble in 1953. Two years later, Lever Brothers responded with Omo. By the late 1950s, there was no functional difference in washing performance between the two brands. Price promotion was rife and ultimately unproductive. Up to 70 per cent of packs carried a '3d off' flash, weakening the perceived value of the brands. There was continuous heavyweight TV advertising. Despite all this activity, market shares seemed locked at 12 per cent for Daz and 9 per cent for Omo.

How could Procter & Gamble break through the 12 per cent share ceiling? How could it escape the price warfare? The answer when it came was a classic of promotional marketing. Nearly 40 years on it carries lessons for any brand in any sector facing similar market conditions.

Procter & Gamble tested alternatives to the '3d off' packs in a panel of 88 stores across the country. Dozens of alternatives were tested – and the clear winner was the offer of plastic roses as a near-pack. Rolled out nationally in 1961, 8 million roses were given away and Daz's market share increased to 18 per cent. Costing around 3d against a perceived value of 6d, the flowers made sense both to the company and the consumer. The scope for retail prominence was immense. The promotion was repeated in the next two years, scoring brand shares of 16 per cent and 14 per cent respectively. By then, Omo had responded with plastic daffodils, effectively turning the detergent price war into a flower war.

Plastic flowers were then – as now – considered naff by many people. They had very little to do with brand values, but rigorous testing showed that they worked. And they did – for a while. Price warfare then resumed and, by the mid-1970s, was again normal.

The lesson of the Procter & Gamble roses is that promotional innovation can have massive impact on brand share, but no single promotional technique lasts forever.

What parallels to the Procter & Gamble and Lever price warfare can you see in the market today, and how could premium promotions change the situation?

In which retail sectors could you now use near-packs, and in which retail sectors would it be impossible?

CASE STUDY 34. CLEARBLUE ONE STEP

What kind of promotion is right for a pregnancy test? Different women hope for very different outcomes, and some may approach the test with considerable anxiety. By 1994, the pregnancy testing market was crowded with technically similar products. Clearblue One Step faced a major competitor that had recently been relaunched with a full support programme. In a crowded market, loss of brand share soon leads to loss of distribution and a cycle of decline sets in.

Clearblue One Step identified four objectives for the promotion: to offset competitor activity; add value to the product; affirm the brand's position on women's health issues; and offer an item of relevance irrespective of the test result. The product cost £10.75 and the cost of any promotional item had to be in proportion to that price.

SMP's promotion had both trade and consumer targets. In pharmacies, it is often the pharmacy assistant who recommends which pregnancy test to buy, so the promotion had to appeal to them. In multiples, such as Boots, consumers self-select, so if the offer was to work, it had to be clearly marked on the pack.

The solution was to band a Well Woman diary to the pack. This featured relevant and helpful information, irrespective of the test result, and a host of other health advice. It worked: sales in autumn 1994 were up 20 per cent on the same period in 1993 – a volume increase of nearly 12,000 units a month.

This was a workable, practical solution rather than a piece of creative genius. What shines through is the clear link between market conditions, brand values, promotional objectives and the promotional solution. It deserved to work and to win an ISP Award for the company and its agency, SMP.

What other options for an on-pack premium could have been considered by Clearblue One Step? What would their advantages and disadvantages be?
Why would a free mail-in promotion or a price offer not be appropriate for this product?
Are there other promotional mechanics Clearblue One Step could have considered?

CASE STUDY 35. ELECTROLUX

Convincing buyers to stock a product is crucial for any new entrant. These 'gatekeepers' are the first hurdle any new product has to overcome on the road to success.

In 1994, Electrolux launched a new micro cleaner, the X8. 'It is very difficult to create buyer interest in the vacuum cleaner market and to make the product promise that bit different', commented Simon Mahoney of sales promotion agency SMP. The objectives of the trade launch were, nevertheless, to create interest and awareness among buyers, gain listings and increase market share.

Building on the name X8, Electrolux sent out a series of Xtraordinary mailers to buyers. The rep then visited the buyer carrying a security box that looked as if it was made of stainless steel and which was emblazoned with top secret messages. On removing the lid, a cassette player played a personalized message to the buyer about the top secret mission he was about to embark on. After the message was played, the box revealed the X8 in all its 'micro' glory. The cassette player was left with the dealer.

Daft or what? It certainly worked, creating a great deal of interest and amusement in the trade. All existing Electrolux outlets listed the X8, and the firm gained several new accounts. Electrolux's share in the cylinder cleaner sector increased by 50 per cent over 1993, and overall it moved into brand leadership.

Marketing is a serious business. Electrolux no doubt had a stack of technical and market research reports to show just how successful X8 would be, but you can't bore someone into buying – amusing people often works better.

Does leaving the tape recorder with the dealer create a conflict of interest in companies where there are rules against gifts? If so, what steps could you take to deal with it?
In what kinds of markets does creating a special premium of this kind make sense, and in what kinds would it not work?

CASE STUDY 36. SMIRNOFF

Smirnoff is the UK's leading brand of vodka, but it faces a constant battle to persuade its core 18–24-year old consumers to ask for it by name in pubs and clubs. It's not an easy market: there are severe restraints on the involvement of staff in promotions at a crowded bar and the age group is promotionally sophisticated. It is often immune to promotional incentives and easily bored.

The agency Marketing Principles looked closely at the question, 'Who do I want to do what?' The key answer was to encourage groups of friends to talk about Smirnoff. This is how the objective was achieved.

On asking for Smirnoff, consumers were given a foil sachet that contained a pin badge replica of a Smirnoff bottle. The consumer then 'cracked' the badge to turn it from opaque to one of four luminous colours. It literally glowed for up to four hours. Two of the colours could also be exchanged over the bar for a baseball cap or T-shirt.

The promotion achieved its objectives. Outlet participation was 60 per cent and sales of Smirnoff's vodka were up by an average of 16 per cent. Nearly a million Smirnoff consumers participated.

Two things characterize this promotion. First, the mechanic was simplicity itself – a small item handed over the bar to those who asked for Smirnoff. The bright and extensive promotional material had a simple message: 'Ask for it!' Second, the promotion relied on conversation among consumers to reveal its real nature and they were all asking questions. Why is your badge red? Why have you won a T-shirt? Are there any other colours? How long will this go on glowing? The promotion picked up the key nature of youth pubs: a busy bar, a great deal of chat among friends and a keen interest in working out something that is not immediately obvious.

What other premiums could Smirnoff have considered as items for the bar staff to hand over?
What particular issues in the Codes of Advertising and Sales Promotion Practice did Smirnoff have to take into account in designing this promotion?
In what other markets is it crucial to encourage groups of friends to talk about the product?

SUMMARY

Premium promotions are the most important way companies can compete promotionally without altering the price. There are four main mechanics –

on-pack, near-pack, free mail-in and self-liquidator. The boundaries between them are becoming blurred with the growth of brand extension promotions.

There are considerable opportunities for promoting, enhancing and extending brand value, but companies must be careful to remember their main priorities. Business gifts should not be considered a separate category, but an extension of thinking about 'Who do I want to do what?' in the business-to-business field.

There are practical and operational issues to consider in sourcing premiums, organizing, handling and dealing with redemption rates, further details of which are given in Chapter 7.

14

Prize Promotions

Prize promotions differ from every other mechanic discussed in this book in that the benefit to the consumer depends on whether they win or not. A 20p coupon is a guarantee of 20p off the product specified on it. A free mail-in is an undertaking by the promoter to provide a premium in return for a certain number of proofs of purchase. With prize promotions, there is no such guarantee. Three other characteristics distinguish prize promotions:

- they are offers where the maximum cost can be predicted in advance and does not vary with the numbers who participate;
- a far bigger benefit can be given in a prize promotion than in a promotion where the benefit is available to everyone who participates;
- they are heavily regulated by the British Codes of Advertising and Sales Promotion, by the Lotteries and Amusement Act 1976 and by other legislation, which is far from simple to interpret.

There is a difficult balance to be struck in writing about prize promotions. On the one hand, they are staggeringly successful. The chance to win a car, a holiday or a substantial sum of money at little or no cost is permanently attractive to consumers. *Reader's Digest* has built its business on this basis, giving away nearly £3 million a year. On the other hand, they are a legal minefield. The complicated pattern of law regulating lotteries and gaming recognizes its attractiveness. Historically, government has restricted the opportunity to gamble. Although government is easing restrictions on casinos and betting shops, and has gone into the business itself with the National Lottery (now Lotto), the older laws still remain.

Too much stress on legal niceties can lead promoters to regard it as a no-go area. Too much stress on promotional effectiveness can lead promoters to forget the need for caution. This chapter is designed to show you that it is a minefield, but one that is worth getting through – just watch your step.

There are five types of prize promotion – competitions, free draws, instant wins, games and lotteries. They are distinct in legal terms, subject to different legal and code of practice restrictions, and offer different mechanisms for winning the prize. The distinctions are not immediately obvious, and it is worth spending some time making sure you fully understand them:

- Competitions offer prizes for the successful exercise of a significant degree of mental or physical skill or judgement. Participants may be required to pay or make a purchase to enter.
- Free draws make available prizes by distribution of random chances. The selection of the winning ticket is separate and later, not instantaneous with its distribution. No skill or judgement is involved, and participants cannot be asked to pay or make a purchase to enter.
- Instant wins offer prizes by distributing a predetermined number of winning tickets. Consumers know instantly whether they have won or lost. No skill or judgement is involved, and consumers cannot be asked to pay or make a purchase to enter.
- Games are forms of free draw or instant win that give the appearance of requiring skill but, in fact, rely on probability. They can be based on brand name games, such as Monopoly or Trivial Pursuit, or on generic games, such as bingo or snakes and ladders. Because no significant degree of skill or judgement is called for, no purchase or payment can be required in order to enter.
- Lotteries work in the same way as free draws or instant wins, but participants pay to enter. They are strictly regulated under the Lotteries and Amusements Act 1976, and are, in practice, restricted to small-scale, local, non-commercial schemes.

These distinctions become clear if we take an example of a prize promotion a local travel agent might put on. The promotion could be headlined, 'Win a weekend break with Sunshine Travel':

- It would be a competition if it required entrants to identify the capitals of five countries and to complete a tie-breaker. It would be legal to sub-head the promotion 'when you book your next holiday with Sunshine Travel'.
- It would be a free draw if it said 'Just drop your name and address in the box'. It would be illegal to subhead it 'when you book your next holiday with Sunshine Travel'. Anyone walking through the door must be allowed to enter.

- It would be an instant win if Sunshine Travel overprinted its booking confirmation with numbers that could be revealed by scratching off a latex panel, and a particular combination of numbers instantly won the prize. To be legal, anyone walking through the door should be given an equal chance of winning.
- It would be a game if the promotion read 'Play snakes and ladders at Sunshine Travel and win a weekend break'. The game may require the use of a dice, even a certain amount of skill. The rules for a free draw would still apply to it.
- It would be a lottery if the subheading read 'Raffle tickets available at just 10p each'. It would be legal only if it was promoted by a local charity or voluntary association registered with the local authority.

To all intents and purposes, lotteries are a no-go area for commercial promoters. The only exceptions are small-scale lotteries, held at a single event (such as a dinner) with non-cash prizes below £50 in total value, and where the proceeds are entirely devoted to charity. For this reason, lotteries are not considered further in this chapter.

The other four types of prize promotion are subject to specific rules relating to the closing date, the judging process, the description of prizes, the announcing of winners, and so forth. The key features are described in the sections that follow, and in more detail in section 40 of the British Codes of Advertising and Sales Promotion Practice. Philip Circus, formerly the Director of Legal Affairs at the Institute of Practitioners in Advertising and legal adviser to the ISP, has written an invaluable book entitled *Sales Promotion Law: A practical guide* and writes a regular column in *Incentive Today* that provides a running commentary on legal developments. Anyone running prize promotions needs to be absolutely clear that they follow the complicated laws that govern them, and the best way to do that is to have your copy checked by the ISP, the ASA or a specialist lawyer.

COMPETITIONS

The offer

To qualify as a competition – and therefore for it to be legal to ask for a purchase to be made – the winner must be determined by the skill or judgement shown. There are many forms of competition, the main ones being:

- Order of merit: 'List the following five items in order of importance.'
- Complete a slogan: 'Complete this sentence in not more than 10 words.'
- Question plus slogan: 'Answer these five questions and complete this sentence in not more than 10 words.'

- Spot the difference: 'Identify 12 differences between pictures a and b.'
- Estimate: 'Estimate how many packs of this product will fit inside this car.'
- Spot the ball: 'Mark the position of the football on this photograph.'
- Identify: 'Identify these famous people from the photographs of their eyes.'
- Be creative: 'Draw a picture, take a photograph or write a story.'
- Treasure hunt: 'Use the clues to find the hidden treasure.'

By far the most common type of test is the question plus slogan. It is the easiest to fit into the limited amount of space available to communicate most competitions, the easiest to explain and the easiest to judge. Its benefit over a slogan-only test is that the questions filter the number of slogans that have to be judged.

That said, there is a simplicity to promotions that do not have a filter to reduce the number of tie-breakers. It makes the competition easier to enter for consumers, and can increase participation. Captioning a photograph is a good one-shot test of skill and judgement that many people enjoy entering.

About 3 per cent of the population always enter competitions and 40 per cent do so from time to time. The scale of competitions used to be enormous. *Reader's Digest* estimated in 1988 that, at any one time, there is £1 million in competition prizes waiting to be won. The November 1988 issue of *Competitors Companion* listed 27 competitions running in Tesco alone over the autumn, and 63 competitions with a closing date of 30 November. Prizes included 40 holidays, £60,000 in cash, 12 cars and 40,000 smaller prizes.

Today, competitions are much less frequent, having been replaced in many cases by instant-win promotions and put in the shade in respect of the prizes they offer by Lotto. Radio stations frequently run competitions that ask a number of simple questions, but have no tie-breaker: the winning entry is the first correct set of answers drawn from a hat. These are, in reality, free draws. It is the skill and judgement in the tie-breaker that is the criterion of skill and judgement in the competition as a whole.

Competitions are known for attracting the professional competition entrant. These are obviously small in number, but it is wrong to think of a clear divide between professional competition entrants on the one hand and non-entrants on the other. The secret of good design is to make your competition attractive to the 40 per cent who sometimes enter, and not just the 3 per cent who always do.

How they work

Competitions tend to have a low level of entry – 0.5 per cent of opportunities to participate would be considered high. Hugh Davidson, the former European Vice-President of Playtex, considers that they 'absorb management and sales force time to no object'. However, this ignores 'promotional slippage' – the number who are attracted by an offer, but do not enter. Competitions can be effective in creating awareness, interest and impact at point of purchase well beyond the number who enter. These are legitimate sales promotion objectives, and they do have a bearing on sales. Unusual prizes can attract significant levels of publicity, and there is still scope for more run-of-the-mill prize publicity in local papers. Competitions are beneficial on these grounds. Competitions can also be useful ways of drawing attention to a product's characteristics. The Zantac 75 promotion (Case study 7) used an imaginative competition mechanic for exactly that purpose.

There is a major benefit in running a promotion that has a fixed level of costs and makes limited demands in terms of premium supply. Once you have established the competition prizes and paid for the communication materials, you know the limit of your costs. This is a characteristic shared by other types of promotion described in this chapter, and is of particular value when a company's budgeting procedure makes it difficult to cope with open-ended costs.

There are various guidelines it is wise to follow when designing a competition. Remember that it is not a mastermind test. Some competitions require entrants to jump through hoops that would have left Magnus Magnusson gasping. There is no point in making the test obscure and difficult. There is, however, considerable purpose in making it fun and amusing for your target audience. Competitions continue to be attractive to children, and very often in specialist markets, for these reasons.

Once you have selected the type of competition you want to run, design it so that there is an identifiable winner. A competition that consists of only a series of questions is likely to result in a great many correct solutions. The winner cannot be selected at random, otherwise it becomes a draw. This is the reason for the common use of the tie-breaker slogan. Creative tests are also capable of yielding a single winner. Every other kind of test needs a method of judging between those who get the correct answer to the estimate, the identification, the order of merit or the questions.

It is essential to set it up from the beginning so that a judge is able to judge. The requirement in a competition is for the exercise of 'skill and judgement'. These are prone to subjective interpretation. It is therefore important to indicate on what grounds 'skill and judgement' will be assessed. This is the reason for the inclusion in tie-breaker instructions of phrases such as 'in the most apt and original way' or 'in the most amusing way'. Any independent judge will want to know the grounds on which the selection of a winner is to be made, so it is sensible to build this into the structure of the competition from the beginning.

When you come to write the copy, make sure everything that the entrant has to do, from obtaining the necessary number of proofs of purchase to completing a tiebreaker, is as clear as possible. The events that follow, from the judging process through to any obligation to participate in publicity activity, must also be made clear from the beginning. Section 40 of the British Codes of Advertising and Sales Promotion sets out what must be included.

The level of response to competitions is strongly influenced by the prizes on offer. The best starting point is to fix the budget available. There are then several ways in which you can think about the prizes you offer.

There is an argument that a single, major prize creates the greatest interest; another, that the greater chance of winning one of many lesser prizes is more attractive. There is no absolute answer to this. Partly in response to Lotto, there has been a decline in the conventional system of a complicated and graduated prize structure: a big first prize, three second prizes, five third prizes, and so forth. This structure dissipates impact and increases costs. The best solution is probably a single, major prize and a large number (perhaps 100 or more) of runners-up prizes. It can be possible to use a variant in which everyone gains an item of some value – for example, a coupon for money off future purchases. If you are doing this, be careful not to describe it as a prize. Something that every entrant obtains is not a 'prize' but a 'gift'.

There are several tried and tested prizes. Holidays and cars are always top of the list because everyone likes them, and it is easy to provide a better version than most people would buy of their own accord. However, your holiday does tend to be lost among the many other holiday prizes simultaneously available. Hence the reason for specials, such as Golden Wonder's offer of 'your own tropical island' or the prize of becoming Lord of the Manor of an English village. Specials tend, by their nature, to be things no one really wants, however. The best solution is probably a twist to a standard prize – for example, 'get your hair cut in New York'. This combines a good standard prize with a special that (importantly) relates to the item in question – in this case, a hair care product.

Many competition rules specify that there is no cash alternative. There are two reasons for doing this: that you have already bought the prize in question or that you will be buying it at a substantial discount to the normal price, and prefer not to disclose the actual cost to you. If the rules do not exclude a cash alternative, arguments about the value of a prize can be difficult, and a refusal to give a cash alternative can seem unreasonable. Conversely, there are cases where a cash alternative is essential, for example, in the case of the delightful but impractical tropical island. In that case, the amount of the cash alternative should be specified upfront.

It is worth seeking publicity for the prize-winner. Local papers are normally happy to run a photograph and caption of a local prize-winner, and it is generally possible to obtain coverage in your relevant trade press. Prize-winners are sometimes reluctant to be used in this way, and it is important to respect their sensitivities. However, if you intend to use the prize-winner for publicity purposes, it is important to make this point in the competition rules, and to specify it as a condition of entry.

What to look out for

There are several things to look out for when running a competition, and some require very careful thought. Asking entrants to predict a future event, such as the outcome of a football match, is considered forecasting, and is illegal in a competition. Asking them to predict when the first goal will be scored is also illegal in a competition, but on the different grounds that it is a matter of chance. Asking them to predict the weather at the London Weather Centre on the day the match will be played may not be illegal because the weather is a state of affairs and not an event; its legality will depend on whether or not a substantial degree of skill is required. No wonder lawyers are needed!

Judging is an area of administration that causes headaches, particularly if you are faced with thousands of entries. Resist the temptation to treat it as a draw – choosing the first tie-breaker slogan that catches your fancy. You could find a dozen other entrants providing evidence that they had submitted the same slogan. Be clear before you start judging how you are going to interpret the rules. Is '100' two words ('one hundred'), one word or not allowed because it is not a word? Do hyphenated words count as one word or two? A good guide is to reduce the number of potential winners by making a strict interpretation of the instruction to complete a sentence in '12 words or fewer'. Being strict also protects you against those who may complain that, if they had known that 'words' meant 'words or numbers' they would have submitted a different entry.

Slogans are often required to be 'apt and original'. There is a trap for the unwary here. If two entries use the same slogan, neither can be the most original, for how do you choose between the two? Slogans that echo the long-established advertising of a brand ('I love Cadbury's Roses because they grow on you') are unlikely ever to be original, however flattering they may be to the advertiser.

James Porteous, a veteran of the judging business, advises using a team of eight people in a judging session. The first stage is to take a pile of entries, choose the ones you like and pass those you have rejected to your neighbour to do the same. When the process has been carried out by five of the eight, that is a majority. The short-listed entries have been short-listed by a majority. The second stage is to go through all the individual favourites and reverse the process – putting to one side any that any single judge dislikes.

These two stages will have produced a crop of entries that could all be winners. The third stage is to choose the winner or winners by asking the question, 'Is this entry better than that?' This is done by all the judges together. If you need to select one winner, take the entry at the top of the pile as the provisional winner and read out the slogan. Take the next entry, read the slogan and ask, 'Is it better?' If not, discard it. If it is, it becomes the provisional winner. The process continues until all entries that have reached stage three have been reviewed, and the last remaining provisional winner becomes the actual winner. If there are 10 winners to be selected, follow the same process, but select the 10 entries at the top of the pile as provisional winners. If any subsequent entry is better, discard the least good of the 10 and replace it, continuing until all entries that have reached stage three have been reviewed.

A large and apparently daunting task quickly and fairly becomes manageable using this method. Normally, judges come to a consensus choice of the final winner. If you need to take a vote, allocate each judge 10 points to distribute among the entries that are in contention for the prize. Often, everyone's second preference will emerge the winner.

The Code of Practice requires that both an expert and an independent judge are involved in the judging process. They can be one and the same person – for example, a teacher for an art-related competition, a travel agent for a travel competition. They can prove a help in managing the judging as well as demonstrating that the process is fair and seen to be fair.

A large number of entries is a reasonable test of the attractiveness of a competition, but not of its promotional effectiveness. The number of entries can be quite unrelated to the promotional objectives. Attracting entries depends on presenting the competition in the most compelling way for your particular audience – offering a free or low-cost means of entry and making the competition easy. Clever word games will be attractive to some groups, if not to most. It may be, however, that your promotional purpose is trade-related – for example, to gain display. Once that is achieved, the number of entries makes no difference at all. The question, 'Who do I want to do what?' discussed in Chapter 4 is the basis on which you can determine the style of competition you use and how easy and attractive you make it to enter.

FREE DRAWS

The offer

In a free draw, winners are determined entirely by chance and it is not permissible to require any payment or proof of purchase from entrants. Free draws differ from instant win promotions in that people do not know immediately whether they have won or not. Second stages in free draws vary, and include waiting until the closing date to see if your entry is selected; posting a set of numbers into a handling house to be checked against a predetermined list of winners (a practice much favoured by direct mail magazines); and hoping to find the matching half of (for example) a banknote on your next visit to the outlet that hands them out.

Why should promoters use free draws rather than competitions and lose the ability to ask for a proof of purchase? What is the advantage of issuing prizes at random to people who may never be customers? There are four reasons for using free draws:

1. They can be highly effective in generating interest, awareness and participation. In particular, free draws are a strong traffic-builder for retailers and a proven readership-builder for newspapers. The absence of tie-breakers means that free draws attract up to 20 times as many participants as do competitions.
2. They are easy for the promoter to administer, easy for consumers to enter, involve a fixed prize fund and are a quick and easy way of building a customer and prospect database.
3. They can involve an implicit encouragement to purchase. This needs to be treated carefully. Newspapers invariably state (as they are required to) that consumers can check their tickets without buying the newspaper; petrol stations invariably state (as they are required to) that tickets are issued to all those who visit the petrol station, not just those who buy petrol. This is the 'plain paper entry' route. In practice, between 80 and 90 per cent of those who enter also make a purchase.
4. They allow substantial opportunities for creativity. In comparison with competitions, the main alternative for those seeking a mechanic with fixed costs, free draws require far fewer rules, do not require questions or tests, but do allow free rein for games of every kind.

Free draws share some of the features of competitions: a fixed prize fund; a range of prizes; the need to make conditions of entry clear. These points are therefore not repeated here. This section looks at the characteristics particular to free draws, those relating not to the offer itself, but to how it works.

How they work

The simplest way to operate a free draw is to have a pile of cards on which consumers can write their names, addresses and any other information you want to collect from them, a box for them to make their entries and a declared date on which the winner will be drawn from the box. For business customers it is even simpler – simply provide a box into which they can drop their business cards. When you make the draw, it is important that it is done by an independent person and that it is done with witnesses so it is seen to be independent.

Another way is to issue consumers with a card printed with a unique set of random numbers. These numbers are openly displayed and not covered by latex. The winning numbers are announced separately – on a board in a shop or in the pages of a newspaper. Consumers have to check the winning numbers against the number of their card and, if they are the same, contact the promoter to claim the prize. Most newspaper cards operate in this way, with winning numbers displayed daily in the paper. There is a clear advantage of a double hit – first, obtain the card, then check the winning numbers. Note that, to be legal, consumers must have a no-cost way of checking the winning numbers.

Predetermined number cards are a variant on the random number system. Each card is uniquely numbered, but instead of the winning numbers being announced for consumers to check, cards must be returned to the promoter to be matched against predetermined winning numbers. *Reader's Digest* and other direct mail operators often use this format because it encourages consumers to respond to direct mail.

A fourth method is to distribute a series of different cards that have to be matched together to create a set. Only a limited number of the cards needed to complete the set are distributed. Once the set is complete, the win is instant. Petrol stations have used this format to good effect with matching halves of banknotes. The left-hand halves were plentiful and right-hand halves very rare.

These are very much the bare bones of each type of free draw offer. Actual free draws can be very complicated, and can have characteristics of two or three of these types. For example, you can have an instant win card that is also (when mailed in) a predetermined number card and gives the opportunity to match and complete a set. Numbers can be replaced with symbols or words and a whole range of other variants introduced.

What to look out for

Out-of-the-hat draws are perfectly straightforward. They are regularly used by retailers, motor dealers and companies holding exhibitions as a traffic-builder, as a way of capturing names and as a focus of attention. As long as the guidelines in the Code of Practice are followed, they present no terrors. Indeed, they are one of the fastest and simplest forms of promotion to organize, and highly attractive on those grounds alone.

Other types of free draw need careful attention to the mechanisms that prevent fraud and ensure an equitable distribution of winning tickets. You need to use a security printer to make sure that you do not have multiple winning tickets in circulation. A means of verifying the winning ticket via hidden but unique marks is also advisable. You need to carefully seed the winning tickets so that they do not all turn up in the same outlet at the same time. Also, you need to ensure that there is no one involved with the distribution of winning tickets who can take advantage of their knowledge. A good way of doing this is to ask an independent person to do the seeding. That way you are also protected if you are publicly accused of fixing the scheme.

All these factors are manageable if you do three things. First, use a specialist printer (discussed in Chapter 6). Second, consider the use of promotional insurance (also discussed in Chapter 6). Third, make sure your copy is checked by the ASA, the ISP or a specialist lawyer. A good sales promotion agency can help you with all of this as well. These three golden rules for successful prize promotions apply even more strongly to instant wins.

INSTANT WINS

The offer

Instant wins have been around for a number of years in the form of scratch cards overprinted with latex or with perforated windows to hide the winning or losing combinations. Only a limited number of winning cards are distributed, and consumers know instantly whether or not the card they have is a winner.

Instant wins took a major step forward with the launch of the Heinz' 'Win a car a day' and Pedigree Petfoods' 'Is there a car in this can?' promotions in the late 1980s. They are seen by some promoters as the only truly new promotional technique in recent years. The great advantage of these promotions over free draws is that consumers know if they have won a prize as soon as they open the can. The hope that there will be a line drawing of a car on the inside of the lid creates an element of excitement and expectation every time the can is opened. The first time it was used, the consumer interest was colossal. Instant wins converted prize promotions from a delayed to an immediate offer – and the latter is always more effective.

Why had instant wins not been used on grocery products before the late 1980s? The reason was that promoters thought it was illegal because consumers would have to buy the can to see if there was a picture of a car under the lid, making it a lottery. What made these promotions possible was careful legal advice that offering consumers the opportunity to have a can opened by the manufacturer on their behalf meant that they did not have to make a purchase in order to participate. Prior to the Heinz and Pedigree Petfoods promotions, an opportunity to 'Win a car a day' printed on a tin was thought to need a competition mechanic. Free entry or 'plain paper entry' made instant wins a promotional offer that could legally be made on-pack.

Promoters still have to be careful. It is vital that there is a genuine, realistic and unlimited method of free entry. In 1995, Interactive Telephone Services (ITS) was convicted of operating a lottery under the Lotteries and Amusements Act 1976. The promotion was called 'Telemillion' and consisted of phoning a premium rate telephone line, answering a simple question and, if the answer was correct, being entered in a draw. ITS claimed the promotion was not a lottery, because there was a free entry route. The court disregarded this as free entries never exceeded more than 0.184 per cent of entries in any month. If there was a genuine, realistic and unlimited free entry route, the proportion would be much higher. Promoters are cautious about releasing figures for the proportion of free entries they receive, but a figure of 10 to 20 per cent would be considered reasonable.

How they work

Instant wins work best on low-cost, high-volume products that have relatively low product differentiation. This enables large prizes to be offered and for the possibility of winning the prize to be a major factor in the purchase decision. Walkers Crisps lifted its market share in groceries from 57 to 63 per cent between August 1992 and August 1994 on the basis of three separate instant win offers. Walkers' device for the instant win was a twist of blue paper in the crisp packet – harking back to the days when crisps were plain, and the salt was contained in a twist of blue paper. The company went on to achieve further gains by integrating 'Dial-a-prize', 'Instant cheque' and other essentially similar promotional activities with its Gary Lineker theme advertising in 1995/6.

Walkers also noted a decline in response to its instant win promotions each time it used them. This is a standard promotional experience. It has been shared by Camelot with its 'Instants'. To continue working, the instant win principle needs constant refreshing with new formats. Among the best people to advise on new ways of delivering the same concept are the specialist printers of scratch cards and games discussed in Chapter 6. Another good way of keeping at the leading edge of promotional practice is to watch what *Reader's Digest* does: a technique is not worn out the second time it is used, though it may be by the twentieth time.

What to look out for

The considerations that apply to free draws also apply to instant wins, notably in respect of security and seeding. An additional issue to take into account is the possibility that the top prize is won early on in the promotion. From then on, consumers are, in effect, being misled about the possibility of winning. The same applies if the promoter keeps back the pack containing the top prize until late on. It can be advisable to have two or three big prizes, though this militates against the attractiveness of the mega prize.

GAMESW

The offer

'Games' in sales promotion are anything from a newspaper fantasy football league, a word search with prizes, a scratch-off game of Monopoly, to predicting the temperature on Christmas Day. Some require proofs of purchase and some do not. They are distributed variously on-pack, door-to-door, in advertising and as free-standing cards. Everyone knows what these games look like, and they can be hugely successful. However, as we will see below, they are really versions of a free draw, instant win or competition.

How they work

Most people think of a game as something that involves skill. In fact, English law defines a game of skill very restrictively. Most games, including complicated card games such as whist and bridge, count in law as games of chance. Only in such games as duplicate bridge, chess, darts and snooker does the element of skill predominate over the element of chance. If it is a game of chance, as you will know by now, you cannot ask for payment or purchase.

Don't people pay to enter games of chance such as bingo, roulette and the football pools? Yes they do, and these are regulated under the Gaming Act 1968 and other legislation. The general purpose of that legislation is to restrict the availability and attractiveness of gambling and to subject it to taxation and detailed regulation.

Games used in sales promotion are generally of two types. They are a form of instant win or free draw dressed up as 'playing' a version of Monopoly, Scrabble, Trivial Pursuit, ludo or snakes and ladders. Alternatively, they are a form of competition dressed up as 'playing' a word game, predicting a future state of affairs or some other test of skill and judgement. What they are not (because that would be illegal) is the sort of game that the Gaming Board regulates. It follows that 'games' do not really exist as a separate category of prize promotion; rather they are a version of either a free draw/instant win or a competition.

This distinction has been tested in law. In 1995, News International won a case against Customs and Excise, which wanted to charge it pool betting duty of 37.5 per cent or general betting tax of 7.5 per cent on its 'fantasy' promotions. These varied from 'fantasy fund manager' in *The Sunday Times* to the 'Dream team' in *The Sun* and two cricket competitions in *The Times* – a classic case of versioning the same concept for the different interests of different readers. Three of the four promotions operated by premium telephone line. The crucial question was whether the payment that this involved amounted to a bet. If it did, News International would have to pay up. The tribunal held that it did not.

What to look out for

If you are going down the free draw/instant win route, games are in practice a clever and interesting way of dressing them up. All the considerations given in the sections on those two mechanics apply. Above all, ensure there is a free entry route that is genuine and realistic. The opportunities for a great promotion rely on your skill and ingenuity in devising a game theme that is original, simple and exciting.

If you are going down the competition route, and requiring a proof of purchase, the considerations in the section on competitions apply. Be careful not to ask for any payment other than the proof of purchase. It is here that you can take advantage of promotions that are based on probability. These are discussed in the next section.

PROBABILITY PROMOTIONS

The offer

Golf clubs have long enjoyed 'hole-in-one' competitions where an enormous prize is made available in the unlikely event of a hole-in-one being achieved. The possibility is insured against by specialists who have calculated the probabilities and are prepared to underwrite the risk for a fee. Exactly the same principle can be used in sales promotions that require a series of 10 items to be listed in order of priority or the temperature on a given day to be predicted.

How they work

The basic form of this offer requires the entrant to list a number of items in order of importance, such as the world's best cricketers or the factors that make for a good holiday. The 'correct' solution is chosen in advance by an independent judge and placed in a sealed envelope. Skill and judgement must be required on the part of those entering. It would be wrong, for example, to ask entrants to list a series of numbers in order of importance, because that would only require guesswork.

Who can objectively place in order of importance the all-time best cricketers or the factors that make for a good holiday? Objectively, no one can, in the sense that they could list the countries of the world in order of size or population. However, the judgement of an expert amounts to an objective test. It is fair enough, therefore, to ask a cricketing journalist to determine the all-time best cricketers and a top travel agent to determine the list of the factors that make for a good holiday and to use your expert's answer as the correct solution.

The basis of a promotion in which 10 items are listed in order of priority is the probability (or unlikelihood) of anyone listing any set of items in any particular order. The chances of so doing depend on the numbers of items to list, and these are as shown in Table 14.1.

The exponential shape of the curve is obvious. If there are 10 items to list in order of importance, the chance of someone getting it right is 1 in over 3.6 million. It should be possible, therefore, to risk offering a prize of £1 million for the inverse of the probability – just 28p. The risk in letting

Table 14.1 The probabilities of listing items in a certain order for a given numbers of items

Numbers of items	Probabilities of being right
2	1 in 2
3	1 in 6
4	1 in 24
5	1 in 120
6	1 in 720
7	1 in 5040
8	1 in 40,320
9	1 in 362,880
10	1 in 3,628,800
11	1 in 39,916,800
12	1 in 479,001,600

1,000 people enter is around 1,000 times greater, but should still only cost £278. Of course, an insurance company needs to cover its administrative costs, security, re-insurance and the possibility of more people entering than expected. The normal minimum for insuring a £1 million prize is £25,000. A rule of thumb for working out the insurance cost is to divide the expected number of entrants by the odds, multiply by the prize value and double the resulting number.

Increasingly imaginative ways are being found to integrate high-value prizes with high odds and lower-value prizes with lower odds. For example, an offer with a football theme could promise a huge prize for getting three questions right:

- the number of goals in a match (odds 4 to 1);
- how many players will be booked in the match (odds 20 to 1);
- the time in minutes before the first goal (odds 90 to 1).

The odds of getting all three questions right are several million to one, but you could offer a voucher or merchandise prize to those getting one or two of the questions right. You could also risk – and insure – the possibility of offering more than one huge prize on the basis that fewer than half the people who win a prize actually check that they have done so.

What to look out for

Promoters using this mechanic should remember that these offers can produce substantial negative publicity and give an impression of sharp practice. Case study 42 shows how Faber & Faber dealt with this possibility by offering a prize of such high value and high odds that it was unlikely anyone would win.

Brooke Bond was less fortunate with its 1995 promotion headlined 'Millionaire tomorrow?' Consumers were asked to select their own combination of numbers and letters and enter them in a free draw. If their sequence matched that drawn on TV, the winner would receive £1 million. Complaints were made to the ASA that the probability of winning was 6,760 million to one. Brooke Bond was censured by the ASA on the grounds that 'Readers would neither readily appreciate the substantial odds against selecting the correct combination nor realize that unless this was achieved no prize at all would be awarded'.

Particular care needs to be taken with promotions that involve predicting the future. The distinction between predicting an event (illegal) and predicting a state of affairs (legal) needs to be borne in mind if a competition format is being used and a proof of purchase is asked for. Note that if no proof of purchase is required, both are legal. In all these cases, a specialist insurer, such as PIMS, can quote a price for insuring the prize you want to offer. It can also work the calculation backwards, telling you, for example, what prize and what odds you could offer if you had (say) £30,000 available to pay for the insurance and a reasonable estimate of the likely number of entrants (how these firms work is described in Chapter 6).

The golden rule, as in any other promotion, is to think about the people who will enter the competition as being people with whom you want to build a long-term relationship. People don't mind high odds – they are high enough in Lotto – but they do mind being misled.

CASE STUDIES

An element of prize promoting comes into many of the case studies in this book: the main mechanic in the Maxwell House promotion (Case study 3) was a free draw; a competition was used by Zantac 75 (Case study 7) and by Rover Group (Case study 15); Gale's Honey used an instant win technique (Case study 29) as did Smirnoff (Case study 36). These all give a sense of the wide variety of prize promotions.

The two case studies selected for this chapter focus on a particular way of integrating an instant win into a product and on an effective probability promotion.

CASE STUDY 37. SARSON'S

Vinegar is not an exciting product. Sarson's, the brand leader, is constantly looking for reasons to maintain its grocery display and justify its price premium over own-label vinegars. Its one distinguishing characteristic is its 'shaker' top, reflected in its advertising line, 'Shake on the Sarson's'.

This, plus the emergence of new ink technologies, gave the basis for a promotion by SMP that won an ISP Award in 1995. Collarettes were printed with a special ink that reacted with vinegar. When sprinkled with vinegar, they revealed cash prizes of £1 to £1000, a £1 McCain's voucher or a 20p off next purchase coupon.

The promotion had extensive objectives: increase sales, arrest market decline, add interest, justify price premium, encourage repeat purchase, add value, differentiate from own-label vinegars, and reinforce the advertising message. It succeeded in lifting share. Its characteristic was a clever use of emerging ink technology to deliver a standard range of prizes in an interesting and relevant way.

Could Sarson's have referred to the 20p off next purchase coupon as a prize? If Sarson's had wanted to offer a £1 million top prize, what would it have needed to do?

CASE STUDY 38. *THE TIMES* FANTASY SHARE GAME

In 2001, PIMS-SCA joined forces with *The Times* newspaper and Bloomberg to run a Fantasy Share Trading Game, offering players the chance to become a millionaire. With over 154,000 players and more than 300,000 registered portfolios, the promotion was a resounding success for *The Times,* Bloomberg and its participants.

In order to play the online game entrants obtained a password from *The Times.* By logging on to the Web site www.thetimes.co.uk/fantasy-shares entrants registered their portfolio containing 10 shares with a fund value of £1 million. Entrants were able to register as many portfolios as they wanted, at any time of the game. For the following 10 weeks, participants traded shares, trying to gain the highest profit.

Mr Tim Mitchell won £100,000 having increased the value of his virtual portfolio by 30 per cent during the 10-week period. If Tim had also been amongst the top performers in any three categories, he would have been awarded a further £900,000 bonus, and reached millionaire status.

Weekly prizes were awarded for those participants who held the portfolio that rose the furthest within the share rankings. These bonus prizes, worth up to £250,000, were insured by PIMS-SCA, and included a Sunseeker yacht, a luxurious gourmet weekend at Hennesy's Chateau de Bagnotet and a garage full of Lotus cars. Overall the total value of prizes available in the promotion was £3 million.

PIMS-SCA helped *The Times* and Bloomberg to achieve their objectives by assisting in constructing the game in a secure online environment and leveraging the budget to maximize prizes, all at a fixed cost.

CASE STUDY 39. WORTHINGTON CUP FINAL KICK FOR £1 MILLION

On 25 February 2001, Worthington Beer, the sponsor of the UK football League Cup, offered three lucky consumers the chance to win £1 million.

At half time, the finale to Worthington Beer's largest ever promotion, with prize money cover, construction and evaluation covered by PIMS/SCA, was played out in front of 80,000 spectators. Two contestants had won the chance to participate in the activity via an on-pack promotion on Worthington's Cream Flow Bitter.

To win the £1 million the contestant needed to complete five football skill tests:

Test 1: Kick a football into the net from the 25-yard line.
Test 2: The contestants competed against each other in a sudden death penalty shoot out against Chris Woods ex-England football goalkeeper. The winner of this round automatically won £25,000 and progressed alone to the third test.
Test 3: The contestant kicked the ball through a target to win £50,000.
Test 4: Identical to test 3, but the diameter of the target was reduced and the prize increased to £200,000.
Test 5: The contestant needed to score five penalties, against Chris Wood, out of five, to win the £1 million.

With the spectators' support the contestant won £50,000 and Worthington Beer generated huge awareness and PR for their brand.

CASE STUDY 40. CADBURY'S TXT N' WIN PROMOTION

When Cadbury decided to run an on-pack promotion on its chocolate bars, moving away from the traditional promotional techniques and incorporating new technologies, it approached PIMS-SCA and Triangle Communications.

With over 1 billion text messages sent in the UK every month, and the increasing popularity of text messaging among all age groups, companies are now incorporating this mean of communication into their promotional activities. Cadbury is one of the first large companies to take advantage of such a medium and incorporate it into its own Txt n' Win promotion.

To be in with a chance of winning cash prizes or PlayStations, Palm pilots, DVDs or TVs, contestants simply purchased a Cadbury chocolate bar with a promotional wrapper and sent off the text message that appeared inside the wrapper, from their mobile phone. Winners were notified via an SMS text message of their prize.

Cadbury was able to take advantage of the PIMS-SCA expertise and maximize its brand awareness while minimizing costs and taking away the financial risk. Not only is this mechanic a fun promotion to enter from the consumers' point of view, but it also firmly positions the Cadbury's brand at the leading edge of consumer interactivity.

As this book goes to press, Cadbury's have announced a repeat of this promotion linked to the Commonwealth Games.

CASE STUDY 41. DIAGEO

Diageo has carried out sales promotions of its Guinness and Smirnoff brands using SMS advertising. These have included a three-question competition with the prize as free drinks or two for the price of one at certain bars between certain times on certain nights. The prizes are awarded on presentation of the text message sent to the winning competitors on their mobile phones at the bar.

These can in future be in code tied into a code reader kept behind the bar. Many promoters are content to allow much wider broadcasting of offers through viral activity and are happy with the extra trade generated.

CASE STUDY 42. FABER & FABER

Some sectors are relatively low users of sales promotion and so give an opportunity for the creative use of techniques that are familiar elsewhere. One of those is the book trade. Publishers face the challenge that 60 per cent of bookshop visitors leave without making a purchase, that consumers buy on impulse and that the saliency of individual titles on bookshelves is low. The solution is to provide a range of key titles with maximum in-store prominence and encourage consumers to browse among them and make a purchase.

Triangle Communications addressed this for Faber & Faber with a self-assembly 'book tower' containing four copies of each of 25 titles heavily flagged 'How to become a millionaire'. Consumers were asked to enter a competition based on clues among the books and complete a tie-breaker. This was to write the title for a book with a given synopsis. The winner was guaranteed a £10,000 prize and the opportunity to turn this into £1 million at a prize-giving event hosted by Melvyn Bragg. At this event, the winner was asked to select from a tower containing 100 books, 99 of them containing £10,000 cheques and one a £1 million cheque.

The need to grip intermediaries was not neglected and followed the theme of the promotion. Retailers were invited to submit photographs of their displays for a £500 reward, which they could turn into £10,000 by means of the same mechanism used with consumers. The highest achieving rep also won £500 that could be turned into £10,000.

The promotion took the book trade by storm, increasing Faber & Faber's sales during the period of the promotion by 15 per cent. Support from both independents and multiples was considerable, with Dillons featuring it for a two-month period. It also received extensive PR coverage – including speculation about whether or not TS Eliot, one of the featured authors, would have approved of the promotion (his widow said he would have done).

Competitions are a relatively unusual mechanic today as consumers are considered not to enjoy the literary effort involved. However, book buyers are among those for whom writing tie-breakers is a pleasure. Using a competition enabled a proof of purchase to be required. The mechanic required them both to browse and make a purchase – central to the promotion's objectives.

Faber & Faber made no secret of the low probability of anyone winning £1 million. The press carried stories of how the risk was being offset by the company having placed a bet with Ladbrokes. The firm was right to be upfront about this: book buyers would have worked it out anyway, with potentially negative PR coverage. Being upfront avoided this and added to the positive PR coverage.

In many sectors, this promotion would have seemed old hat. In the book trade, it was both innovative and effective – and closely focused on the firm's objectives at every point.

What other retail sectors can you see using the type of promotion Faber & Faber used, and in what ones would it not work?
Do you think an instant win would work with books, and a tiebreaker competition with vinegar?

SUMMARY

The five types of prize promotion each have their strengths and can be used to achieve different promotional objectives. It is vital to be clear about the differences between them. They are among the most powerful promotional techniques, but are subject to quick wear-out.

The administrative rules are well covered in the codes of practice and should be followed in detail. Copy should always be checked, and insurance is often a good idea.

Prize promotions offer particular opportunities for creativity, and have the major advantage of largely fixed costs.

The law in this area is particularly complicated and uncertain. Parliament has legislated separately for gaming, lotteries and betting, and in none of this law did it specifically address the needs of sales promoters.

Prize promotions are an enormously successful promotional device, as major national newspapers from *The Times* to *The Sun* have discovered. Like them, you should take specialist advice before using all but the simplest forms.

International Sales Promotion

When we speak of international promotions, we usually think of major, worldwide activity promoting a branded product in many countries, at the same time, under the same theme. Pepsi-Cola's worldwide link-up with the Spice Girls in 1997 is an example. However, a great deal more international promotion comprises activity that is designed in one country and then also implemented in another. It is multi-local rather than global.

In the early 1970s, it was quite common for companies throughout the world to employ UK sales promotion consultants to create promotions in their own countries – rather as UK TV producers were recruited in the 1990s to develop soaps in Eastern Europe. This was because UK consultancies were far more experienced than the non-specialists in other countries. Such promotions are not truly international as they appear in only one country, but they are included in this chapter as they still occur quite frequently, particularly in emerging markets.

A truly international promotion should appear in a number of countries, though not necessarily at the same time, nor in exactly the same form. This is the direction in which promotional activity has developed in multinational companies.

TYPES OF INTERNATIONAL PROMOTION

International promotions started with a highly successful, transferable promotion run in one country. The success of this promotion becomes known throughout the sales and marketing community, both within the company and often its competitors. Quite quickly the promotion, or a very close approximation, is run in another country, either by the original company or, perhaps, by its competitor. If it is successful again, it is repeated again and again in as many markets as possible. This is how the famous Shell 'Make Money' promotion first travelled the world in the 1950s, long before internationally integrated marketing was an everyday topic.

It is not a long step for marketing people within the company to recognize that they should meet or at least communicate with their opposite numbers in other countries in order to pass on details of their successful promotions. These promotions may then be replicated in other countries by the originating company before their competitors can do so. Relationships between these marketing people soon form to the point at which one manager discusses a potential promotion with one of their colleagues in another country. The usual stimulus for this discussion is money: the desire to split the origination costs with another group of people. Three things can be a particular focus of cost-saving promotion activity: the development of unique premiums, the use of character licences, such as Disney, and the exploitation of celebrity links, such as the Spice Girls.

Corporate pressure for the standardization of promotions has also been powerful. This has been driven by concern about the impact of varied promotional strategies on international brand identity, doubts about whether or not all subsidiaries have an equal capability to design, implement and evaluate promotions, and the integration of retail customers on a regional basis.

The increasing importance of sales promotion in the marketing mix and the growing sophistication of promotional techniques led many companies during the 1980s to conclude that it was no longer possible to regard it as a locally determined activity supported by a certain amount of cross-frontier information sharing. However, the pace of internationalization has been slower than was forecast. There are aspects of sales promotion that remain determinedly local.

By the late 1990s, the structure for managing the local/global balance in sales promotion had taken one of two forms. In one model, a worldwide promotions planning group is created that is responsible for all promotions throughout the world – a pattern followed by Coca-Cola and Pepsi-Cola. In the other, an essentially country- or region-based network becomes more proactive and, as a group, tries to find promotional solutions that will fit the needs of several countries. This is the pattern followed by Nestlé and a number of other leading companies. In both cases, the promotions will be planned in concept and outline in one country, allowing other countries to manage the local details within a global theme.

The primary difference is not one of sales promotional effectiveness, but of corporate culture. The first structure tends to dictate global strategy, while the second is far more consultative. In the one, there is a strong belief in the efficacy of central control, while in the other of the value of harnessing diversity. What has been proven in both circumstances is that the economies of scale can be very attractive.

Whichever structure a firm has adopted, there remain three quite different forms of international promotion activity. These are promotions that are planned in one country, but run in another country; the almost, but not quite, mythical pan-European or pan-world promotions; and the relatively new phenomenon of promoting within a well-defined market that just happens to be global. These three types can be described in shorthand as 'single country', 'multiple country' and 'borderless'.

The difference is very important. The approach you will have to take initially will be different in each case. After that the details of creation and implementation will be the same.

Single country

The process for promoting in another country is little different to that for promoting in your home country, but you do have to imagine a totally different 'village' to answer the question, 'Who do I want to do what?' Crucially, you must make sure that you really know what that village is like. You need to know the people, the way they do business, their expectations and what is allowed by law and by custom, just as you do automatically at home.

Not all that long ago, an English company decided to promote its products in an Irish chain of supermarkets by offering a free draw for a tea set to be won in each store, every day for one week. By 11 o'clock on the first day, all the free draw entry forms had been used up. All the stores were so jammed with people that no business could be done until new entry forms had been delivered and the crowds dispersed. It is hard to believe, but it is true. Not a good promotion! If only the promoter had realized that house-wives in Eire were far less promotionally sophisticated than in the UK.

Another example can be found in the fashion mail-order business. Freemans has agents in many different countries, all using a modified form of the UK catalogue. An important sales opportunity is presented each year by the need to buy new clothes for growing children at the beginning of the school year in September. Thus, a form of 'Back to school' promotion has proved successful in every market. The promotion itself may be simple and similar in every market. What is different is the timing. In Japan and Europe it is possible to promote in August, when mothers are beginning to think of the peace and quiet that lies ahead when the children return to school. In the Middle East, families tend to stay abroad on holiday until much later and therefore the timing of the promotion needs to be as much as two months later, in late September/early October.

Multiple country

If a promotion is to run across several countries, it is likely that the greater the number of countries that you include, the simpler will be your promotion. Often it will become a basic theme that may then be implemented locally using a variety of techniques. Coca-Cola and Pepsi-Cola are well known for their global promotional themes.

In 1996, Shell became the world's largest distributor of die-cast model cars, selling over 26 million via its worldwide 'Colleczione' promotion. The international objective was to reinforce Shell's sponsorship of the Ferrari Formula One team. The model Ferrari cars were offered by the local Shell companies in any appropriate way they saw fit. Some gave them away with oil purchases, some redeemed them free on petrol sales while others offered only a discount on the car in return for a smaller purchase of petrol. The promotional objectives were selected locally as the local situation dictated. In this type of international promotion, the global theme provides a stronger tool than any of the individual companies could afford to provide for themselves as advantage can be taken of tremendous economies of scale.

In 1997, this promotional activity was researched in South America, the Far East and in Europe, and a new range of variations on a theme was developed for 1998. You could expect to collect your Lego Ferrari toy, only at your local Shell station, wherever you were in the world.

Multiple country promotions on a regional basis are becoming increasingly possible as trading groups harmonize their laws and companies set up a single structure to market their products across a group of countries. This has long been the pattern in Northern Europe, and will be extended by the completion of the Single Market. It is also more and more the case in South East Asia. If, as some argue, the fundamental building block of the future is regions rather than individual countries, sales promotion will increasingly take place on a multiple country basis rather than either globally or nationally.

Borderless

The world is shrinking rapidly. There are now well-defined markets that cross geographical borders. While the customers may be from many different countries, they are often more similar to each other than they are to their fellow citizens.

These markets may well increase rapidly once the Internet becomes a true marketplace but, until then, perhaps the best example is that of the frequent business traveller. These people stay at the same hotels and fly on the same aeroplanes. The brands to be found in international airports are already identical across the world, and hotel chains are similarly interchangeable from country to country. Loyalty is what the hotels and airlines want to promote, and they do this by a variety of frequent flyer and frequent visitor promotions. The key point is that the structure for truly global promotion is in place. The communication appears mainly at the point of use or by direct mail. Customers are more similar than different. 'Who do I want to do what?' can be asked and answered of frequent business travellers as a single 'village' across the world, and campaigns can be implemented on a truly global basis. All that needs changing is the language – and, in some cases, not even that.

Other well-defined, cross-frontier markets are achieved by the spread of identical retail formats. Benetton, Marks & Spencer (now withdrawing from the global scene but a good example while they were global) and McDonald's are among three very different retail formats that are identical across frontiers and appeal in each location to fundamentally similar people.

However, it remains the case that there are fewer markets that are truly global than was expected 10 years ago, and that the cultural factors governing behaviour remain persistently different. Even within business-to-business markets, there are radically different approaches to the relationship between groups and individuals, the taking of personal benefits from business transactions and the use of time. The disparities are even greater in consumer markets. For these reasons, sales promotion more than any other part of the marketing mix needs to be planned globally, but implemented locally.

LOCALIZING THE GLOBAL

Once you have identified which of the three types of international promotion you are to implement, you will be able to set realistic and achievable objectives. As with all promotions, it is better to keep it simple, especially when it is to happen halfway around the world. When you start getting down to the details, you should follow exactly the same process as outlined elsewhere in this book. However, you must take account of the particular characteristics of culture and law that continue to differ between countries in most consumer markets.

Every country has laws that may affect your promotion. Table 8.1 indicates what is legal and what is not in some European countries. It is a guide, but no more. Please check the information. You will see that in Germany it is possible to run a competition or a sweepstake, but not a cash back offer. The rules are more subtle. If you run a competition, the answers must be easy to find on the competition form. You may then award the prize to the sender of the first correct entry received – a free draw in all but name. What's more, you are not supposed to have the entry forms near to the promoted product. That's the law, but it is normally flouted. Thus, to operate promotions effectively, you need not only a knowledge of the law, but also that of local practice and culture.

Again, in Germany if you wish to band a premium to your product, you must ensure that it is very product-related and worth not more than a small percentage of the price of the main product. As a consequence, banded offers are hardly used and the consumer's expectation is that such offers may well be useful, but are of limited value. Should you introduce a banded offer that is more exciting than is allowed, then not only will you have broken the law, but you will run the risk of generating an unusually high demand that could create an 'out of stock' situation. Check the latest information with an expert or through a Web site.

There are also differences in trade expectations and in the logistics required to support promotions. If a market is experienced in promotions, the trade will be equipped to handle and implement them. If not, your best ideas may never see the light of day due to confusion and lack of discipline. It is surprising how many support services we take for granted when we run promotions – post offices that are reliable, retailers who will redeem coupons fairly, literate consumers. The absence of these are just a few of the things that could sink your promotion.

If you decide to supply the promoting companies with promotional items, find out about the customs regulations and the way the customs people really work. It is not unknown for items that are known to be urgent to fall into some suddenly created and highly expensive import category if they are to be released within a year. If you use local suppliers, and it is often a good idea, make sure you have a local contact capable of managing them if things go wrong.

Often cultural differences require different techniques. In some countries, people want, and expect, an immediate reward: they live for today, not tomorrow. Thus, a collector scheme is less likely to succeed than a banded or free product offer. A free mail-in might seem attractive, but will be totally useless in most developing countries.

Differences in practices of payment for drinks affect the way in which on-trade promotions can be run. The Smirnoff promotion (Case study 36) assumed UK practice – that people go to the bar to order their drinks and then pay for them immediately. In France, the traditional practice is to sit at a table and be waited on or, if at the bar, to remain there. It is also the practice to collect a number of receipts and pay for them all when you leave. These differences in behaviour would have meant a fundamental rethink of the Smirnoff promotion.

However, different practices also create different opportunities. There are greater numbers of small, counter-service retailers in some countries than in others – the UK included. This means that promotions no longer possible in countries where the grocery trade is dominated by superstores can still be run in countries where the former situation persists. Great promotions of the past in one country can be a new opportunity in another. How can you make the most of them and avoid the other pitfalls we have discussed? The answer is to know the behaviour of your 'village' – both intermediaries and final consumers.

If you are promoting in a foreign country, you need allies who will act as your eyes and ears. Provided you ask the right questions, they will be able to come up with the answers. The difficult part is knowing which questions to ask. Also, whether you are promoting in a single country, across a range of borders or dealing with a truly global market, the additional challenge makes promoting even more fun than on your home ground.

CASE STUDIES

The following three case studies illustrate the two primary forms of international promotion – one that is borderless because the market makes it possible to be so and one that operates across multiple, but different, markets. The third case is a sales promotion that ran in Canada, but it could have been anywhere.

CASE STUDY 43. TONY STONE IMAGES

Tony Stone Images has long been the UK's leading supplier of stock photography, used by generations of art directors. By the mid-1990s it faced a classic marketing challenge. Competition was increasing and it had little brand differentiation. The solution, devised by agency IMP, was to demonstrate that the company understands creative needs and is not just another stock photography supplier. The strategy was to associate Tony Stone Images with 'creative visual solutions' and to position the company as a partner rather than a supplier.

The core idea was the 'scamp', or scribbled drawing that 'creatives' use to indicate the picture they have in mind – it being a poorly kept trade secret that drawing is not always their greatest strength. The campaign began in April 1996 with a series of trade press ads featuring single-colour scamps in place of the traditional full-colour photography used by competitors. It was extended to a range of merchandise incentives such as Post-it Notes and a sweatshirt with a rough outline of a jogger helpfully arrowed 'jogger'. The campaign continued at Christmas 1996 with a calendar for the following year showing both scamps and the photographs that matched them, one for each month.

To launch Tony Stone Images' 1997 generic stock photography catalogue, IMP devised a competition offering a two-night break in New York. It featured a scribbled drawing of a skyline marked 'sunrise/sunset, wide angle skyscrapers'. Entrants were asked to identify the matching photograph in the catalogue, mark on a map where it had been taken and fax back their entries. A follow-up mailing offered a night out for two for identifying a 'lovey dovey shot' in the catalogue and, as a tiebreaker, completing a half-drawn scamp. These competitions meant that the catalogue was browsed and that the product therefore stood out.

The mailing was translated into French, German, Danish and Flemish. It worked internationally because creatives are creatives the world over, photography is similarly international and the creative concept had universal appeal to the target audience. This is more than an illustration of international sales promotion: it is a fine example of using carefully thought-out and relevant incentives to make a wacky but deeply serious point about the positioning of a company and its relationship to its customers.

How did IMP answer the question, 'Who do I want to do what?' in this promotion?
What other ideas could you suggest to extend the campaign for future years?

CASE STUDY 44. UMBRO

Every football fan dreams of walking out of a tunnel into a stadium filled with 80,000 supporters. If you can't achieve that, at least you can enjoy the gear that goes with it. This is the background to Umbro's positioning itself as being as passionate about football as the fans. It was the specific impetus for an in-store promotion devised by IMP to run internationally with the retail chain Footlocker in the run up to Euro '96.

The objectives were to extend the Umbro brand personality through sales promotion and to increase sales through Footlocker on a pan-European basis to the benefit of both companies. The promotion was to use the humorous, mickey-taking tone of voices familiar on terraces and in dressing rooms.

The core idea was to give purchasers of Umbro products an electronic swipe card that they took through a freestanding 'tunnel' in the shop. It would play one of two messages: 'You came, you won, you're walking out a winner. Claim your Euro '96 T-shirt from the cash desk', or, 'What grief, what pain, you haven't won, but you can still win Euro '96 T-shirts with your game card.' Messages were recorded by recognizable football commentators from each country.

Football is a game of two halves whatever the country. Footlocker would not operate across Europe if specialist retailing was not remarkably similar. After all, fans watched the same games during Euro '96. However, sales promotion is not yet similarly international. In Germany, cards had to be made available to shoppers who did not make a purchase. In Italy, the promotion had to be registered with the Finance Ministry for tax purposes. In Holland, winners would hear a cheer in the 'tunnel' and then had to go to the cash desk and answer a simple question before they could obtain their T-shirt.

The variances are important, but so is the transferability of the core concept of tunnel, swipe card and football razzamatazz. The promotion worked for Footlocker and Umbro because the hard work had been undertaken to devise an offer that simultaneously worked across countries and adapted to their specific rules. It also illustrates a feature of the internationalization of sales promotion: that promotions are increasingly tailor-made to specific retailers, which know the particularities of their own markets as well or better than the promoter.

What dangers, if any, do you see in trying to devise retail promotions that will work in several different EU countries?
If budgets had allowed, are there any other marketing activities that you would have recommended to support this promotion?

CASE STUDY 45. VISIBLE VAULT

When radio station CFCW in Edmonton, Canada was looking to boost its ratings, it approached SCA for its traffic-building Visible Vault.

CFCW Radio had a vault filled with a moneybag worth $1 million. Contestants simply had to punch in a six-digit combination in an attempt to crack the code and win the prize.

Day 20 of the promotion saw a $1 million winner, as a woman punched in the correct six digits that opened the vault. Marty Stevens, Promotions Director at CFCW, notified SCA of the winner and relaxed, safe in the knowledge that SCA would pay the prize in full. 'SCA gave us million dollar exposure without our having to pay a million dollars.'

The Vault is very portable, which enabled CFCW to take it to different locations increasing their awareness and visibility. With the prize of $1 million, CFCW radio was the first radio station to offer such a high prize in Canada. The added bonus of having a winner provided plenty of exposure and was covered by all three major television stations and two major newspapers in the area, as well as achieving greater ratings.

'We wanted something that would make an impact' Stevens noted. With the SCA Visible Vault, CFCW Radio certainly achieved its aim.

SUMMARY

International sales promotion came about to achieve cost savings and ensure consistency. It differs depending on whether companies are centralized or decentralized in their structures, but the nature of sales promotion means that there are always cultural and legal factors to take into account.

Borderless promotions work where there is a single international target audience. In most cases, international promotions are multiple-country ones, and vary in terms of timing and detail from country to country.

Succeeding requires close attention to be paid to the behaviour and culture of each market in which you are promoting.

Self-study Questions and Feedback

SELF-STUDY QUESTIONS

If you are doing one of the courses on sales promotion, you'll find that these questions help you meet the course requirements. If you're using the book to help you in your day-to-day work, you'll find they help you get the most out of what you've read. You can also use them as a 'trivia quiz'!

Introduction and Chapter 1

Why do you start with the customer?
What are the six Cs – the offer you make to the customer, the marketing mix – and why are they expressed using a customer focus?
What are the main reasons for the growth in sales promotion?

Chapter 2

Describe the process of getting from business objectives to a marketing plan.
What do the letters of the mnemonic SMART stand for?
What are the tools available in the promotional mix?
What is the difference between price and value promotions, and what sort of promotions fit into each category?

Chapter 3

What are the 10 promotional objectives that sales promotion tackles?

Chapter 4

How can sales promotion be planned strategically?
What are the main points to include in a promotional brief?
What sorts of promotion are best for encouraging trial?
What sorts of promotion are best for encouraging repeat purchase?
What are the pros and cons of delayed and immediate promotions?

Chapter 5

What are some of the leading techniques for developing creative ideas?
How would you go about answering the question, 'Who do I want to do
what?'

Chapter 6

What issues should you take into account when organizing a pitch among
sales promotion agencies?
What are the main things needed in a brief for a handling house?
What things can you use promotional insurance for, and why should you
do so?

Chapter 7

What are the different ways in which you can set a budget for sales
promotion?
If you offer a premium with three proofs of purchase on 150,000 packs, how
many opportunities to apply will there be?
What are some of the main issues to watch in contracts for sales promotional
supply?

Chapter 8

How do you make sure your promotional copy accords with the codes of
practice?
What are the most frequent causes of promotions being criticized by the
ASA?
What are the main principles of the Codes of Advertising and Sales
Promotion Practice?

Chapter 9

What is the process of obtaining marketing accountability?
What must you record for effective evaluation?
What are the main types of research you can use in sales promotion?
Why do you think so little research goes on into sales promotion?

Chapter 10

What do you need to watch for if you are organizing a free flight offer?
How do free rooms offers work?
What issues do you need to take into account if you are using discount coupons?
Why can insurance be offered in a promotion at a much lower cost than the consumer would pay for it from a broker?
How do fixed-fee promotions work?

Chapter 11

What major problems tend to arise in joint promotions?
What should you take into account in looking for a joint promotion partner?
What can you do and what can't you do if you want to promote on the back of a major event licensed to another company?
What particular rules apply to promoting with charities?

Chapter 12

What are the key features of segment pricing and how does it differ from other types of pricing?
What are the pros and cons of multi-buys?
What are the pros and cons of reduced price offers?
What alternative means of coupon distribution are available, and what are the typical redemption rates for each?
If a 10p coupon is placed in a newspaper with a circulation of 2,300,000 and a readership of 3,900,000, and you expect a 1 per cent redemption rate, how many coupons will be redeemed?
What are the main types of trade price promotion?
What key things should you look out for if you are using a 0 per cent finance offer?

Chapter 13

What are the pros and cons of on-pack offers?
What do you need to take into account if you are planning a near-pack?

What contribution can you ask the consumer to make if you are running a free mail-in?

Why have self-liquidators fallen out of favour?

How can sales promotion extend a brand into new distribution outlets?

Chapter 14

What are the main differences between a competition and a free draw?

What is it essential to include in an instant win if it is not to be considered to be a lottery?

What types of prize promotion do games actually consist of?

What sorts of lotteries are legal for promoters to run?

How can companies offer a £1 million prize without having £1 million to give away?

Chapter 15

What are the main types of international promotion?

What must you take into account in planning a promotion that is going to run in several countries?

SUMMARY

If sales promotion is a major part of your job, there's a lot to be said for doing the full range of courses arranged by CAM, the CIM and the ISP. Together, they give you a good grounding in communications and marketing, and specialist knowledge in sales promotion. If sales promotion is less central to what you do, at least make sure you keep up with the magazines.

If this all seems like a lot of work, do not worry. This book has been written to help you design and implement promotions that really work. There's no substitute for experience and for keeping your eyes open, and the best form of learning is doing.

FEEDBACK

Measuring the effectiveness of this book

The author and the publisher would welcome feedback on this book.

Feedback may take any number of forms – please write or e-mail (roddywpmullin@hotmail.com) or visit the Kogan Page Web site (www. koganpage.com); please also answer our nine questions given below.

The key measurement we would like to know from you is that we have met this book's purpose, that is, we have provided you with what you need to carry out sales promotion. So please write or e-mail and let us know whether:

1. You are now able to carry out or supervise sales promotion as a result of reading this book.
2. You found the book stimulating and as a plus now go for sales promotion with enthusiasm and confidence.

We tried to provide in the first part of the book sufficient background and understanding of marketing to deploy sales promotion successfully.

3. Did you feel the first part provided enough background and understanding of marketing?

The chapters in the second part each covered a technique of sales promotion.

4. Was the cover of each sales promotion technique sufficient for you to carry out that activity? If not please elaborate on any shortfalls.
5. Was the chapter format helpful?
6. Are there any other activities peripheral to sales promotion activities which we should include?

Finally, we included in this book suggestions for measuring marketing accountability to confirm the effectiveness of sales promotions for use by you, or for use by those responsible to you for marketing activity.

7. Did you or those responsible to you find measurement mechanisms for all your sales promotions?
8. What was the most useful measurement mechanism and why?
9. As a result have you been able to persuade others outside marketing of the effectiveness and value for money of your sales promotions?

We would appreciate any additional general comments you have.

Further Information

USEFUL ADDRESSES

Trade associations

Advertising Standards Authority (ASA) and Code of Advertising Practice Committee (CAP), 2 Torrington Place, London WC1E 7HW; ASA: Tel 0207 580 5555; Fax 0207 631 3051; Web site www.asa.org.uk. Offers copy advice by e-mail. CAP's Copy Advice Service: Tel 0207 580 4100; Fax 0207 580 4072; Web site www.cap.org.uk. Offers advice online, plus related cases.

Association of Promotion Marketing Agencies Worldwide (APMA World-wide), 750 Summer Street, Stamford CT 06901, USA; Tel 00 1 203 3253911; Fax 00 1 203 969 1499; Web site www.apmaw.org; e-mail mccapma@aol.com.

British Committee of the International Chamber of Commerce, 14–15 Belgrave Square, London SW1X 8PS; Tel 0207 823 2811; Fax 0207 235 5447; Web site www.icc.uk.net; e-mail info@icc.org.co.uk. A business policy organization. Offers publications on sale and list purchase. Sales promotion is covered in the work of one of the area committees.

British Promotional Merchandise Association, Bank Chambers, 15 High Street, Byfleet, Surrey KT14 7QH; Tel 01932 355660; Fax 01932 355662; Web site www.bpma.co.uk; e-mail enquiries@bpma.co.uk. Has a list of members' products and services.

British Retail Corporation, 5 Grafton Street, London W1X 3LB; Tel 0207 647 1510; Fax 0207 647 1599.

CAM Foundation, Moor Hall, Cookham, Maidenhead, Berkshire SL6 9QH; Tel 01628 427192; Fax 01628 427399; Web site www.camfoundation.com; e-mail info@camfoundation.com. Covers specific areas of marketing communication and promotional aspects of marketing for those pursuing a career in advertising, PR, media, market research direct marketing or sales promotion through examinations.

Chartered Institute of Marketing, Moor Hall, Cookham, Maidenhead, Berkshire SL6 9QH; Web site www.cim.co.uk. Tel 01628 427500 The home of the professional practitioner in marketing. Offer training courses on most marketing subjects.

Chartered Institute of Purchasing and Supply, Easton House, Easton on the Hill, Stamford, Lincolnshire PE9 3NZ; Tel 01780 756777; Fax 01780 751610; Web site www.cips.org.uk; e-mail info@cips.org.uk.

Code of Advertising Practice Committee (CAP), see under Advertising Standards Authority, above.

Direct Marketing Association, 70 Margaret Street, London W1W 8SF; Tel 0207 291 3300; Fax 0207 291 3301; Web site www.dma.org.uk; e-mail dma@dma.org.uk. The Direct Marketing Association (DMA) is Europe's largest trade association in the marketing and communications sector, with around 900 corporate members. On behalf of its membership, the DMA promotes best practice and self-regulation, through its codes, in order to maintain and enhance consumers' trust and confidence in the direct marketing industry. The DMA has set up the Direct Marketing Authority as an independent body to monitor industry compliance. Offers an extensive range of assistance on its Web site including codes of practice.

European Marketing and Promotion Association, PO Box 47, Banbury, Oxfordshire OX15 6AS; Tel 01295 678150; Fax 01295 678155. Offers individual consultancy on other countries.

Incorporated Society of British Advertisers (ISBA), 44 Hertford Street, London W1J 7AA; Tel 0207 499 7502; Fax 0207 629 5355; Web site www.isba. org.uk; e-mail info@isba.org.uk. Trade association for advertisers.

Institute of Practitioners in Advertising, 44 Belgrave Square, London SW1X 8QS; Tel 0207 235 7020; Fax 0207 245 9904; Web site www.ipa.co.uk ; e-mail mark@ipa.co.uk. Getting into advertising is not easy! But we also know what a great career it can be. So for those of you who really want to know more, the IPA can give you a better understanding of what it is like to work in the advertising world, the variety of jobs that exist, what sort of skills you will need (and what you will learn), how to go about getting into the industry and which agencies are actively looking for graduates. The IPA is the trade body and professional institute for leading agencies in the UK's advertising, media and marketing communications industry.

Institute of Sales Promotion, Arena House, 66–68 Pentonville Road, London N1 9HS; Tel 0207 837 5340; Fax 0207 837 5326; Web site www.isp.org.uk; e-mail enquiries@isp.org.uk. Web site has 25,000 pages and 200 examples of sales promotions – see awards. Offers plenty of advice on content of sales promotion, examples are the layout, copy and design of coupons. Keen to educate the public on sales promotion. ISP's purpose is to protect and promote professional and effective sales promotion.

Marketing Communications Consultants Association, 2nd Floor, 47/48 Margaret Street, London W1W 8SD; Tel 0207 580 8225; Fax 0207 580 8189; Web site www.mcca.org.uk; e-mail info@mcca.org.uk (formerly Sales Promotion Consultants Association). Offers communications agencies supplying a range of services, recruitment and training information. Will help find an agency through its Portfolio service.

Point of Purchase Advertising Institute (POPAI) Europe, 6 Square de l'Opera, 75009 Paris; Tel +33 1 53 75 16 87; Fax +33 1 53 75 16 88. See UK site: POPAI Europe – UK Office, Devonshire House, Bank Street, Lutterworth, Leicestershire LE17 4AG; Tel 01455 554848; Fax 01455 554421;Web site www.popai.co.uk; e-mail info@popai.co.uk. Trade association for point of purchase, point of sale.

Voucher Association. Twenty-two full members and 11 associate members representing a £1.15bn annual business offering 160 different vouchers available for sales promotions or employee incentives. Call Jo Bell on 0207 608 3222. Visit www.voucherassociation.co.uk.

Agencies that have supplied case studies

The Blue-Chip Marketing Consultancy, St Peter's Court, 8 Trumpet Street, Manchester M1 5LW; Tel 0161 833 4300; Fax 0161 833 4200; e-mail bc@blue chipmarketing.co.uk.

Clarke Hooper Consulting, Parliament House, St Lawrence Way, Slough, Berkshire SL1 2BW; Tel 01753 577767; Fax 01753 823664; Web site www.chc. co.uk; e-mail info@chc.co.uk.

The Communications Agency, 11 Bingham Place, London W1V 2HY; Tel 0207 224 3456; Fax 0207 224 3565; Web site www.t-c-a.com.

The Continuity Company, Unit 1, Berkeley Business Park, Wainwright Road, Warndon, Worcester WR4 9FA; Tel 01905 342100; 01905 342101; e-mail name@contco.com. Also London office 0208 742 3880.

IMP, Waraick Building, Kensington Village, Avonmore Road, London W14 8HQ; Tel 0207 751 1662; Fax 0207 348 3856; Web site www.implondon.co.uk.

SMP, Castle House, 27 London Road, Tunbridge Wells, Kent TN1 1BX; Tel 01892 548282; Fax 01892 538996; e-mail smp@smp.uk.com. Supplies direct marketing and sales information.

Tequila London, 82 Charing Cross Road, London WC2H 0QB; Tel 0207 557 6100; Fax 0207 557 6111; Web site www.tequila-uk.com; e-mail info@tequila-uk.com.

Triangle Communications Limited, 23 Newman Street, London W1P 3HD; Tel 0207 637 0322; Fax 0207 255 2021.

Promotional suppliers

Fotorama, Fotorama House, Icknield Way Estate, Tring, Hertfordshire MK14 6LY; Tel 01442 828383; Fax 01442 822415; Web site www.fotorama.co.uk. Handles promotions, market sourcing and fixed fee promotions.

P&MM Services, Rockingham House, Linford Wood, Milton Keynes WD2 4AG; Tel 01923 255355; Fax 01923 235324; Web site www.p-mm.co.uk; e-mail sheona.hemmings@p-mm.co.uk. Performance and motivation management, manages promotions for others.

PIMS/SCA, Quadrant House, 80–82 Regent Street, London W1B 5RP; Tel 0207 434 3046; Fax 0207 434 0384; Web site www.pims.promo.co.uk; e-mail ideas@pims.promo.co.uk. Interesting case studies. New media capable; text-and-win promotions.

General

Consumers Association, 2 Marylebone Road, London NW1 4DF; Tel 0207 486 5544; Fax 0207 770 7600; Web site www.which.net; e-mail which@which.net.

National Consumer Council, 20 Grosvenor Gardens, London SW1W 0DH; Tel 0207 730 3469; Fax 0207 730 0191; Web site www.ncc.org.uk; e-mail info@ncc.org.uk.

National Statistical Office, Press and Information Office, 1 Drummond Gate, London SW1V 2QQ; Tel 0207 233 9233; Fax 0207 533 6261; Web site www.statistics.gov.uk.

Magazines

Incentive Business (see *Sales Promotion*) bi-monthly, an educational title with tips for success, best ways, Q&As, how to use premiums, how to buy premiums.

Incentive Today, 3rd Floor, Broadway House, 2–6 Fulham Broadway, London SW6 1AA; Tel 0207 610 3001; Fax 0207 610 3566; Web site www.incentive today.com.

Marketing, 174 Hammersmith Road, London W6 7JP; Tel 0207 413 4150; Fax 0207 413 4504; Web site www.marketing.magazine.co.uk.

Marketing Week, 12–26 Lexington Street, London W1R 4HQ; Tel 0207 970 4000; Fax 0207 970 6721; Web site www.marketing-week.co.uk.

Promotions & Incentives, 174 Hammersmith Road, London W6 7JP; Tel 0208 267 4152; Fax 0208 267 4447; Web site www.pandionline.com; subscriptions: 0208 606 7500.

Sales Promotion, Archant Specialist, The Mill, Bearwalden Business Park, Wendens Ambo, Saffron Walden, Essex CB11 4JX; Tel 01799 544200; Fax 01799 544203; Web site www.salespromo.co.uk. Monthly; an up-to-date monthly magazine covering promotional marketing and incentive strategy. Subscriptions: 0845 6014651.

LEARNING MORE ABOUT SALES PROMOTION

Considering the scale of sales promotion, there are still relatively few books about it, a relatively low level of teaching about it in university and professional courses and relatively little academic research into it. However, the situation is better than it was 10 years ago, and can only go on improving. Below is a guide to finding out more in books and magazines and from exhibitions, conferences and courses.

Books

Author's recommendations

Dr John Williams has written an A4 format book of nearly 500 pages entitled *The Manual of Sales Promotion*. First published in 1983, and completely revised in 1996, it is privately published by his company, Innovation Licensing Limited, and costs £40. It provides checklists for techniques and administration, reprints most codes of practice and provides draft copy for many types of promotion. It is an excellent source of reference for the details of sales promotion.

Alan Toop, founder of The Sales Machine, is one of the most prolific writers on sales promotion. His first book, long out of print, entitled *Choosing the Right Sales Promotion* was published by Crosby Lockwood in 1966. Kogan Page published his *European Sales Promotion: Great campaigns in action* in 1992, which comprises more than 40 case studies under broad headings such as awareness, brand value and repeat purchase. The examples are good, and his comments are pithy. If you can find it anywhere, his earlier book, *Just £3.95?!* published privately by The Sales Machine in 1978, contains powerful case studies of brand-enhancing promotions that are still relevant today. Together with Pran Choudhury and Ricky Elliott, he wrote *Successful Sales Promotion* (Sangram Books, 1992), which mainly consists of 26 sales promotions from India on brands including Horlicks, Palmolive and Bournvita.

Christian Petersen, co-founder of KLP, wrote one of the best of the earlier generation of books – *Sales Promotion in Action* (Associated Business Press, 1979). Shortly before his untimely death, he teamed up with Alan Toop to write *Sales Promotion in Post-modern Marketing* (Gower, 1994). It is expensive to buy, but well worth borrowing for its intelligent discussion of the changing face of marketing and the evolution of sales promotion techniques.

For the legal side, you cannot do better than Philip Circus' *Sales Promotion Law: A practical guide* (Butterworth, 1996).

The publisher of this book, Kogan Page, has also published Chris Brown's *Sales Promotion Handbook* (1993). It is complementary to this book, containing useful checklists for many aspects of sales promotion.

One of the few academics to take sales promotion seriously is John Quelch of the Graduate School of Business Administration at Harvard and Dean at LBS (he has now returned to the US). His book *Sales Promotion Management* (Prentice Hall, 1989) is mainly concerned with price promotion, is wholly US-focused, and fairly demanding. If you like statistical analysis, it provides an important basis for thinking seriously about price promotions.

Knowing more about a subject needs to go hand in hand with knowing how it fits into the broader scheme of things. Here there is a problem. The established industry view is that sales promotion is just one part of one of the four Ps. In the seventh edition of his classic book, *Marketing Management* (Prentice Hall, 1997), Philip Kotler is less dogmatic about this classification than in earlier editions, but he still goes on using it. Kotler does not refer to the alternative way of seeing sales promotion in the marketing mix advanced by Waterschoot and Van den Bulte. The mechanical model of marketing developed in the 1950s and 1960s is collapsing under the weight of reality, but the textbooks have yet to develop a new model. In the interim, readers have to develop their own way of fitting the various elements of marketing into a coherent whole, and refer to books such as *Sales Promotion in Post-modern Marketing*. The textbooks get longer and longer, but don't give the answer. The solution used in this book is to consider the marketing mix in terms of the six Cs. How that is communicated to the customer is through the promotional mix, which includes sales promotion alongside advertising, direct marketing and publicity all considered together in integrated fashion.

One popular model covering this is 'integrated marketing'. P R Smith's *Marketing Communications: An integrated approach* (Kogan Page, 1993) provides an accessible example covering all the communications tools. The trouble is that integration is easier to talk about than to do, and you still have to know what the separate bits are that you are trying to integrate. In practice, integrated marketing is a buzzword that cuts little ice with most companies. Far better to understand sales promotion thoroughly, and then try to ensure that your campaigns reinforce and do not undermine everything else the company is trying to do. Integration is wider than marketing, and absolute integration a dream we seldom achieve.

Books mentioned or from which reference is taken in the text

Baguley, P (1995) *Managing Successful Projects*, Pitman Publishing, London

Chisnall, P (1991) *The Essence of Marketing Research*, Prentice Hall, Englewood Cliffs, NJ

Collins, J C and Porras, J I (1996) *Built to Last: Successful habits of visionary companies*, Century Business, London

Davidson, H (1987) *Offensive Marketing*, Penguin, Harmondsworth

Ehrenberg, A S C, Hammond, K and Goodhart, C A E (1991) *The After-effects of Large-scale Consumer Promotions*, Centre for Marketing and Communications, London Business School, London

Finney, J (1992) *Finding Faith Today*, Bible Society/Churches Together in England, London

Fletcher, W (1992) *A Glittering Haze: Strategic advertising in the 1990s*, NTC Publications, Henley-on-Thames

Hague, P and Jackson, P (1992) *Marketing Research in Practice*, Kogan Page, London

Hague, P and Jackson, P (1996) *Market Research: A guide to planning, methodology and evaluation*, Kogan Page, London

Hampden-Turner, C and Trompenaars, F (1993) *The Seven Cultures of Capitalism*, Piatkus, London

Kashani, K (1997) 'Why marketing still matters', in *Mastering Management*, ed G Bickerstaffe, Financial Times/Pitman Publishing, London

Kay, J (1993) *Foundations of Corporate Success*, Oxford University Press, Oxford

Kotler, P (1997) *Marketing Management: Analysis, planning, implementation and Control* (9th edn), Prentice Hall, Englewood Cliffs, NJ

Mahoney, S (1995) 'The carrot and the stick', *Sales Promotion*, February

Mullin R (2001) *Value for Money Marketing*, Kogan Page, London

Nevett, T R (1982) *Advertising in Britain: A history*, Heinemann, Oxford

Ogilvy, D (1983) *Ogilvy on Advertising*, Pan, London

Ohmae, K (1996) *The End of the Nation State: The rise of regional economies*, Free Press Paperbacks, Simon & Schuster, New York

Quelch, J (1989) *Sales Promotion Management*, Prentice Hall, Englewood Cliffs, NJ

RSA (1995) *Tomorrow's Company: The role of business in a changing world*, Gower, Aldershot

Trompenaars, F (1993) *Riding the Waves of Culture: Understanding cultural diversity in business*, Nicholas Brealey, London

van Waterschoot, W, and Van den Bulte, C (1992) 'The 4P classification of the marketing mix revisited', *Journal of Marketing*, **56**, October

Warren, R (1995) *Signs of Life: How goes the decade of evangelism?*, Church House Publishing, London

Wicks, A (1990) 'Advertising research', in *A Handbook of Market Research Techniques*, ed R Burn, P Hague and P Vangelder, Kogan Page, London

Magazines and Web sites

If you've got time to look at academic marketing magazines, there are, periodically, articles on sales promotion in the *Journal of Marketing* and *Journal of Marketing Research*. Most of them are mind-numbingly statistical, US-based, focused on price promotions and very difficult to draw practical conclusions from. If that doesn't put you off, the easiest way to access them is not through electronic media, but by going into a business school's library and looking in the index of the bound volumes.

There are several popular magazines published in the UK that are relevant, of which *Promotions & Incentives* and *Incentive Today* are the best. Both are controlled-circulation magazines, so you should try to get yourself on their distribution lists. However, beware the bias that their dependency on advertising creates. There is almost nothing in them on price promotion (other than coupons) because price promotion does not attract advertisers. There are endless, repetitive features on vouchers, travel and luxury gifts because they do attract advertisers. The features on sales promotion that occur in *Marketing* and *Marketing Week* follow a similar pattern, but occasionally carry very useful in-depth analysis.

The ISP publishes a useful newsletter, which is particularly good on developments in EU regulations, which is now echoed on the Web site. In 2002 there is particular concern about EU sales promotion legislation. The ISP also publishes an awards brochure each year, also available on the Web site, which gives photographs and brief write-ups of that year's winners. It is an excellent way of keeping in touch with what the industry regards as best current practice. (At the time of going to press – April 2002 – the 2002 Award winners lists have been published but not what they did in detail. You can still see the 2001 award winners details of their promotions in full.)

The MCCA also puts the winners of its best awards on its Web site. Not all are related to sales promotion but quite a number are. Worth a look.

There is, sadly, no equivalent in sales promotion of the monthly magazine *Admap* or the biennial *Advertising Works*, both published by NTC Publications and containing serious analysis of advertising effectiveness that is accessible to practitioners. These publications have a dual role: serious research and advancing the cause of advertising. They tend to underestimate the significance of sales promotion, if they mention it at all.

Exhibitions and conferences

The major events in the sales promotion calendar is the marketing *Incentive Today* exhibition held in London in May. Other exhibitions are held in different parts of the country, notably the Sales Promotion and Incentives exhibition held every two years in Manchester. These are particularly good for keeping up to date with the latest in premiums.

Conferences are organized periodically by the ISP, the MCCA and by commercial providers. These tend to be expensive, but bring out the insights of those at the leading edge of the business. If you want to keep up to date in this way, meetings of the ISP (mainly in London) are particularly useful.

Courses

The top-level course in sales promotion is run by the ISP with support from Kingston Business School. See www.isp.org.uk for full details.

The ISP also runs an intensive three-day course entitled (from its town of origin) The Brighouse Weekend. Sadly, it has migrated from West Yorkshire, but it continues to provide first class training and the opportunity to devise and present a promotion to senior marketing managers.

The Chartered Institute of Marketing (CIM) runs three-day residential courses – Sales Promotion and Sales Promotion for Retail – at intermediate level (two to five years' experience) at its headquarters near Maidenhead. Visit its Web site for full details.

The CIM's Postgraduate Diploma, Diploma and Certificate courses include sales promotion within its papers on Marketing Communications.

This only provides the most general introduction to each of the communications disciplines. The CIM courses are valuable for their strategic approach to marketing and for putting what you know about communications in a broader context.

The Communications Advertising and Marketing Foundation (CAM) offers a course culminating in a Certificate for which you need to sit six papers that focus more on the communications disciplines – marketing, advertising, PR, media, sales promotion and direct marketing, and research and behavioural studies. The CAM Diploma allows students who have taken the certificate to specialize in one of the communications disciplines. The ISP Diploma is recognized by CAM as the specialist qualification in sales promotion. To achieve the CAM Diploma you need to take the ISP Diploma and the CAM paper in Management and Strategy. Again the Web sites give the latest details.

For a career in sales promotion, again this is covered in the ISP Web site. To find out the sort of things that sales promotion people do, time spent visiting ISP awards and ISP member Web sites will reap a real benefit, demonstrating what you might one day do.

Index

'added value' 25, 77
Admap 15, 249
advertising xiii–xv, xvii, xviii, 2–4, 12, 14,
    22–23, 25–26, 29, 37–40, 42–43, 57–58,
    72–73, 78–80, 86–87, 90, 101–03, 110, 117,
    131, 176–78, 186, 193, 195, 200, 203, 205,
    208–09, 214, 236, 247–48
Advertising Association 3
Advertising Effectiveness Awards 57
Advertising Regulations Act (1907) 101
Advertising Standards Authority (ASA) 5,
    17, 102, 218
  case studies 106–08
  complaints 102, 116, 218
  Copy Advice Service 103
Advertising Works 249
agency relationships 99
Air Miles xiv, 39, 133, 149
Ammaritis Puris Istas 69
American Adventure Theme park 128
Asda 56, 142, 150, 159
Association of Promotion Marketing
    Agencies Worldwide 241
attitude *see* customer attitude
Avista 195

Balkan Holidays 107
  case study 108
banded offers 230
banded packs 164

Barclays Bank 127, 129, 133
Barclaycard 125, 142
Barnardo's 147–48
behaviour *see* customer behaviour
Benetton 229
Bloomberg 219
Blue-Chip Marketing Consultancy 51–53
BMW 193
Body Shop, The 38
Bonusbreaks 130
Boot, Jesse 37–38
Boots 38, 130, 142, 180, 198
'bounce-back' offer 131, 134–35
Bovril 35, 43, 152
  case study 43
brand xiii–xvi, 2, 4, 12–16, 22, 24–25, 28–29,
    34–39, 44, 48, 62–63, 66–67, 77–79, 81,
    86, 89, 91, 94–95, 101, 113–15, 117, 127,
    130, 132, 142, 145, 147, 152, 157–58, 163,
    168, 178–79, 183, 185–86, 188–90,
    192–96, 201, 204, 209, 225–26, 238, 248
'brand equity' 14
brand extension promotions 186, 193, 201
Branson, Richard 16, 38
British Airways 38
British Codes of Advertising and Sales
    Promotion 203, 208
British Gas 102, 142
British Heart Foundation 148
British Midland 120, 129

British Premium Merchandise Association
(BPMA)   85, 104
British Telecom (BT)   138, 147, 195
case study   138
Brooke Bond   218
Brown, Chris   246
Brylcream   15, 193
budget   90
Burger King   151
business gifts   194
suppliers   85
business objectives   xvi, 19–21, 29, 48, 51,
90, 235
business to business (B2B)   10
buying process and behaviour   13
'buy one, get one free' (BOGOF) offers   151,
164, 167
Buzz   129

Cadbury's   16, 38, 79–80, 115, 194, 209
case study   221
Camelot   214
Campaign   117
Canadian Moosehead lager   79
case study index   ix
Charities Aid Foundation   147
charity promotions   146
Chartered Institute of Marketing (CIM)   xiii,
1, 238, 242
Cherry Blossom   61
case study   60
Choudhury, Pran   246
Circus, Philip   205
Clarke Hooper Consulting   55
Classic FM   52
Clearblue One Step   198
Coca-Cola   193, 226, 228
case study   106
Code of Advertising Practice Committee
(CAP)   102, 103, 241
Code of Sales Promotion Practice   203, 208
codes of practice in UK   102
collector promotions   35, 105, 147
Communications, Advertising and
Marketing Foundation (CAM)   242
communications mix   22
competitions   103, 150, 204–10
competitive advantage   15, 27
competitive differentiation   158
Competitors Companion   206
Consumers Association   104
Consumer Credit Act   173
'container' promotions   25
Continuity Company   55

Control of Misleading Advertisements
Regulations (1988)   104
Co-operative Retail Trading Group   36, 55,
152
coupons   169
covermounts   187
creative techniques   65
creativity   57–70
credit card companies   142
customer
attitudes   xv, 4, 13–14, 26, 111, 114
behaviour   xvi, 4, 9, 13–14, 17, 24–26, 44,
61, 80, 89, 111, 118, 194, 229
needs   9, 11, 44
profile   10, 21, 143
relationships   1–2, 16, 24, 101, 157
customer loyalty market   133
customer relationship management (CRM)
10, 12
Customs and Excise   196, 215

Daewoo   158
Daily Mail   131
Davidson, Hugh   206
Daz   5, 187
'dealer loaders' see business gifts
Debenhams   130
Deep Pan Pizza   128
delayed discounts   166
Department of Transport and Industry (DTI)
Code of Practice for Traders on Price
Indications   104
Design and Art Direction Association
(D&AD)   57
differential advantage   29, 45
direct mail   73, 77, 81, 93, 169–71, 212, 229
direct marketing   xv, xviii, 3, 21, 23–24, 29,
90, 110, 246
Direct Marketing Association   3, 27, 72, 78,
84, 93, 102
Code of Practice   104
discount coupons   127
discounting   161, 176, 192
distributors   40, 83
distribution chain   61
Dixons   153
DMIS   3
Do It All   142
Dollond & Aitchison   147
Dream Works   30

Easyjet   24, 129
Ehrenberg, Andrew   247
Electrolux   41, 195

case study   199
Elliott, Ricky   246
EMI   186
Esso   26, 38, 134, 153
Euromonitor   117
European Promotional Marketing
    Association (EPMA)   242
evaluation *see* research
Eversheds   38, 195, 197
  case study   69
extra fill packs   166

Faber & Faber   34, 217
  case study   222
Financial Times   128
Flora   148
Flymo   151
Footlocker   232
Ford   36, 94
Fosters   128
'four Ps'   12, 15
free draws   210
free film promotions   134
free samples   145
Freemans   227

Gale's Honey   35, 39, 190
  case study   222
games   214
Gaming Act (1968)   214
Gaming Board   214
'gift with purchase' (GWP)   188
Go   129
Golden Wonder   68
Green Shield stamps   39, 150, 179
Guinness   15, 24, 129, 193, 221
Guinness Book of Records   194

Haagen-Dazs   38, 193
  case study   186
Halfords   142
handling houses   77
'Hayfever Survival' campaign *see* Kleenex
Heineken   38
Henley Centre   xvi
HFC Bank   142
high street vouchers   130
Hoover   xiv, 17, 28
  case study   139
HMV stores   136, 153
HP Foods   148
HSBC   160

IMP   231

implementing a promotion   89–101
  budget   90
  communication   92
  legalities   94
  logistics   94
  stages   95–99
  timings   92
'in-pack' promotion   169
Incentive Today   74, 117
Incentive World   87
Incorporated Society of British Advertisers
    (ISBA)   74
Independent Committee for the Supervision
    of Standards of Telephone Services Code
    of Practice   104
influencers, role of   14
Innovation Licensing Limited   246
Institute of Directors   40
Institute of Practitioners in Advertising
    (IPA)   57
Institute of Purchasing and Supply
    Code of Practice   104
Institute of Sales Promotion (ISP)   xvii, 3, 6,
    24, 53, 59, 72, 74, 93, 102–03, 108, 114,
    117, 153, 171, 182, 198, 205, 219
  Legal Advice Service   205
insurance   81–82
insurance offers   130
'integrated marketing'   xv
Interactive Telephone Services (ITS)   213
intermediaries   230
intermediary support   33, 40, 111
International Code of Sales Promotion
    Practice   104
international sales promotion   225–34
  types   225
Internet   xiii–xv, 13, 21, 24, 69, 79, 130, 195,
    229
ITVC Digital   39

Jacob's Club   36, 152
  case study   55
Japan   148
Jet   26
joint promotions   99
  case studies   152–54
  charities   146
  loyalty schemes   149
  phantom partnerships   151
  planning principles   141
  referral coupons   145
  sample promotions   145
Journal of Marketing   248
Journal of Marketing Research   248

Kay, John   27
Kellogg   154
key performance indicator (KPI)   29–30, 46,
    48, 89, 95, 97, 99, 109–14, 119
Kimberley-Clark   51–53
Kinder Surprise   193
Kit Kat   24, 56, 186
Kleenex   25, 28, 40, 51, 197
    case study   51
Kotler, Philip   2, 247
knowledge management   11

law   101
    EU   105
    international   105
    UK   104
Lee & Perrins   37, 182
    case study   182
Lever Brothers   25–26, 154
Liberal Democrats   174
Lloyds Bank   132
Lombard Group   174
London Business School   163
London Marathon see Flora
Lotto   203, 218
Lotteries and Amusements Act (1976)
    203
loyalty schemes   141, 149
Lucozade   15

magazine covermount   187
Mahoney, Simon   199
Mail Order Traders' Association Code of
    Practice   104
mail-in premiums   189
Marketing   117
marketing accountability   109–13
marketing department   xv, 9, 15
market intelligence   117
marketing objectives   19–22
marketing mix   11–12, 15, 20, 24, 27, 29, 33,
    42, 45, 157, 193, 226, 229
Marketing Principles   200
Marketing Week   117
Marks & Spencer   130, 157, 229
Mars   37
Maxwell House   34–35, 42
    case study   42
Mazda   67
MCCA   72, 74
    Code of Conduct   74
McDonald's   151, 229
MEAL   39
'mechanics' see promotional mechanics

'member get member' schemes   40
million pound competitions   31
Mintel   117, 194–195
money off coupons   25, 182, 185
multibuys   163
Mutton, Edwin DG ISP   3

National Lottery 203 see also Lotto
Natwest   133
    case study   138
NCH Promotional Services   170–71
NCH (National Children's Home)   146
'near-packs'   188
needs see customer needs
Nescafé   42
Nestlé   42, 86, 181, 187, 192, 226
Nissan   30
    case study   30
Norweb   26
NSPCC   147

Oddbins   171
off-the-shelf offers   123–40
    case studies   136–39
    discount coupons   127
    free film promotions   134
    free hotel accommodation   124
    high street vouchers   130
    holiday vouchers   125
    insurance offers   130
    packaged schemes   133
Omo   197
on-pack offers   48
operational plan   68, 95, 97
opportunities to apply (OTA)   134–35
Osram   61
'Cash box and key' promotion case study   59
overriders   176
oxo   148

P&MM services   129, 133, 138
P & O ferries   128
packaged schemes   133
partnerships see joint promotions
'partnership sourcing'   71
pence off flashes   25, 35
Pepsi-Cola   225–26, 228
Persil   146
Petersen, Christian   246
petrol promotions   26
phantom partnerships   151
Pilot Fashion   128
PIMS/SCA   81, 131, 218–20
Playtex   206

Point of Purchase Advertising Institute
    (POPAI) 78, 80
point of purchase manufacturers 78
Porteous, Jim 209
premium promotions 185–201
  brand extension promotions 193
  business gifts 194
  case studies 186, 191, 197–200
  covermounts 187
  free mail-ins 189
  on-pack offers 186
  self-liquidators 192
  with purchase premiums 188
premiums 185–98
price
  'going rate' 159
  segmentation 157
  setting 157
  'target mark-up' 159
pricing policies
  psychological 159
  segment 159
  value 159
price promotions 25
  case studies 179–82
  coupons 169
  delayed discounts 166
  finance deals 172
  immediate discounts 161
price setting 159
segment pricing 160
trade price promotions 175
price wars 161
Prince's Trust 136
printers see specialist printers
prize promotions 203–23
  case studies 218–223
  competitions 205
  free draws 210
  games 214
  instant wins 213
  lotteries 203–205
probability promotions 216
Procter & Gamble 25–26, 151, 154, 185
  case study 197
profile see customer profile
promotional brief 45–47, 95–96
Promotional Campaigns Group 43–44, 54
Promotional Handling Association
  Code of Practice 104
promotional insurers 81
  over-redemption insurance 81
printers' errors and omissions insurance 81
product liability and recall insurance 81

promotional mechanics 49–51 see also
    premium promotions
promotional objectives 20, 33–44
  list of 10 core 33
promotional offers
  off-the-shelf 123
  joint 141
  price 157
  premium 185
  prize 203
Promotional Sourcing Association
  Code of Practice 104
Promotions & Incentives 74, 117
publicity 23

Quelch, John 246
questionnaires 235

Ramada 64, 67
  case study 60
Reader's Digest 203, 206
Red or Dead 128
redemption rate 81–82, 169, 171
redemption systems 171
reduced price offers (RPOs) 165
referral coupon promotions 145
relationships see customer relationships
repertoire purchasing 35
repurchase offers 168
resale price maintenance 158
research 114
response rate 115, 117, 190
retailers 26–27, 34, 39, 78, 81, 85, 130, 159,
    162–63, 165–66, 169, 172–77, 187–88,
    211–12, 230
Revlon 193
risk management see promotional insurers
Rover Group 174
  case study 67
Royal British Legion 142
Royal Mail xvi, 93
Royal Society of Arts 16
  'Tomorrow's Company' report 16
Ruddles 127

Saatchi&Saatchi 2
Safeway 133, 180
Sainsbury's xiv, 17, 133, 150, 152, 180
  case study 43–44
sales promotion
  agencies 72
  books 246
  conferences 249
  courses 249

definition   22, 24 (ISP)
evaluation   1
exhibitions   249
extent   2
implementation   89
international   225
law   101
magazines   248
reasons for growth   3
research   114
strategies   27
tactics   27
Sales Promotion Consultants Association
        (SPCA) *see* MCCA
Sarson vinegar   48, 83
   case study   154
scratchcards   83, 214
segment pricing   159–61
   principles   161
   rules of thumb   161
self-liquidator promotion (SLP)   192
Sellotape   48, 107, 154
   case study   154
Shark   31
   case study   31
Shell   26, 36, 61, 134, 228
   case study   60, 153
Shelter   147
Sheraton Securities   59, 67
   case study   59
Shrek   30
'six Cs'   11–14, 24, 29
SMART criteria   20–21, 47
Smarties   24, 86, 187
Smirnoff   38
Smith PR   247
Smithkline Beecham
   case study   191
SMP   39, 198–99
SMS   xviii, 80
Sony Music   128
specialist printers   213
Spillers Petfoods   79
Stone, Merlin   xv
suppliers   71–87
Swatch   38

Talk Radio   53
Tango
   case study   136
'Tango Bash'   35, 39, 136
telemarketing   xvii, 3
Tequila   xv, 30, 31, 136, 153–54
Tesco   26, 48, 133, 150–51, 179, 206

   case study   179
   Clubcard   149, 180
text messaging   xviii, 80
The Express   53
   case study   107
The Guardian   24
The Independent   24
The Sun   154, 215
   case study   107, 137
The Sunday Times   215
The Times   215
   case study   219
Thomas Cook   146
Toyota   133
trade price promotion   175
trade promotion   133
'tribal marketing'   143
trial promotions   35
Triangle Communications   42, 221–22

UCI Cinemas   138, 153
Umbro
   case study   232
Unilever   115

Value Added Tax   196
value for money marketing   29, 110, 248
value promotions   25
Van den Burgh   148
Vauxhall Motors   36, 52, 106
   case study   106
Virgin   17, 38
Virgin Atlantic 129
Visa   125
Visible Vault
   case study   233
Vodafone   133
Voucher Association   233

Walkers Crisps   214
Wal-Mart   159
Warner Bros   129
Which?   132
Williams, John   104
Willott Kingston Smith (WKS)   29, 90
Woolworths   157
Worthington
   case study   220

Yellow Pages   196
Youth Hostel Association   128

Zantac   41, 54, 207
   case study   54